Threefold Lotus Kwoon

Sifu Sylvain Chamberlain, Nyudo

Nichiren Gosho Study

All contents of this book are intended as reference material for the study of Nichiren School Buddhism.

Information is from many sources and public access archives from the World Wide Web for the scholarship of Buddhist studies.

Copyright applies only to this formatting and collection along with commentaries of the study material.

Threefold Lotus Kwoon Press with LULU.com prints this book in order to facilitate learning and study for students of the Nichiren school lineage of Buddhism.

Table of Contents

On Attaining Buddhahood in This Lifetime .. 7
    Background 10
A Ship to Cross the Sea of Suffering 13
On Establishing the Correct Teaching for the Peace of the Land 19
The Postscript to "On Establishing the Correct Teaching for the Peace of the Land" 91
    Background 92
The Izu Exile 95
    Background 100
The Universal Salty Taste 105
    Background 108
The Four Debts of Gratitude 111
    Background 125
The Teaching, Capacity, Time, and Country 129
    Background 144
Questions and Answers about Embracing the Lotus Sutra 149
    Background 175
The Recitation of the "Expedient Means" and "Life Span" Chapters 185
    Background 198
Encouragement to a Sick Person 207
    Background 224

The Essence of the "Medicine King" Chapter 247
Background 265
Conversation between a Sage and an Unenlightened Man 271
    Part One 271
    Part Two 319
    Background 370

On Attaining Buddhahood in This Lifetime

IF you wish to free yourself from the sufferings of birth and death you have endured since time without beginning and to attain without fail unsurpassed enlightenment in this lifetime, you must perceive the mystic truth that is originally inherent in all living beings. This truth is Myoho-Renge-Kyo. Chanting Myoho-Renge-Kyo will therefore enable you to grasp the mystic truth innate in all life.

The Lotus Sutra is the king of sutras, true and correct in both word and principle. Its words are the ultimate reality, and this reality is the Mystic Law (Myoho). It is called the Mystic Law because it reveals the principle of the mutually inclusive relationship of a single moment of life and all phenomena. That is why this sutra is the wisdom of all Buddhas.

Life at each moment encompasses the body and mind and the self and environment of all sentient beings in the Ten Worlds as well as all insentient beings in the three thousand realms, including plants, sky, earth, and even the minutest particles of dust. Life at each moment permeates the entire realm of phenomena and is revealed in all phenomena. To be awakened to this principle is itself the mutually inclusive relationship of life at each moment and all phenomena. Nevertheless, even though you chant and believe in Myoho-Renge-Kyo, if you think the Law is outside yourself, you are embracing not the Mystic Law but an inferior teaching. "Inferior teaching" means those other than this [Lotus] sutra, which are all expedient and provisional. No expedient or provisional teaching leads directly to enlightenment, and without the direct path to enlightenment you cannot attain Buddhahood, even if you practice lifetime after lifetime for countless kalpas. Attaining Buddhahood in this lifetime is then impossible. Therefore, when you chant Myoho and recite renge,1 you must summon up deep strong mind of determination that Myoho-Renge-Kyo is your life itself.

You must never think that any of the eighty thousand sacred teachings of Shakyamuni Buddha's lifetime or any of the Buddhas and bodhisattvas of the ten directions and three existences are outside yourself. Your practice of the Buddhist teachings will not relieve you of the sufferings of birth and death in the least unless you perceive the true nature of your life. If you seek enlightenment outside yourself, then your performing even ten thousand practices and ten thousand good deeds will be in vain. It is like the case of a poor man who spends night and day counting his neighbor's wealth but gains not even half a coin. That is why the T'ien-t'ai school's commentary states, "Unless one perceives the nature of one's life, one cannot eradicate one's grave offenses."2 This passage implies that, unless one perceives the nature of one's life, one's practice will become an endless, painful austerity. Therefore, such students of Buddhism are condemned as non-Buddhist. Great Concentration and Insight states that, although they study Buddhism, their views are no different from those of non-Buddhists.

Whether you chant the Buddha's name,3 recite the sutra, or merely offer flowers and incense, all your virtuous acts will implant benefits and roots of goodness in your life. With this conviction you should strive in strong mind of determination. The Vimalakīrti Sutra states that, when one seeks the Buddhas' emancipation in the minds of ordinary beings, one finds that ordinary beings are the entities of enlightenment, and that the sufferings of birth and death are nirvana. It also states that, if the minds of living beings are impure, their land is also impure, but if their minds are pure, so is their land. There are not two lands, pure or impure in themselves. The difference lies solely in the good or evil of our minds.

It is the same with a Buddha and an ordinary being. When deluded, one is called an ordinary being, but when enlightened, one is called a Buddha. This is similar to a tarnished mirror that will shine like a jewel when polished. A mind now clouded by the illusions of the innate darkness of life is like a tarnished mirror, but when polished, it is sure to become like a clear mirror, reflecting the essential nature of phenomena and the true aspect of reality. Arouse deep strong mind of determination, and diligently polish your mirror day and night. How should you polish it? Only by chanting Nam-Myoho-Renge-Kyo.

What then does myō signify? It is simply the mysterious nature of our life from moment to moment, which the mind cannot comprehend or words express. When we look into our own mind at any moment, we perceive neither color nor form to verify that it exists. Yet we still cannot say it does not exist, for many differing thoughts continually occur. The mind cannot be considered either to exist or not to exist. Life is indeed an elusive reality that transcends both the words and concepts of existence and nonexistence. It is neither existence nor nonexistence, yet exhibits the qualities of both. It is the mystic entity of the Middle Way that is the ultimate reality. Myō is the name given to the mystic nature of life, and hō, to its manifestations. Renge, which means lotus flower, is used to symbolize the wonder of this Law. If we understand that our life at this moment is myō, then we will also understand that our life at other moments is the Mystic Law.4 This realization is the mystic Kyo, or sutra. The Lotus Sutra is the king of sutras; the direct path to enlightenment, for it explains that the entity of our life, which manifests either good or evil at each moment, is in fact the entity of the Mystic Law.

If you chant Myoho-Renge-Kyo with deep strong mind of determination in this principle, you are certain to attain Buddhahood in this lifetime. That is why the sutra states, "After I have passed into extinction, [one] should accept and uphold this sutra. Such a person assuredly and without doubt will attain the Buddha way."5 Never doubt in the slightest.

Respectfully.

Maintain your strong mind of determination and attain Buddhahood in this lifetime. Nam-Myoho-Renge-Kyo, Nam-Myoho-Renge-Kyo.

Nichiren

Background

This letter was written to Toki Jōnin in the seventh year of Kenchō (1255), two years after Nichiren Shonin established his teaching of Nam-Myoho-Renge-Kyo. At the time of this letter, the Shonin was thirty-four years old and was living in Kamakura, the seat of the military government. Toki was a staunch follower of the Shonin who lived in Wakamiya in Shimōsa Province. He received some thirty letters, including Letter from Sado and one of the major treatises, The Object of Devotion for Observing the Mind. A retainer of Lord Chiba, the constable of Shimōsa, Toki had become a follower of the Shonin around 1254.

Of all his writings from the mid-1250s, On Attaining Buddhahood in This Lifetime focuses most clearly on the tenets of the Shonin's Buddhism; many of the other works of this period are aimed chiefly at refuting the erroneous doctrines of other schools and discussing theoretical questions. This short essay not only reflects the theories T'ien-t'ai formulated based on the Lotus Sutra, but also reveals the concrete practice for attaining Buddhahood—namely, chanting Nam-Myoho-Renge-Kyo—that is missing in T'ien-t'ai's theoretical framework.

Myoho-Renge-Kyo is the title of the Lotus Sutra, but to the Shonin it is much more; it is the essence of the sutra, the revelation of the supreme Law itself. Apparent in this work are both the depth of his thought and his conviction that Nam-Myoho-Renge-Kyo is the only teaching that can lead people to Buddhahood in this lifetime.

Notes

1. "Chant Myoho and recite Renge" means to chant the Daimoku of the Mystic Law, or Nam-Myoho-Renge-Kyo.

2. The Annotations on "Great Concentration and Insight."

3. As used here, "the Buddha's name" denotes Nam-Myoho-Renge-Kyo.

4. This sentence can also be interpreted to read, "If one understands that one's life is myō, then one also understands that others' lives are all entities of the Mystic Law."

5. Lotus Sutra, chap. 21.

A Ship to Cross the Sea of Suffering

WHEN I asked him about what you told me the other day, I found it to be exactly as you said. You should therefore strive in strong mind of determination more than ever to receive the blessings of the Lotus Sutra. Listen with the ears of Shih K'uang and observe with the eyes of Li Lou.[1]

In the Latter Day of the Law, the votary of the Lotus Sutra will appear without fail. The greater the hardships befalling him, the greater the delight he feels, because of his strong mind of determination. Doesn't a fire burn more briskly when logs are added? All rivers flow into the sea, but does the sea turn back their waters? The currents of hardship pour into the sea of the Lotus Sutra and rush against its votary. The river is not rejected by the ocean; nor does the votary reject suffering. Were it not for the flowing rivers, there would be no sea. Likewise, without tribulation there would be no votary of the Lotus Sutra. As T'ien-t'ai stated, "The various rivers flow into the sea, and logs make a fire burn more briskly."[2]

You should realize that it is because of a profound karmic relationship from the past that you can teach others even a sentence or phrase of the Lotus Sutra. The sutra reads, "Nor will they hear the correct Law—such people are difficult to save."[3] The "correct Law" means the Lotus Sutra; it is difficult to save those who are deaf to the teachings of this sutra.

A passage from the "Teacher of the Law" chapter reads: "If one of these good men or good women [in the time after I have passed into extinction is able to secretly expound the Lotus Sutra to one person, even one phrase of it, then you should know that] he or she is the envoy of the Thus Come One." This means that anyone who teaches others even a single phrase of the Lotus Sutra is the envoy of the Thus Come One, whether that person be priest or layman, nun or laywoman. You are already a lay practitioner and therefore one of the "good men" described in the sutra. One who listens to even a sentence or phrase of the sutra and cherishes it deep in one's heart may be likened to a ship that crosses the sea of the sufferings of birth and death. The Great Teacher Miao-lo stated, "Even a single phrase cherished deep in one's heart will without fail help one reach the opposite shore. To ponder one phrase and practice it is to exercise navigation."[4] Only the ship of

Myoho-Renge-Kyo enables one to cross the sea of the sufferings of birth and death.

The Lotus Sutra speaks of "someone finding a ship in which to cross the water."[5] This "ship" might be described as follows: As a shipbuilder of infinitely profound wisdom, the World-Honored One of Great Enlightenment, the lord of teachings, gathered the lumber of the four flavors and eight teachings, planed it by honestly discarding the provisional teachings, cut and assembled the planks, forming a perfect unity of both right and wrong,[6] and completed the craft by driving home the spikes of the one true teaching that is comparable to the flavor of ghee. Thus he launched the ship upon the sea of the sufferings of birth and death. Unfurling its sails of the three thousand realms on the mast of the one true teaching of the Middle Way, driven by the fair wind of "the true aspect of all phenomena,"[7] the vessel surges ahead, carrying aboard all people who can "gain entrance through strong mind of determination alone."[8] The Thus Come One Shakyamuni is at the helm, the Thus Come One Many Treasures takes up the mooring rope, and the four bodhisattvas led by Superior Practices row quickly, matching one another as perfectly as a box and its lid. This is the ship in "a ship in which to cross the water." Those who are able to board it are the disciples and lay supporters of Nichiren. Believe this wholeheartedly. When you visit Shijō Kingo, please have an earnest talk with him. I will write you again in more detail.

With my deep respect,

Nichiren

The twenty-eighth day of the fourth month

To Shiiji Shirō

Background

Nichiren Shonin wrote this letter at Kamakura in the first year of Kōchō (1261), about two weeks before he was exiled to Itō in Izu. Virtually nothing is known about the recipient, Shiiji Shirō, other than that he lived in the province of Suruga and was acquainted with two of the Shonin's leading disciples, Shijō Kingo and Toki Jōnin.

The title of this letter is drawn from a passage in the "Medicine King" chapter of the Lotus Sutra that speaks of "a ship in which to cross the water." In this letter, the Shonin teaches that the Daimoku of the Lotus Sutra is the "ship" that can unfailingly transport one across the sea of life's inevitable sufferings to the distant shore of enlightenment.

Notes

1. Shih K'uang, in Chinese legend, was a court musician whose sense of hearing was so keen that he could judge the quality of a newly cast bell, where ordinary musicians could not. Li Lou's sight was so acute that he could see the tip of a hair at a hundred paces.

2. *Great Concentration and Insight.*

3. Lotus Sutra, chap. 2.

4. *The Annotations on "The Words and Phrases of the Lotus Sutra."* "The opposite shore" represents nirvana, or enlightenment, while this shore where we live represents illusion.

5. Lotus Sutra, chap. 23.

6. "Forming a perfect unity of both right and wrong" means that both good and evil are eternally inherent in life. Provisional sutras hold that wicked people cannot attain enlightenment, but the Lotus Sutra reveals that even such people possess the Buddha nature, giving the example of Devadatta attaining Buddhahood.

7. Lotus Sutra, chap. 2.

8. Ibid., chap. 3.

On Establishing the Correct Teaching for the Peace of the Land

ONCE there was a traveler who spoke these words in sorrow to his host:

In recent years, there have been unusual disturbances in the heavens, strange occurrences on earth, famine and pestilence, all affecting every corner of the empire and spreading throughout the land. Oxen and horses lie dead in the streets, and the bones of the stricken crowd the highways. Over half the population has already been carried off by death, and there is hardly a single person who does not grieve.

All the while some put their whole strong mind of determination in the "sharp sword"[1] of the Buddha Amida and intone the name of this lord of the Western Land; others believe that hearing the name of the Buddha Medicine Master will "heal all ills"[2] and recite the sutra that describes this Thus Come One of the Eastern Region. Some, putting their trust in the passage in the Lotus Sutra that says, "His illness will be wiped out and he will know neither old age nor death,"[3] pay homage to the wonderful words of that sutra; others, relying upon the sutra passage that reads, "The seven disasters will instantly vanish, and the seven blessings will instantly appear,"4 conduct ceremonies at which a hundred priests expound the sutra at a hundred preaching platforms.5 There are those who follow the esoteric teachings of the True Word school and conduct rituals in which they fill five jars with water,6 and others who devote themselves entirely to seated meditation and try to perceive the emptiness of all phenomena as clearly as the moon.7 Some write out the names of the seven guardian spirits8 and paste them on a thousand gates, others paint pictures of the five mighty bodhisattvas9 and hang them over ten thousand thresholds, and still others pray to the heavenly gods and earthly deities in ceremonies conducted at the four corners of the capital and on the four boundaries of the nation. Taking pity on the plight of the common people, the rulers carry out government on the national and local levels in a benevolent manner.

But despite all these efforts, they merely exhaust themselves in vain. Famine and epidemics rage more fiercely than ever, beggars are everywhere in sight, and scenes of death fill our eyes. Corpses pile up in mounds like observation platforms, and dead bodies lie side by side like planks on a bridge.

If we look about, we find that the sun and moon continue to move in their accustomed orbits, and the five planets10 follow the proper course. The three treasures of

Buddhism continue to exist, and the period of a p.7hundred reigns has not yet expired.11 Then why is it that the world has already fallen into decline and that the laws of the state have come to an end? What is wrong? What error has been committed?

The host then spoke: I have been brooding alone upon this matter, indignant in my heart, but now that you have come, we can lament together. Let us discuss the question at length.

When a man leaves family life and enters the Buddhist way, it is because he hopes to attain Buddhahood through the teachings of the Buddha. But attempts now to move the gods fail to have any effect, and appeals to the power of the Buddhas produce no results. When I observe carefully the state of the world today, I see people who give way to doubt because of the lack of understanding [on the part of eminent priests]. They look up at the heavens and mouth their resentment, or gaze down at the earth and sink deep into despair.

I have pondered the matter carefully with what limited resources I possess, and have looked a little at the scriptures for an answer. The people of today all turn their backs upon what is right; to a person, they give their allegiance to evil. This is the reason that the benevolent deities have abandoned the nation and departed together, that sages leave and do not return. And in their stead devils and demons come, and disasters and calamities occur. I cannot keep silent on this matter. I cannot suppress my fears.

The guest said: These disasters that befall the empire, these calamities of the nation—I am not the only one pained by them; the whole populace is weighed down with sorrow. Now I have been privileged to enter the orchid room12 and listen to these enlightening words of yours. You speak of the gods and sages taking leave, and of disasters and calamities arising in sequence—upon what sutras do you base your views? Could you describe for me the passages of proof?

The host said: There are numerous passages that could be cited and a wide variety of proofs. For example, in the Golden Light Sutra we read: "[The four heavenly kings said to the Buddha], 'Though this sutra exists in the nation, its ruler has never allowed it to be propagated. In his heart he turns away from it, and he takes no pleasure in hearing its teachings. He neither makes offerings to it, honors it, nor praises it. Nor is he willing to honor or make offerings to the four kinds of Buddhists who embrace the sutra. In the end, he makes it impossible for us and the other countless heavenly beings who are our followers to hear this profound and wonderful teaching. He deprives us of the sweet dew of its words and cuts us off from the flow of the correct teaching, so that our majesty and strength are drained away. Thus the number of beings who occupy the evil paths increases, and the number who dwell in the human and heavenly realms decreases. People fall into the river of the sufferings of birth and death and turn their backs on the road to nirvana.

"'World-Honored One, we, the four heavenly kings, as well as our various followers and the yakshas and other beings, observing this state of affairs, have decided to abandon this nation, for we have no heart to protect it. And it is not we alone who cast aside this ruler. All the great benevolent deities who guard and watch over the countless different regions of the country will also invariably reject him. And once we and the others abandon and desert this nation, then many different types of disasters will occur in the country, and the ruler will fall from power. Not a single person in the entire population will possess a heart of goodness; there will be nothing p.8but binding and enslaving, killing and injuring, anger and contention. People will slander each other or fawn upon one another, and the laws will be twisted until even the innocent are made to suffer. Pestilence will become rampant, comets will appear again and again, two suns will come forth side by side, and eclipses will occur with unaccustomed frequency. Black arcs and white arcs will span the sky as harbingers of ill fortune, stars will fall, the earth will shake, and noises will issue from the wells. Torrential rains and violent winds will come out of season, famine will constantly occur, and grains and fruits will not ripen. Marauders from many other regions will invade and plunder the nation, the people will suffer all manner of pain and affliction, and no place will exist where one may live in safety.'"

The Great Collection Sutra says: "When the teachings of the Buddha truly become obscured and lost, then people will all let their beards, hair, and fingernails grow long, and the laws of the world will be forgotten and ignored. At that time, loud noises will sound in the air, and the earth will shake; everything in the world will begin to move as though it were a waterwheel. City walls will split and tumble, and all houses and dwellings will collapse. Roots, branches, leaves, petals, and fruits will lose their medicinal properties. With the exception of the heavens of purity, 13 all the regions of the world of desire will become deprived of the seven flavors 14 and the three kinds of vitality, 15 until not a trace of them remain any more. All the good discourses that lead people to emancipation will at this time disappear. The flowers and fruits that grow in the earth will become few and will lose their flavor and sweetness. The wells, springs, and ponds will all go dry, the land everywhere will turn brackish and will crack open and warp into hillocks and gullies. All the mountains will be swept by fire, and the heavenly beings and dragons will no longer send down rain. The seedlings of the crops will all wither and die, all the living plants will perish, and even the weeds will cease to grow any more. Dust will rain down until all is darkness and the sun and moon no longer shed their light.

"All the four directions will be afflicted by drought, and evil omens will appear again and again. The ten evil acts will increase greatly, particularly greed, anger, and foolishness, and people will think no more of their fathers and mothers than does the roe deer.16 Living beings will decline in numbers, in longevity, physical strength, dignity, and enjoyment. They will become estranged from the delights of the human and heavenly realms, and all will fall into the paths of evil. The wicked rulers and monks who perform these ten evil acts will curse and destroy my correct teaching and make it difficult for those in the human and heavenly realms to stay there. At that time the benevolent deities and heavenly kings, who would ordinarily take pity on living beings, will abandon this impure and evil nation, and all will make their way to other regions."

The Benevolent Kings Sutra states: "When a nation becomes disordered, it is the spirits that first show signs of rampancy. Because the spirits become rampant, all the people of the nation become disordered. Invaders come to plunder the country, and the common people face annihilation. The ruler, the high ministers, the crown prince, the other princes, and the hundred officials all quarrel with one another over right and wrong. Heaven and earth manifest prodigies and strange occurrences; the twenty-eight constellations, the stars, and the sun and moon appear at irregular times and in irregular positions; and numerous outlaws rise up."

The same sutra also states: "Now when I use the five types of vision to clearly perceive the three existences, I see that in their past existences all the rulers served five hundred Buddhas, and that is the reason that they were able to become emperors and sovereigns. And that also is the reason that all the various sages and Arhats are born in their nations and bring great benefits. But if a time should come when the good fortune of these rulers runs out, then all the sages will abandon them and depart. Once the sages have departed, then the seven disasters are certain to arise."

The Medicine Master Sutra states: "If disasters and calamities should befall members of the ruling Kshatriya class and anointed kings,17 such disasters will be as follows: the calamity of disease and pestilence among the populace; the calamity of invasion from foreign lands; the calamity of revolt within one's own domain; the calamity of irregularities and strange occurrences among the stars and constellations; the calamity of eclipses of the sun and moon; the calamity of unseasonable wind and rain; and the calamity of rain that fails to fall even when the season for it has come and gone."

In the Benevolent Kings Sutra [the Buddha addresses King Prasenajit with these words]: "Great King, the region where my teachings now hold sway consists of one billion Sumeru worlds with one billion suns and moons. Each of these Sumeru worlds comprises four continents. In the southern continent of Jambudvīpa, there are sixteen great states, five hundred middle-sized states, and ten thousand small states. In these states, seven types of fearful disasters may occur. All the rulers of these states agree that these are indeed disasters. What, then, are these disasters?

"When the sun and moon depart from their regular courses, when the seasons come in the wrong order, when a red sun or a black sun appears, when two, three, four, or five suns appear at the same time, when the sun is eclipsed and loses its light, or when one, two, three, four, or five coronas appear around the sun, this is the first disaster.

"When the twenty-eight constellations do not move in their regular courses, when the Metal Star,18 the Broom Star, the Wheel Star, the Demon Star, the Fire Star, the Water Star, the Wind Star, the Ladle Star, the Southern Dipper, the Northern Dipper, the great stars of the Five Garrisons, and all the many stars that govern the ruler, the three high ministers, and the hundred officials—when each of these stars manifests some peculiar behavior, this is the second disaster.

"When huge fires consume the nation, and the people are all burned to death, or when there are outbreaks of demon fire, dragon fire, heavenly fire, mountain god fire, human fire, tree fire, or bandit fire19—when these prodigies appear, this is the third disaster.

"When huge floods drown the population; when the seasons come out of order and there is rain in winter, snow in summer, thunder and lightning in winter, and ice, frost, and hail in the sixth month;20 when red, black, or green rain falls; when mountains of dirt and stones come raining down, or when it rains dust, sand, or gravel; when the rivers and streams run backward; when mountains are afloat and boulders are washed away—when freakish happenings of this kind occur, this is the fourth disaster.

"When huge winds blow the people to their death, and the lands, the mountains and rivers, and the trees and forests are all at one time wiped out; when great winds come out of season, or when black winds, red winds, green winds, heavenly winds, earthly winds, fire winds, and water p.10winds blow21—when prodigies of this kind occur, this is the fifth disaster.

"When heaven and earth and the whole country are stricken by terrible heat so that the air seems to be on fire, when the hundred plants wither and the five kinds of grain22 fail to ripen, when the earth is red and scorched and the inhabitants all perish—when prodigies of this kind occur, this is the sixth disaster.

"When enemies rise up on all four sides and invade the nation, when rebels appear in the capital and the outlying regions, when there are fire bandits, water bandits, wind bandits, and demon bandits,23 and the population is subjected to devastation and disorder, and fighting and plundering break out everywhere—when prodigies of this type occur, this is the seventh disaster."

The Great Collection Sutra says: "Though for countless existences in the past the ruler of a state may have practiced the giving of alms, observed the precepts, and cultivated wisdom, if he sees that my teaching is in danger of perishing and stands idly by without doing anything to protect it, then all the inestimable roots of goodness that he has planted through the practices just mentioned will be entirely wiped out, and his country will become the scene of three inauspicious occurrences. The first is high grain prices, the second is warfare, and the third is epidemics. All the benevolent deities will abandon the country, and although the ruler may issue commands, the people will not obey them. The country will constantly be invaded and vexed by neighboring nations. Violent fires will rage out of control, fierce winds and rains will abound, the waters will swell and overflow, and the inhabitants will be blown about by winds or swept away by floods. The paternal and maternal relatives of the ruler will join in plotting revolt. Before long, the ruler will fall gravely ill, and after his life has come to an end, he will be reborn in the great hell. . . . And the same fate will befall the ruler's consort, his heir, the high ministers of the state, the lords of cities, the village heads and generals, the magistrates of districts, and the other officials."

The passages I have quoted from these four sutras are perfectly clear—what person in ten thousand could possibly doubt their meaning? And yet the blind and the deluded recklessly trust to distorted doctrines and fail to recognize the correct teaching. Therefore, throughout the empire these days people are inclined to turn away from the Buddhas and the sutras, and no longer endeavor to protect them. Because of this, the benevolent deities and sages abandon the nation and leave their accustomed places. As a result, demons and evil spirits24 bring about disasters and cause calamities.

The guest thereupon flushed with anger and said: Emperor Ming of the Later Han dynasty, having comprehended the significance of his dream of a golden man, welcomed the teachings [of Buddhism] brought by white horses.25 Prince Jōgū, having put down the rebellion of Moriya [an opponent of Buddhism],26 proceeded to construct temples and pagodas. Since that time, from the ruler on down to the common people, all have worshiped the Buddha images and devoted their attention to the scriptures. As a result, in the monasteries of Mount Hiei and the southern capital at Nara, at the temples of Onjō-ji and Tō-ji, throughout the land bounded by the four seas, in the five provinces of the capital area and along the seven marches, Buddha images and Buddhist scriptures have been ranged like stars in the sky, and halls of worship have spread like clouds. Those who belong to the lineage of Shāriputra meditate on the moon atop Eagle Peak, while those p.11who adhere to the traditions of Haklenayashas transmit the teachings of Mount Kukkutapāda.27 How, then, can anyone say that the teachings of the Buddha's lifetime are despised, or that the three treasures of Buddhism have ceased to exist? If there is evidence to support such a contention, I would like to hear all the facts.

The host, anxious to clarify his words, replied: To be sure, Buddhist halls stand rooftop to rooftop, and sutra storehouses are ranged eave to eave. Priests are as numerous as bamboo plants and rushes, monks as common as rice and hemp seedlings. The temples and priests have been honored from centuries past, and every day respect is paid them anew. But the monks and priests today are fawning and devious, and they confuse the people and lead them astray. The ruler and his subjects lack understanding and fail to distinguish between what is correct and what is erroneous.

The Benevolent Kings Sutra, for example, says: "Evil monks, hoping to gain fame and profit, in many cases appear before the ruler, the crown prince, or the other princes, and take it upon themselves to preach doctrines that lead to the violation of the Buddhist Law and the destruction of the nation. The ruler, failing to perceive the truth of the situation, listens to and puts strong mind of determination in such doctrines, and proceeds to create regulations that are perverse in nature and that do not accord with the rules of Buddhist discipline. In this way he brings about the destruction of Buddhism and of the nation."

The Nirvana Sutra states: "Bodhisattvas, have no fear of mad elephants. What you should fear are evil friends! . . . Even if you are killed by a mad elephant, you will not fall into the three evil paths. But if you are killed by an evil friend, you are certain to fall into them."

The Lotus Sutra says: "In that evil age there will be monks with perverse wisdom and hearts that are fawning and crooked who will suppose they have attained what they have not attained, being proud and boastful in heart. Or there will be forest-dwelling monks wearing clothing of patched rags and living in retirement, who will claim they are practicing the true way, despising and looking down on all humankind. Greedy for profit and support, they will preach the Law to white-robed laymen and will be respected and revered by the world as though they were Arhats who possess the six transcendental powers. . . . Because in the midst of the great assembly they constantly try to defame us, they will address the rulers, high ministers, Brahmans, and householders, as well as the other monks, slandering and speaking evil of us, saying, 'These are men of perverted views who preach non-Buddhist doctrines!' . . . In a muddied kalpa, in an evil age there will be many things to fear. Evil demons will take possession of others and through them curse, revile, and heap shame on us. . . . The evil monks of that muddied age, failing to understand the Buddha's expedient means, how he preaches the Law in accordance with what is appropriate, will confront us with foul language and angry frowns; again and again we will be banished."28

The Nirvana Sutra says: "After I have passed away and countless hundreds of years have gone by, the sages of the four stages29 too will have all passed away. After the Former Day of the Law has ended and the Middle Day of the Law has begun, there will be monks who will give the appearance of abiding by the rules of monastic discipline. But they will scarcely ever read or recite the sutras, and instead will crave all kinds of food and drink to nourish their bodies. Though they wear the clothes of a monk, they will p.12go about searching for alms like so many huntsmen who, narrowing their eyes, stalk softly. They will be like a cat on the prowl for mice. And they will constantly reiterate these words, 'I have attained arhatship!' Outwardly they will seem to be wise and good, but within they will harbor greed and jealousy. [And when they are asked to preach the teachings, they will say nothing,] like Brahmans who have taken a vow of silence. They are not true monks—they merely have the appearance of monks. Consumed by their erroneous views, they slander the correct teaching."

When we look at the world in the light of these passages of scripture, we see that the situation is just as they describe it. If we do not admonish the evil priests, how can we hope to do good?

The guest, growing more indignant than ever, said: A wise monarch, by acting in accord with heaven and earth, perfects his rule; a sage, by distinguishing between right and wrong, brings order to the world. The monks and priests of the world today enjoy the confidence of the entire empire. If they were in fact evil monks, then the wise ruler would put no trust in them. If they were not true sages, then worthies and learned persons would not look up to them. But now, since worthies and sages do in fact honor and respect them, they must be nothing less than paragons of their kind. Why then do you pour out these wild accusations and dare to slander them? To whom are you referring when you speak of "evil monks"? I would like an explanation.

The host said: In the time of the Retired Emperor Gotoba there was a priest named Hōnen who wrote a work entitled The Nembutsu Chosen above All. He contradicted the sacred teachings of the Buddha's entire lifetime and brought confusion to people in every direction. Nembutsu Chosen above All states: "Regarding the passage in which the Meditation Master Tao-ch'o distinguished between the Sacred Way teachings and the Pure Land teachings and urged people to abandon the former and immediately embrace the latter, first of all, there are two kinds of Sacred Way teachings, [the Mahayana and the Hinayana]. . . . Judging from this, we may assume that the esoteric Mahayana teachings and the true Mahayana teachings are both included in the Sacred Way. If that is so, then the eight present-day schools—the True Word, Zen, Tendai, Flower Garland, Three Treatises, Dharma Characteristics, Treatise on the Ten Stages Sutra, and Summary of the Mahayana—all are included in the Sacred Way that is to be abandoned.

"The Dharma Teacher T'an-luan in his Commentary on 'The Treatise on Rebirth in the Pure Land' states, 'I note that Bodhisattva Nāgārjuna's Commentary on the Ten Stages Sutra says, "There are two ways by which a bodhisattva may reach the state of avaivartika, or non-retrogression. One is the difficult-to-practice way, the other is the easy-to-practice way."'

"The difficult-to-practice way is the same as the Sacred Way teachings, and the easy-to-practice way is the Pure Land teachings. Students of the Pure Land School should first of all understand this point. Though they may be people who have previously studied the Sacred Way teachings, if they wish to become followers of the Pure Land teachings, they must discard the Sacred Way and give their allegiance to the Pure Land teachings."

Hōnen also says: "Regarding the passage in which the Reverend Shan-tao distinguished between correct and sundry practices and urged people to abandon the sundry and embrace the correct: Concerning the first of the sundry practices, that of reading and reciting sutras, with the exception of p.13the recitation of the Meditation on the Buddha Infinite Life Sutra and the other sutras that preach rebirth in the Pure Land, the embracing, reading, and recitation of all other sutras, whether Mahayana or Hinayana, exoteric or esoteric, is to be regarded as a sundry practice. . . . Concerning the third of the sundry practices, that of worshiping, with the exception of worshiping the Buddha Amida, the worshiping or honoring of any other Buddha or bodhisattva, or deity of this world is to be regarded as a sundry practice. . . . In the light of his statement, I declare that one should abandon such sundry practices and concentrate upon the practice of the Pure Land teachings. What reason would we have to abandon the correct practices of the Pure

Land teachings, which insure that out of a hundred persons all one hundred will be reborn in the Pure Land, and cling instead to the various sundry practices and procedures, which could not save even one person in a thousand? Followers of the way should ponder this carefully."

Hōnen further states: "In The Chen-yüan Era Catalog of the Buddhist Canon we find it recorded that, from the 600 volumes of the Great Wisdom Sutra to the Eternity of the Law Sutra, the exoteric and esoteric sutras of Mahayana, or the great vehicle, total 637 works in 2,883 volumes. The phrase [from the Meditation Sutra] 'reading and reciting the great vehicle' should be applied to all these works. You should understand that, when the Buddha was preaching according to the capacity of his various listeners, he for a time taught the two methods of concentrated meditation and un-concentrated meditation.30 But later, when he revealed his own enlightenment, he ceased to teach these two methods. The only teaching that, once revealed, shall never cease to be taught is the single doctrine of the Nembutsu."

Hōnen also states: "Regarding the passage that says that the practitioner of the Nembutsu must possess three kinds of mind,31 it is found in the Meditation Sutra. In his commentary on that sutra [Shan-tao says]: 'Someone may ask, "If there are those who differ in understanding and practice from the followers of the Nembutsu, persons of distorted and mistaken belief, [how should we confront them]?" I will now make certain that their perverse and differing views will not cause trouble. These persons of evil views with different understanding and different practices are compared to a band of robbers who call back the traveler who has already gone one or two steps along his journey.' In my opinion, when this commentary speaks of different understanding, different practices, varying doctrines, and varying beliefs, they are referring to the teachings of the Sacred Way."

Finally, in a concluding passage, Hōnen says: "If one wishes to escape quickly from the sufferings of birth and death, one should confront these two superior teachings and then proceed to put aside the teachings of the Sacred Way and choose those of the Pure Land. And if one wishes to follow the teachings of the Pure Land, one should confront the correct and sundry practices and then proceed to abandon all of the sundry and devote one's entire attention to the correct."

When we examine these passages, we see that Hōnen quotes the erroneous explanations of T'an-luan, Tao-ch'o, and Shan-tao, and establishes the categories of the Sacred Way and the Pure Land teachings, and of the difficult-to-practice and the easy-to-practice ways. He then takes all the 637 works in 2,883 volumes that comprise the Mahayana teachings of the Buddha's lifetime, including those of the Lotus Sutra and the True Word sutras, along with all the Buddhas and bodhisattvas and the deities of this world, p.14and assigns them all to the categories of the Sacred Way teachings, the difficult-to-practice way, and the sundry practices, and urges people to "discard, close, ignore, and abandon" them. With these four injunctions, he leads all people astray. On top of that, he groups together all the sage monks of the three countries [of India, China, and Japan] as well as the students of Buddhism of the ten directions, and calls them a "band of robbers," causing the people to insult them.

In doing so, he turns his back on the passage in the three Pure Land sutras, the sutras of his own school, which contains Amida's vow to save the people "excepting only those who commit the five cardinal sins and those who slander the correct teaching."32 More fundamentally, he shows that he fails to understand the warning contained in the second volume of the Lotus Sutra, the heart and core of the entire body of teachings the Buddha expounded in the five periods of his preaching life, which reads, "If a person fails to have strong mind of determination but instead slanders this sutra . . . When his life comes to an end he will enter the Avīchi hell."33

Now we have come to this latter age, when people are no longer sages. Each enters his own dark road, and all alike forget the direct way. How pitiful that no one cures them of their blindness! How painful to see them taking up these false beliefs in vain! As a result, everyone from the ruler of the nation on down to the common people believes that there are no true sutras outside the three Pure Land sutras, and no Buddhas other than the Buddha Amida with his two attendants.34

Once there were men like Dengyō, Gishin, Jikaku, and Chishō who journeyed ten thousand miles across the waves to China to acquire the sacred teachings, and there visited the mountains and rivers to pay reverence to Buddhist statues [and carry them back]. In some cases they built holy temples on the peaks of high mountains in which to preserve those scriptures and statues; in other cases they constructed sacred halls in the bottoms of deep valleys where such objects could be worshiped and honored. As a result, the Buddhas Shakyamuni and Medicine Master35 shone side by side, casting their influence upon present and future ages, while the bodhisattvas Space Treasury and Earth

Repository brought benefit to the living and the dead. The rulers of the nation contributed districts or villages so that the lamps might continue to burn bright before the images, while the stewards of the great estates gave their fields and gardens as an offering.

But because of this book by Hōnen, this Nembutsu Chosen above All, the lord of teachings, Shakyamuni, is forgotten, and all honor is paid to Amida, the Buddha of the Western Land. The transmission of the Law [from Shakyamuni Buddha] is ignored,36 and Medicine Master, the Thus Come One of the Eastern Region, is neglected. Attention is paid only to the three Pure Land sutras in four volumes, and all the other wonderful scriptures that Shakyamuni expounded throughout the five periods of his preaching life are cast aside. If temples are not dedicated to Amida, then people no longer have any desire to support them or pay honor to the Buddhas enshrined there; if priests are not practitioners of the Nembutsu, then people quickly forget all about giving those priests alms. As a result, the halls of the Buddha have fallen into ruin, scarcely a wisp of smoke rising above their moss-covered roof tiles; and the priests' quarters have become empty and dilapidated, the dew deep on the grasses in their courtyards. And in spite of such conditions, no one gives a thought to protecting the Law or to restoring the temples. Hence the sage priests who once presided over the p.15temples leave and do not return, and the benevolent deities who guarded the nation depart and no longer appear. This has all come about because of this Nembutsu Chosen above All by Hōnen. How pitiful to think that, in the space of a few decades, hundreds, thousands, tens of thousands of people have been deluded by these devilish teachings and in so many cases confused as to the true teachings of Buddhism. If people favor what is only incidental and forget what is primary, can the benevolent deities be anything but angry? If people cast aside what is perfect and take up what is biased, can the world escape the plots of demons? Rather than offering up ten thousand prayers for remedy, it would be better simply to outlaw this one evil .

This time the guest was truly enraged and said: In the ages since our original teacher, the Buddha Shakyamuni, preached the three Pure Land sutras, the Dharma Teacher T'an-luan had originally studied the four treatises,37 but abandoned them and put all his strong mind of determination in the Pure Land teachings. Similarly, the Meditation Master Tao-ch'o ceased to spread the varied practices of the Nirvana Sutra and devoted all his attention to propagating the practice that leads one to the Western Pure Land. The Reverend Shan-tao discarded the sundry practices and established the single practice of the Nembutsu, and the Supervisor of Priests Eshin collected essential passages from various sutras to form his work, making the single practice of the Nembutsu the essence of his teaching. Such was the manner in which these men honored and respected the Buddha Amida, and uncountable numbers of people as a result were able to gain rebirth in the Pure Land.

Of particular note was the Sage Hōnen, who as a child entered the monastery on Mount Hiei. By the time he was seventeen, he had worked his way through all sixty volumes of Tendai literature,38 and had investigated all the eight schools and mastered their essentials. In addition, he had read through the entire body of sutras and treatises seven times, and exhausted all the works of exegesis and biography. His wisdom shone like the sun and moon, and his virtue exceeded that of the earlier teachers.

In spite of all this, he was in doubt as to the proper path to emancipation and could not make out the true meaning of nirvana. Therefore, he read and examined all the texts he could, pondered deeply and considered every possibility, and in the end put aside all the sutras and concentrated on the single practice of the Nembutsu. In addition, he received confirmation of his decision when Shan-tao miraculously appeared to him in a dream,39 and he proceeded to spread his doctrines among friends and strangers in all four corners of the land. Thereafter, he was hailed as a reincarnation of Bodhisattva Great Power, or was revered as Shan-tao reborn. In every quarter, people of eminent and lowly birth alike bowed their heads in respect, and men and women from all over Japan sought him.

Since that time, the springs and autumns have succeeded each other, and the years have piled upon years. And yet you insist upon putting aside the venerable teachings of Shakyamuni Buddha [contained in the Pure Land sutras] and willfully speak evil of the passage describing the oath of the Buddha Amida. Why do you try to blame the sacred age of Hōnen for the disasters of recent years, going out of your way to slander the former teachers of Pure Land doctrines and to heap abuse on the Sage Hōnen? You are, as the saying goes, deliberately blowing back the fur and hunting for flaws in the leather, deliberately piercing the skin in hopes of drawing blood. From ancient times to the present, the world has p.16never seen such a speaker of evil. You had better learn a little caution and restraint. When you pile up such grave offenses, how can you hope to escape punishment? I am afraid even to sit here in your company. I must take up my staff and be on my way!

The host, smiling, restrained his guest and said: Insects that live on smartweed forget how bitter it tastes; those who stay long in privies forget how foul the smell is. Here you listen to my good words and think them wicked, point to a slanderer of the Law and call him a sage, mistrust a correct teacher and take him for an evil priest. Your confusion is great indeed, and your offense anything but light. Listen to my explanation of how this confusion arose, and let us discuss the matter in detail.

Shakyamuni Buddha expounded the five periods of doctrines, established the order in which they were preached, and divided them into the provisional and the true teachings. But T'an-luan, Tao-ch'o, and Shan-tao embraced the provisional teachings and forgot about the true ones, went by what had been taught in the earlier period of the Buddha's life and discarded what was taught later. They were not the kind of men who delve into the deep places of Buddhist doctrine.

Hōnen in particular, though he followed the practices advocated by these earlier men, was ignorant as to their source. How do we know this? Because he lumped together all the 637 Mahayana scriptures in 2,883 volumes and along with them all the Buddhas and bodhisattvas and the deities of this world, and urged people to "discard, close, ignore, and abandon" them, with these four injunctions corrupting the hearts of all people. Thus he poured out perverted words of his own invention and took absolutely no cognizance of the explanations put forth in the Buddhist scriptures. His is the worst kind of baseless talk, a clear case of defamation. There are no words to describe it, no way to censure it that is not too mild. And yet people all put strong mind of determination in this baseless talk of his, and without exception pay honor to his Nembutsu Chosen above All. As a consequence, they revere the three sutras of the Pure Land and cast all the other sutras aside; they look up to one Buddha alone, Amida of the Land of Perfect Bliss, and forget about the other Buddhas. A man such as Hōnen is in truth the archenemy of the Buddhas and the scriptures, and the foe of sage priests and ordinary men and women alike. And now his distorted teachings have spread throughout the eight regions of the country, permeating the ten directions.

You became quite horrified when I blamed an earlier period[40] for the disasters that have occurred in recent years. Perhaps I should cite a few examples from the past to show you that you are mistaken in your feelings.

The second volume of Great Concentration and Insight quotes a passage from Records of the Historian that says, "In the closing years of the Chou dynasty, there were persons who let their hair hang down, went about naked to the waist, and did not observe the rites and regulations." The Annotations on "Great Concentration and Insight," in the second volume, explains this passage by quoting from Tso's Commentary on "Spring and Autumn Annals" as follows: "When King P'ing of the Chou first moved his capital to the east, he saw men by the Yi River who let their hair hang down and performed sacrifices in the fields. Someone who had great understanding said, 'In less than a hundred years the dynasty will fall, for the rites are already neglected.'" From this it is evident that the portent appears first, and later the disaster itself comes about.

[The Great Concentration and Insight p.17passage goes on to say:] "Juan Chi41 was a man of extraordinary talent, but he let his hair grow like a mass of brambles and left his belt undone. Later, the sons of the aristocracy all imitated him, until those who behaved in a churlish and insulting manner were thought to be acting quite naturally, and those who were restrained and proper in their behavior were ridiculed as mere peasants. This was a sign that the Ssu-ma family [the rulers of the Western Chin dynasty] would meet with their downfall."

Similarly, The Record of a Pilgrimage to China in Search of the Law by the Great Teacher Jikaku states that, in the first year of the Hui-ch'ang era (841), Emperor Wu-tsung of the T'ang dynasty commanded the priest Ching-shuang of Chang-ching-ssu temple to transmit the Nembutsu teachings of the Buddha Amida in the various temples. Ching-shuang spent three days in each temple, going about from one temple to another without ever ceasing.

In the second year of the same era, soldiers from the land of the Uighurs42 invaded the borders of the T'ang empire. In the third year of the same era, the regional commander in the area north of the Yellow River suddenly raised a revolt. Later, the kingdom of Tibet once more refused to obey orders from China, and the Uighurs repeatedly seized Chinese territory. On the whole, the conflicts and uprisings were like those that prevailed at the time when the Ch'in dynasty and the military leader Hsiang Yü were overthrown, and the towns and villages were devastated by fire and other disasters. What was even worse, Emperor Wu-tsung carried out a vast campaign to wipe out Buddhist teachings and destroyed a great many temples and pagodas. He was never able to put down the uprisings and died in agony shortly after. (This is the essence of Jikaku's original passage.)

In view of these events, we should consider the fact that Hōnen belonged to the time of the Retired Emperor Gotoba, around the Kennin era (1201–1204). And what happened to the retired emperor is evident before our very eyes.43 Thus T'ang China provided an earlier example of the fall of an emperor, and our own country offers similar proof. You should neither doubt this nor consider it strange. The only thing to do now is to abandon the evil ways and take up those that are good, to cut off this affliction at the source, to cut it off at the root.

The guest, looking somewhat mollified, said: Though I have not yet probed deeply into the matter, I believe I understand to some degree what you are saying. Nevertheless, throughout the area from Kyoto, the capital, to Kamakura, the headquarters of the shogun, there are numerous eminent Buddhist leaders and key figures in the clergy. And yet none of them has so far appealed to the shogun concerning this affair, or submitted a memorial to the throne. You, on the other hand, a person of humble position, think nothing of spewing out offensive accusations. Your assertion goes too far and your behavior is unreasonable.

The host said: Though I may be a person of little ability, I have reverently given myself to the study of the Mahayana. A blue fly, if it clings to the tail of a thoroughbred horse, can travel ten thousand miles, and the green ivy that twines around the tall pine can grow to a thousand feet. I was born as the son of the one Buddha, Shakyamuni, and I serve the king of scriptures, the Lotus Sutra. How could I observe the decline of the Buddhist Law and not be filled with emotions of pity and distress?

Moreover, the Nirvana Sutra states: "If even a good monk sees someone destroying the teaching and disregards him, failing to reproach him, to oust p.18him, or to punish him for his offense, then you should realize that that monk is betraying the Buddha's teaching. But if he ousts the destroyer of the Law, reproaches him, or punishes him, then he is my disciple and a true voice-hearer."

Although I may not be a "good monk," I certainly do not want to be accused of "betraying the Buddha's teaching." Therefore, in order to avoid such charges, I have cited a few general principles and given a rough explanation of the matter.

Earlier, in the Gennin era (1224–1225), petitions to the throne were submitted time and again by the two temples of Enryaku-ji and Kōfuku-ji. And as a result, an imperial command and a letter of instruction from the shogunate were handed down, ordering that the woodblocks used in printing Hōnen's Nembutsu Chosen above All be confiscated and brought to the Great Lecture Hall of Enryaku-ji. There they were burned in order to repay the debt owed to the Buddhas of the three existences. In addition, orders were given that the menials at Kanjin-in Shrine should dig up and destroy Hōnen's grave. Then, Hōnen's disciples Ryūkan, Shōkō, Jōkaku, Sasshō, and others were condemned by the imperial court to exile in distant regions and were never pardoned.

In view of these facts, how can you say that no one has submitted a complaint to the authorities concerning these matters?

The guest, continuing to speak in a mild manner, replied: One could hardly say that Hōnen is the only one who disparages sutras and speaks ill of other priests [since you do the same thing yourself]. However, it is true that he takes the 637 Mahayana scriptures in 2,883 volumes, along with all the Buddhas and bodhisattvas and the deities of this world, and urges people to "discard, close, ignore, and abandon" them. There is no doubt that these four injunctions are his very words; the meaning of the passage is quite clear. But you keep harping on this one little "flaw in the jewel" and severely slandering him for it. I do not know whether he spoke out of delusion or out of enlightenment. Between you and Hōnen, I cannot tell which is wise and which is foolish, or determine whose assertions are right and whose are wrong.

However, you assert that all the recent disasters are to be traced to Nembutsu

Chosen above All, speaking quite volubly on that point and elaborating on the meaning of your assertion. Now surely the peace of the world and the stability of the nation are sought by both ruler and subject and desired by all the inhabitants of the country. The nation achieves prosperity through the Buddhist Law, and the Law is proven worthy of reverence by the people who embrace it. If the nation is destroyed and the people are wiped out, then who will continue to pay reverence to the Buddhas? Who will continue to have strong mind of determination in the Law? Therefore, one must first of all pray for the safety of the nation and then work to establish the Buddhist Law.44 Now if you know of any means whereby disasters can be prevented and troubles brought to an end, I would like to hear about it.

The host said: There is no doubt that I am the foolish one—I would never dare claim to be wise. However, I would just like to quote some passages from the scriptures and offer some brief thoughts. Concerning the means for insuring order in the nation, there are numerous passages in both Buddhist and non-Buddhist texts, and it would be difficult to cite them all here. Since taking up the study of Buddhism, however, I have frequently given thought to this matter, and it seems to me that restraining those who slander the Law and respecting the followers of the correct way will assure p.19 stability within the nation and peace in the world at large.

In the Nirvana Sutra, we read: "The Buddha said, 'With the exception of one type of person, you may offer alms to all kinds of persons, and everyone will praise you.'

"Chunda said, 'What do you mean when you speak of "one type of person"?'

"The Buddha replied, 'I mean the type described in this sutra as violators of the precepts.'

"Chunda spoke again, saying, 'I am afraid I still do not understand. May I ask you to explain further?'

"The Buddha addressed Chunda, saying, 'By violators of the precepts, I mean the icchantika. In the case of all other types of persons, you may offer alms, everyone will praise you, and you will achieve great rewards.'

"Chunda spoke once more, asking, 'What is the meaning of the term icchantika?'

"The Buddha said: 'Chunda, suppose there should be monks or nuns, lay men or women who speak careless and evil words and slander the correct teaching, and that they should go on committing these grave acts without ever showing any inclination to reform or any sign of repentance in their hearts. Persons of this kind I would say are following the path of the icchantika.

"'Again there may be those who commit the four grave offenses45 or are guilty of the five cardinal sins, and who, though aware that they are guilty of serious faults, from the beginning have no trace of fear or contrition in their hearts or, if they do, give no outward sign of it. When it comes to the correct teaching, they show no inclination to protect, treasure, and establish it over the ages, but rather speak of it with malice and contempt, their words replete with error. People of this kind too I would say are following the path of the icchantika. With the exception of this one group of people called icchantika, however, you may offer alms to all others, and everyone will praise you.'"

Elsewhere in the same sutra, the Buddha spoke in these words: "When I recall the past, I remember that I was the king of a great state in this continent of Jambudvīpa. My name was Sen'yo, and I loved and venerated the great vehicle scriptures. My heart was pure and good and had no trace of evil, jealousy, or stinginess. Good men, at that time I cherished the great vehicle teachings in my heart. When I heard the Brahmans slandering these correct and equal sutras, I put them to death on the spot. Good men, as a result of that action, I never thereafter fell into hell."

In another passage it says, "In the past, when the Thus Come One was the ruler of a nation and practiced the way of the bodhisattva, he put to death a number of Brahmans."

Again it says: "There are three degrees of killings: the lower, middle, and upper degrees. The lower degree constitutes the killing of any humble being, from an ant to any of the various kinds of animals. But the killing of any being that a bodhisattva has chosen to be born as [to help other living beings] is excluded. As a result of a killing of the lower degree, one will fall into the realms of hell, hungry spirits, and animals, and will suffer all the pains appropriate to a killing of the lower degree. Why should this be? Because even animals and other humble beings possess the roots of goodness, insignificant though those roots may be. That is why a person who kills such a being must suffer full retribution for his offense.

"Killing any person from an ordinary mortal to an anāgāmin46 constitutes what is termed the middle degree. As a consequence of such an act p.20of killing, one will fall into the realms of hell, hungry spirits, and animals, and will suffer all the pains appropriate to a killing of the middle degree. The upper degree of killing refers to the killing of a parent, an

Arhat, a pratyekabuddha, or a bodhisattva who has reached the stage of non-retrogression. For such a crime one will fall into the great Avīchi hell. Good men, if someone were to kill an icchantika, that killing would not fall into any of the three categories just mentioned. Good men, the various Brahmans that I have said were put to death—all of them were in fact icchantikas."

In the Benevolent Kings Sutra, we read: "The Buddha announced to King Prasenajit, 'Thus I entrust the protection of my teachings to the ruler of the nation rather than to the monks and nuns. Why do I do so? Because they do not possess the kind of power and authority that the king has.'"

The Nirvana Sutra states: "Now I entrust the correct teaching, which is unexcelled, to the rulers, the ministers, the high officials, and the four kinds of Buddhists. If anyone should vilify the correct teaching, then the ministers and four kinds of Buddhists should reprimand him and bring him to order."

It also states: "The Buddha replied: '[Bodhisattva] Kāshyapa, it is because I was a defender of the correct teaching that I have been able to attain this diamond-like body. . . . Good man, defenders of the correct teaching need not observe the five precepts or practice the rules of proper behavior. Rather they should carry knives and swords, bows and arrows, halberds and lances.'"

Again the Buddha said: "Even though there may be those who observe the five precepts, they do not deserve to be called practitioners of the great vehicle. But even if one does not observe the five precepts, if one defends the correct teaching, then one may be called a practitioner of the great vehicle. Defenders of the correct teaching ought to arm themselves with knives and swords, weapons and staves. Even though they carry swords and staves, I would call them men who observe the precepts."

The Buddha likewise said: "Good man, in past ages in this very city of Kushinagara, a Buddha appeared whose name was the Thus Come One Joy Increasing. After this Buddha passed away, the correct teaching that he had taught remained in the world for countless millions of years. Finally, only forty more years were left before the Buddhist teaching was due to come to an end.

"At that time there was a monk named Realization of Virtue who observed the precepts. There were many monks at this time who violated the precepts, and when they heard this monk preaching, they all conceived evil designs in their hearts and, arming themselves with swords and staves, approached this teacher of the Law.

"At this time the ruler of the kingdom was named Possessor of Virtue. He received reports of what was happening, and, in order to defend the teaching, he went at once to the place where the monk was preaching the Law and fought with all his might against the evil monks who broke the precepts. As a result, the monk who had been preaching was able to escape grievous injury. But the king received so many wounds from the knives and swords, halberds and lances, that there was not a spot on his body the size of a mustard seed that remained unharmed.

"At this time the monk Realization of Virtue praised the king, saying: 'Splendid, splendid! You, O king, are now a true defender of the correct teaching. In ages to come, this body of yours will surely become a boundless vessel of the Law!'

p.21"At that time, the king had already heard the teaching, and he felt great joy in his heart. Thereupon his life came to an end, and he was reborn in the land of the Buddha Akshobhya, where he became the Buddha's principal disciple. Moreover, all the military leaders, citizens, and associates of the king who had fought beside him or had rejoiced in his effort were filled with an unflagging determination to achieve enlightenment, and when they died, all of them were reborn in the land of the Buddha Akshobhya.

"Later, the monk Realization of Virtue also died, and he too was reborn in the land of the Buddha Akshobhya, where he became second among the Buddha's voice-hearer disciples. Thus, if the correct teaching is about to come to an end, this is the way one ought to support and defend it.

"Kāshyapa, the king who lived at that time was I myself, and the monk who preached was the Buddha Kāshyapa.47 Kāshyapa, those who defend the correct teaching enjoy this kind of boundless reward. As a consequence, I have been able to obtain the distinguished characteristics that I possess today, to adorn myself with them, and to put on the Dharma body that can never be destroyed."

Then the Buddha declared to Bodhisattva Kāshyapa: "For this reason, laymen believers and others who wish to defend the Law should arm themselves with swords and staves and protect it in this manner.

"Good man, in the age of impurity and evil after I have passed away, the nation will fall into devastation and disorder, men will plunder and steal from one another, and the common people will be reduced to starvation. Because of hunger, many men at that time will declare their determination to leave their families and become monks. Men such as these may be called shavepates.48 When this crowd of shavepates see anyone who is attempting to protect the correct teaching, they will chase after him and drive him away, or even kill him or do him injury. That is why I now give permission for monks who observe the precepts to associate with and keep company with white-robed laymen who bear swords and staves. Even though they carry swords and staves, I would call them men who observe the precepts. But although they may carry swords and staves, they should never use them to take life."

The Lotus Sutra says: "If a person fails to have strong mind of determination but instead slanders this sutra, immediately he will destroy all the seeds for becoming a Buddha in this world. . . . When his life comes to an end he will enter the Avīchi hell."

The meaning of these passages from the sutras is perfectly clear. What need is there for me to add any further explanation? If we accept the words of the Lotus Sutra, then we must understand that slandering the Mahayana scriptures is more serious than committing the five cardinal sins countless times. Therefore, one who does so will be confined in the great citadel of the Avīchi hell and cannot hope for release for an immeasurable length of time. According to the Nirvana Sutra, even though you may give alms to a person who has committed the five cardinal sins, you must never give alms to a person who has slandered the Law. One who kills so much as an ant will invariably fall into the three evil paths, but one who helps eradicate slander of the Law will ascend to the state from which there can be no retrogression. Thus the passage tells us that the monk Realization of Virtue was reborn as the Buddha Kāshyapa, and that King Possessor of Virtue was reborn as the Buddha Shakyamuni.

The Lotus and the Nirvana sutras represent the very heart of the doctrines that Shakyamuni preached during the five periods of his teaching life. Their warnings must be viewed with the utmost gravity. Who would fail to heed them? And yet those people who forget about the correct way and slander the Law put more trust than ever in Hōnen's Nembutsu Chosen above All and grow blinder than ever in their foolishness.

Thus some of them, remembering how their master looked in life, fashion wooden sculptures and paintings of him, while others, putting strong mind of determination in his perverse teachings, carve woodblocks with which to print his ugly words. These writings they scatter about throughout the area bounded by the seas, carrying them beyond the cities and into the countryside until, wherever honor is paid, it is to the practices of this school, and wherever alms are given, it is to the priests of this school.

As a result, we see people cutting off the fingers of the images of Shakyamuni and refashioning them to form the gesture of Amida, or converting the temples formerly dedicated to Medicine Master, the Thus Come One of the Eastern Region, and replacing his statues with those of Amida, the Thus Come One of the Western Land. Or we find the ceremony of copying the Lotus Sutra, which had been carried out for over four hundred years on Mount Hiei, being suspended and the copying of the three Pure Land sutras substituted in its place, or the annual lectures49 on the doctrines of the Great Teacher T'ien-t'ai being replaced by lectures on the teachings of Shan-tao. Indeed, the slanderous people and their associates are too numerous to count. Are they not destroyers of the Buddha? Are they not destroyers of the Law? Are they not destroyers of the Buddhist Order? And all their distorted teachings derive from Nembutsu Chosen above All.

Alas, how pitiful that people should turn their backs on the true words of prohibition spoken by the Thus Come One [Shakyamuni]! How tragic that they should heed the gross and deluded words of this ignorant priest! If we hope to bring order and tranquility to the world without further delay, we must put an end to these slanders of the Law that fill the country.

The guest said: If we are to put an end to these people who slander the Law and do away with those who violate the prohibitions of the Buddha, then are we to condemn them to death as described in the sutra passages you have just cited? If we do that, then we ourselves will be guilty of inflicting injury and death upon others, and will suffer the consequences, will we not?

In the Great Collection Sutra, the Buddha says: "If a person shaves his head and puts on clerical robes, then, whether that person observes the precepts or violates them, both heavenly and human beings should give him alms. In doing so, they are giving alms and support to me, for that person is my son. But if men beat that person, they are beating my son, and if they curse and insult him, they are reviling me."

If we stop to consider, we must realize that, regardless of whether one is good or bad, right or wrong, if he is a priest, then he deserves to have alms and nourishment extended to him. For how could one beat and insult the son and still not cause grief and sorrow to the father? The Brahmans of the Bamboo Staff School who killed the Venerable Maudgalyāyana have for a long time been sunk in the depths of the hell of incessant suffering. Because Devadatta murdered the nun Utpalavarṇā, he has for a long time gasped in the flames of the Avīchi hell. Examples from earlier ages make the matter perfectly clear, and later ages fear this offense most of all. You speak of punishing those who slander the Law, but to do so would violate the Buddha's p.23prohibitions. I can hardly believe that such a course would be right. How can you justify that?

The host said: You have clearly seen the sutra passages that I have cited, and yet you can ask a question like that! Are they beyond the power of your mind to comprehend? Or do you fail to understand the reasoning behind them? I certainly have no intention of censuring the sons of the Buddha. My only hatred is for the act of slandering the Law. According to the Buddhist teachings, prior to Shakyamuni slanderous monks would have incurred the death penalty. But since the time of Shakyamuni, the One Who Can Endure, the giving of alms to slanderous monks is forbidden in the sutra teachings. Now if all the four kinds of Buddhists within the four seas and the ten thousand lands would only cease giving alms to wicked priests and instead all come over to the side of the good, then how could any more troubles rise to plague us, or disasters come to confront us?

With this the guest moved off his mat in a gesture of respect, straightened the collar of his robe, and said: The Buddhist teachings vary greatly, and it is difficult to investigate each doctrine in full. I have had many doubts and perplexities, and have been unable to distinguish right from wrong.

Nevertheless, this work by the Sage Hōnen, Nembutsu Chosen above All, does in fact exist. And it lumps together all the various Buddhas, sutras, bodhisattvas, and deities, and says that one should "discard, close, ignore, and abandon" them. The meaning of the text is perfectly clear. And as a result of this, the sages have departed from the nation, the benevolent deities have left their dwelling places, hunger and thirst fill the world, and disease and pestilence spread widely.

Now, by citing passages from a wide variety of scriptures, you have clearly demonstrated the rights and wrongs of the matter. Therefore, I have completely forsaken my earlier mistaken convictions, and my ears and eyes have been opened on point after point.

There can be no doubt that all people, from the ruler on down to the general populace, rejoice in and desire the stability of the nation and the peace of the world. If we can quickly put an end to the alms that are given to these icchantikas and insure that continuing support is instead given to the host of true priests and nuns, if we can still these "white waves"50 that trouble the ocean of the Buddha and cut down these "green groves" that overgrow the mountain of the Law, then the world may become as peaceful as it was in the golden ages of Fu Hsi and Shen Nung, and the nation may flourish as it did under the sage rulers Yao and Shun.51 After that, there will be time to dip into the waters of the Law and to decide which are shallow doctrines and which are deep, and to pay honor to the pillars and beams that support the house of the Buddha.

The host exclaimed with delight: The dove has changed into a hawk, the sparrow into a clam.52 How gratifying! You have associated with a friend in the orchid room and have become as straight as mugwort growing among hemp.53 If you will truly give consideration to the troubles I have been describing and put entire strong mind of determination in these words of mine, then the winds will blow gently, the waves will be calm, and in no time at all we will enjoy bountiful harvests.

But a person's heart may change with the times, and the nature of a thing may alter with its surroundings. Just as the moon on the water will be tossed about by the waves, or the soldiers in the vanguard will be cowed by the swords of the enemy, so, although at this moment you may say you believe in my words, I fear that later p.24you will forget them completely.

Now if we wish first of all to bring security to the nation and to pray for our present and future lives, then we must hasten to examine and consider the situation and take measures as soon as possible to remedy it.

Why do I say this? Because, of the seven types of disasters described in the Medicine Master Sutra, five have already occurred. Only two have yet to appear, the calamity of invasion from foreign lands and the calamity of revolt within one's own domain. And of the three calamities mentioned in the Great Collection Sutra, two have already made their appearance. Only one remains, the disaster of warfare.

The different types of disaster and calamity enumerated in the Golden Light Sutra have arisen one after the other. Only that described as marauders from other regions invading and plundering the nation has yet to materialize. This is the only trouble that has not yet come. And of the seven disasters listed in the Benevolent Kings Sutra, six are now upon us in full force. Only one has not yet appeared the calamity that occurs "when enemies rise up on all four sides and invade the nation."

Moreover, as the Benevolent Kings Sutra says: "When a nation becomes disordered, it is the spirits that first show signs of rampancy. Because the spirits become rampant, all the people of the nation become disordered."

Now if we examine the present situation carefully in the light of this passage, we will see that the various spirits have for some time been rampant, and many of the people have perished. If the first predicted misfortune in the sutra has already occurred, as is obvious, then how can we doubt that the later disasters will follow? If, in punishment for the evil doctrines that are upheld, the troubles that have yet to appear should fall upon us one after the other, then it will be too late to act, will it not?

Emperors and kings have their foundation in the state and bring peace and order to the age; ministers and commoners hold possession of their fields and gardens and supply the needs of the world. But if marauders come from other regions to invade the nation, or if revolt breaks out within the domain and people's lands are seized and plundered, how can there be anything but terror and confusion? If the nation is destroyed and people's homes are wiped out, then where can one flee for safety? If you care anything about your personal security, you should first of all pray for order and tranquility throughout the four quarters of the land, should you not?

It seems to me that when people are in this world they all fear what their lot may be in the life to come. So it is that they put their strong mind of determination in distorted doctrines and pay honor to slanderous teachings. It distresses me that they should be so confused about right and wrong, and at the same time I feel pity that, having embraced Buddhism, they should have chosen the wrong kind. With the power of strong mind of determination that is in their hearts, why must they recklessly give credence to distorted doctrines? If they do not shake off these delusions that they cling to but continue to harbor erroneous views, then they will quickly leave this world of the living and surely fall into the hell of incessant suffering.

Thus the Great Collection Sutra says: "Though for countless existences in the past the ruler of a state may have practiced the giving of alms, observed the precepts, and cultivated wisdom, if he sees that my teaching is in danger of perishing and stands idly by without doing anything to protect it, then all the inestimable roots of goodness that he has planted through the practices just mentioned will be entirely wiped p.25out . . . Before long, the ruler will fall gravely ill, and after his life has come to an end, he will be reborn in the great hell. . . . And the same fate will befall the ruler's consort, his heir, the high ministers of the state, the lords of cities, the village heads and generals, the magistrates of districts, and the other officials."

The Benevolent Kings Sutra states: "If persons destroy the teachings of the Buddha, they will have no filial sons, no harmony with their six kinds of relatives,54 and no aid from the heavenly deities and dragons. Disease and evil demons will come day after day to torment them, disasters will descend on them incessantly, and misfortunes will dog them wherever they go. And when they die, they will fall into the realms of hell, hungry spirits, and animals. Even if they should be reborn as human beings, they will be destined to become soldiers or slaves. Retribution will follow as an echo follows a sound, or a shadow follows a form. Someone writing at night may put out the lamp, but the words he has written will still remain. It is the same with the effect of the deeds we perform in the threefold world."

The second volume of the Lotus Sutra says, "If a person fails to have strong mind of determination but instead slanders this sutra . . . When his life comes to an end he will enter the Avīchi hell." And in the "Never Disparaging" chapter in the seventh volume, it says, "For a thousand kalpas they underwent great suffering in the Avīchi hell."

In the Nirvana Sutra, we read: "If a person separates himself from good friends, refuses to listen to the correct teaching, and instead embraces evil teachings, then as a result he will sink down into the Avīchi hell, where the size of his body will become eighty-four thousand yojanas in total length and breadth."55

When we examine this wide variety of sutras, we find that they all stress how grave a matter it is to slander the correct teaching. How pitiful that people should all go out of the gate of the correct teaching and enter so deep into the prison of these distorted doctrines! How stupid that they should fall one after another into the snares of these evil doctrines and remain for so long entangled in this net of slanderous teachings! They lose their way in these mists and miasmas, and sink down amid the raging flames of hell. How could one not grieve? How could one not suffer?

Therefore, you must quickly reform the tenets that you hold in your heart and embrace the one true vehicle, the single good doctrine [of the Lotus Sutra]. If you do so, then the threefold world will become the Buddha land, and how could a Buddha land ever decline? The regions in the ten directions will all become treasure realms, and how could a treasure realm ever suffer harm? If you live in a country that knows no decline or diminution, in a land that suffers no harm or disruption, then your body will find peace and security, and your mind will be calm and untroubled. You must believe my words; heed what I say!

The guest said: Since it concerns both this life and the lives to come, who could fail to be cautious in a matter such as this? Who could fail to agree with you? Now when I examine the passages you have cited from the sutras and see exactly what the Buddha has said, I realize that slandering the Law is a very grave fault indeed that violating the Law is in truth a terrible offense. I have put all my strong mind of determination in one Buddha alone, Amida, and rejected all the other Buddhas. I have honored the three Pure Land sutras and set aside the other sutras. But this was not due to any distorted ideas of my own conception. I was simply obeying the words of the eminent men of the past. And the p.26same is true of all the other persons in the ten directions.

But now I realize that to do so means to exhaust oneself in futile efforts in this life and to fall into the Avīchi hell in the life to come. The texts you have cited are perfectly clear on this point, and their arguments are detailed—they leave no room for doubt. From now on, with your kind instruction to guide me, I wish to continue dispelling the ignorance from my mind. I hope we may set about as quickly as possible taking measures to deal with these slanders against the Law and to bring peace to the world without delay, thus insuring that we may live in safety in this life and enjoy good fortune in the life to come. But it is not enough that I alone should accept and have strong mind of determination in your words—we must see to it that others as well are warned of their errors.

Background

On the twenty-eighth day of the fourth month, 1253, Nichiren Shonin established the teaching of Nam-Myoho-Renge-Kyo at Seichō-ji temple in his native province of Awa, and later he returned to Kamakura, the seat of the military government, to begin propagation. In examining the records, we find that in those days the era names were changed frequently. The year 1253 was in the Kenchō era. Three years later, in 1256, the era name changed to Kōgen, and the next year, to Shōka. Then, two years later, in 1259, it was changed to Shōgen, the following year to Bunnō, and the year after that to Kōchō. In the five years from 1256 to 1261, the era name changed five times. An era name was usually changed only on the accession of a new emperor, or when some natural disaster of severe proportions occurred; the frequency of these changes attests to the magnitude of the disasters that struck Japan during this period.

Soon after the Shonin's arrival, Kamakura and the country as a whole faced a series of disasters and conflicts that served to emphasize his conviction that the Latter Day of the Law had indeed been entered upon. On the sixth day of the eighth month of 1256, torrential rainstorms caused floods and landslides, destroying crops and devastating much of Kamakura. In the ninth month of the same year, an epidemic swept through the city, taking many lives. During the fifth, eighth, and eleventh months of 1257, violent earthquakes rocked the city, and the sixth and seventh months witnessed a disastrous drought. Most frightful of all was an earthquake of unprecedented scale that occurred on the twenty-third day of the eighth month. The year 1258 witnessed no lessening of natural calamities. The eighth month saw storms destroy crops throughout the nation, and floods in Kamakura drowned numerous people. In the tenth month of the same year, Kamakura was visited by heavy rains and severe floods. In the first month of 1258, fires consumed Jufuku-ji temple, and in 1259, epidemics and famine were rampant, and a violent rainstorm decimated crops.

Nichiren Shonin sought answers to the cause of these disasters in the scriptural writings of Buddhism. In an effort to clarify it, he went to

Jissō-ji temple at Iwamoto in Suruga Province, and he stayed there from 1258 through the middle of 1260. As a major temple of the Tendai school in eastern Japan, p.27 Jissō-ji housed many important sutras in its scripture library. The Shonin pored over them all.

As a result, Nichiren Shonin found evidence for his theory in such sutras as the Benevolent Kings, Medicine Master, Great Collection, and Golden Light. He quotes passages from these sutras in the present text, On Establishing the Correct Teaching for the Peace of the Land, chronologically the first of his five major works.

The work was originally written in classical Chinese and submitted to Hōjō Tokiyori through the offices of high-ranking government official Yadoya Mitsunori on the sixteenth day of the seventh month in the first year of Bunnō (1260). Tokiyori was then living in retirement, but was still the most influential member of the ruling Hōjō clan. The work occasioned no immediate reaction, and no official response was made to the Shonin. But the members of the government were incensed at the rational but unrelenting attack that the work made on the Pure Land teachings of Hōnen and his followers. Government officials who were Pure Land followers apparently encouraged an attack made on the Shonin's dwelling at

Matsubagayatsu in Kamakura on the twenty-seventh day of the eighth month. The Shonin narrowly escaped and made his way to the province of Shimōsa to stay at the home of a follower. He returned to Kamakura early in the following year, 1261. He remained continually under the threat of persecution and was summarily banished to Izu on the twelfth day of the fifth month of the same year.

The work consists of a dialogue between a host and a visitor. The host represents Nichiren Shonin, and the visitor, it is thought, represents Hōjō Tokiyori. At the outset, the host lays the blame for the disasters that have befallen the country on the belief in an erroneous religion, the Pure Land teachings of Hōnen. Presented are numerous scriptural references to disasters that will befall a nation that follows false teachings. The Shonin puts particular emphasis on a passage in the Medicine Master Sutra that describes seven types of disasters that will strike such a nation. Of these calamities, he points out, five have already occurred, and two, the "calamity of invasion from foreign lands" and the "calamity of revolt within one's own domain," have yet to occur. The Shonin cautions that these will come about if the doctrines of the Lotus Sutra are not followed. Later, the prophecies of internal strife and foreign invasion were fulfilled when Hōjō Tokisuke revolted against his younger half-brother, Regent Hōjō Tokimune, in 1272, and when the Mongols attacked Japan twice, in 1274 and 1281.

In terms of its view of the relationship between the people's religious beliefs and the realization of a peaceful society, On Establishing the Correct Teaching holds an important position in Nichiren Shonin's writings. The Shonin lived at a time of authoritarian government, and he probably felt that through an appeal to the most powerful members of the government he could help bring about a reformation of society. That his appeal was ignored only spurred his unremitting effort to propagate his teaching for the peace and happiness of society, a task he would pursue to the end of his life.

Notes

1. Reference is to a passage in Shan-tao's praising the Meditation to Behold the Buddha, in which he says that calling on the name of Amida Buddha serves as a sword to cut off earthly desires, karma, and suffering.

p.282. One of the twelve vows of the Buddha Medicine Master, which appear in the

Medicine Master Sutra. As a bodhisattva he made these vows to cure all illnesses and lead all people to enlightenment.

3. Lotus Sutra, chap. 23. This is a reference to a practice of the Tendai school.

4. Benevolent Kings Sutra. This is another reference to the Tendai school, which held a ritual of prayer based on this passage.

5. According to the Benevolent Kings Sutra, a type of ceremony originally held by the god Shakra to defeat the evil king Born from the Crown of the Head.

6. Ritual in which priests of the True Word school placed five jars, colored white, blue, red, yellow, and black, on a platform and put into them, respectively, gold, silver, lapis lazuli, pearls, and crystal. In addition, they placed in these jars the five grains, five herbs, and five types of incense, and then filled them with water and set flowers in them. The ritual of filling the jars in this manner was believed to drive away disasters.

7. Reference is to the practice of the Zen school.

8. The names of the seven guardian spirits appear in the Mysterious Spells for Eliminating the Illnesses of the Five Components Sutra.

9. The five mighty bodhisattvas enumerated in the Benevolent Kings Sutra. According to this sutra, if a ruler embraces the correct teaching of Buddhism, these five powerful bodhisattvas will protect him and the people of his country.

10. Jupiter, Mars, Venus, Mercury, and Saturn.

11. This refers to an oracle said to have been received from Great Bodhisattva Hachiman in the reign of the fifty-first sovereign, Emperor Heizei (r. 806–809). In it Hachiman vowed to protect the nation until the reign of the hundredth sovereign. On Establishing the Correct Teaching for the Peace of the Land was written in the reign of the ninetieth sovereign, Emperor Kameyama (r. 1259–1274).

12. The orchid room indicates the dwelling of a virtuous person.

13. The heavens of purity refer to the five highest heavens in the world of form, the second division of the threefold world, located above the world of desire.

14. Sweet, pungent, sour, bitter, salty, astringent, and faint flavors.

15. The power of earth that nourishes grains and fruits, the power of living beings that raise the people and vitalize human society,

and the power of the Buddhist Law that brings about peace and happiness.

16. In the Great Collection Sutra, the roe deer is described as a small deer so timid that it flees immediately whenever danger approaches, without giving a thought to the welfare of its parents or others.

17. Anointed kings refer to the rulers of major kingdoms. In ancient India, when the ruler of a powerful kingdom ascended the throne, the rulers of smaller kingdoms and their ministers poured water on his head.

18. The Metal Star is Venus. The Broom Star, the Fire Star, and the Water Star refer to comets, Mars, and Mercury, respectively. Most of the other stars mentioned make up parts of the twenty-eight celestial houses.

19. Demon fire refers to fires of unknown origin attributed to the anger of demons. Dragon fire means fires ascribed to the wrath of dragons, who were thought to be able to change water into fire at will. Heavenly fire is said to be caused by the wrath of heaven, and mountain god fire—possibly a reference to volcanic eruptions—by the wrath of mountain gods. Human fire refers to fires caused by human error or negligence. Tree fire probably indicates forest fires, and bandit fire means fires set by invaders.

20. According to the Japanese lunar calendar, the sixth month corresponds to the last month of summer.

21. Black, red, and green winds refer to winds that stir up and convey clouds of sand, while heavenly and earthly winds correspond to tornados or cyclones. Fire winds indicate hot air in the dry season, and water winds refer to rainstorms.

22. Wheat, rice, beans, and two types of millet. Also a generic term for all grains, which is the meaning here.

23. Bandits who do evil amid the confusion of disasters caused by fire, water, and wind, respectively. Demon bandits are said to be abductors.

24. The original word is gedō, which literally means "outside of the way" and usually indicates heretics and non-Buddhists. Here the word means something or someone that brings about p.29disasters. Hence the expression "evil spirits."

25. This refers to the tradition that Emperor Ming (28–75) dreamed of a golden man levitating above the garden. He awakened and asked his ministers about the dream. One of them said that he had once heard of the birth of a sage in the western region (India) during the reign of King Chao of the Chou dynasty, and that this sage had been called the

Buddha. The emperor sent eighteen envoys to the western region in order to obtain the Buddha's teachings. And at the request of these envoys, two Indian Buddhist monks came to China in c.e. 67 with Buddhist scriptures and images on the backs of white horses.

26. In 587, while still a youth, Jōgū, or Prince Shōtoku, is said to have joined with Soga no Umako in attacking and killing Mononobe no Moriya, a powerful minister who opposed Buddhism and the Soga clan.

27. "Those who belong to the lineage of Shāriputra" refers to those who attach greater importance to practicing meditation than to abiding by the teachings. "Those who adhere to the traditions of Haklenayashas" refers to those who hold doctrinal study to be more important than the practice of meditation. Haklenayashas was the twenty-third of Shakyamuni's twenty-four successors. Kukkutapāda is present-day Kurkihar, located about thirty kilometers northeast of Buddhagayā. Mahākāshyapa is said to have transmitted the teachings to Ānanda and to have died on this mountain.

28. Lotus Sutra, chap. 13. This is often called the "twenty-line verse of the 'Encouraging Devotion' chapter," which enumerates the types of persecutions that will be met in propagating the Lotus Sutra in the fearful

latter age. These persecutions were later summarized as the three powerful enemies by Miao-lo of China.

29. The sages of the four stages refer to the Buddhist teachers who embrace and propagate the correct teaching and benefit the people. Often this expression refers to the sages of Hinayana, who are classified into four ranks according to their level of understanding, but generally it indicates those successors of the Buddha who propagate his teachings and lead people to salvation.

30. "Concentrated meditation and un-concentrated meditation" refers to the sixteen types of meditation that are described as practices leading people to rebirth in the Pure Land. In the first thirteen types of meditation, one concentrates one's mind on the splendor of the Pure Land and the features of the Buddhas and bodhisattvas. These are regarded as "concentrated meditation." The other three types of meditation can be carried out even if one's mind is not focused. Therefore, they are called "un-concentrated meditation."

31. The three kinds of mind refer to the three requisites for reaching the Pure Land: a sincere mind, a mind of deep strong mind of determination, and a mind resolved to attain the Pure Land.

32. This refers to the eighteenth of the forty-eight vows, described in the Buddha Infinite Life Sutra, that Bodhisattva Dharma Treasury, the name of Amida Buddha before his enlightenment, made to bring all people to the Pure Land, except those mentioned here.

33. Lotus Sutra, chap. 3.

34. The two attendants are the bodhisattvas Perceiver of the World's Sounds and Great Power.

35. Shakyamuni and Medicine Master were Buddhas whose images were enshrined in the head temple of the Tendai school on Mount Hiei. The images of the bodhisattvas Space Treasury and Earth Repository were also enshrined on Mount Hiei. Space Treasury is a bodhisattva said to possess immeasurable wisdom and blessings. Earth Repository is a bodhisattva entrusted by Shakyamuni Buddha with the mission of saving people.

36. At the ceremony of the Lotus Sutra, Shakyamuni Buddha transferred his teachings to the bodhisattvas of the theoretical teaching led by Medicine King and entrusted them with the mission of propagating them in the Middle Day of the Law. It is said that Bodhisattva Medicine King was later born as the Great Teacher T'ien-t'ai in China and the Great Teacher Dengyō in Japan. On the basis of the parable of the skilled physician in the "Life Span" chapter of

the Lotus Sutra, T'ien-t'ai and Dengyō used the Buddha Medicine Master, the lord of the Pure Emerald World in the eastern part of the universe, as an object of devotion for their school. In this sense, to neglect the Buddha Medicine Master and revere the Buddha Amida is to ignore Shakyamuni Buddha's transmission.

37. The four treatises refer to Nāgārjuna's Treatise on the Middle Way and Treatise on the Twelve Gates, and The Treatise on the Great Perfection of Wisdom also attributed to Nāgārjuna, as well as The One-Hundred-Verse Treatise attributed to Āryadeva.

38. T'ien-t'ai's three major works: Great Concentration and Insight, The Words and Phrases of the Lotus Sutra, and The Profound Meaning of the Lotus Sutra, consisting of thirty volumes, and Miao-lo's three commentaries on them, which also consist of thirty volumes.

39. According to Hōnen's biography, in a dream he received permission from Shan-tao to spread the practice of calling on the name of Amida and was entrusted with the Pure Land teachings.

40. "An earlier period" refers to the period in which Hōnen propagated the Pure Land teaching.

41. Juan Chi (210–263) was one of the Seven Worthies of the Bamboo Grove, a group of scholars who, in the troubled political times at the end of the Wei dynasty, are said to have gathered in a bamboo grove to drink, play music, write poems, and discuss philosophy, particularly the Taoist philosophy of Lao Tzu and Chuang Tzu. Juan Chi is also known as a noted poet.

42. Uighurs: A Turkish people of Central Asia who prospered from the eighth through the mid-ninth century.

43. In 1221, the Retired Emperor Gotoba played a leading role in a struggle for power between the imperial court in Kyoto and the Hōjō clan in Kamakura, an incident known as the Jōkyū Disturbance. The imperial forces were defeated, and he and two other retired emperors were sent into exile.

44. This statement by the guest, who represents the highest political authority in the land, reflects his position as a ruler who puts matters of government first. In contrast, the Shonin teaches that the refutation of misleading teachings and the propagation of the correct teaching are the surest way to establish the true security of the nation.

45. The four grave offenses are those particularly grave among the ten evil offenses: killing, stealing, committing adultery, and lying.

46. An anāgāmin, or "non-returner," is one who has reached the third of the four stages that voice-hearers can attain. The fourth and highest stage is that of Arhat.

47. Kāshyapa was one of the seven ancient Buddhas or Buddhas of the past. Of these seven, the Buddha Kāshyapa was the sixth to appear, and Shakyamuni Buddha was the seventh.

48. Shavepate refers here to someone who has received tonsure and become a monk for self-serving reasons, such as to gain personal security or financial comfort, and is negligent in the practice and study of Buddhism.

49. Lectures held on the anniversary of T'ien-t'ai's death on the twenty-fourth day of the eleventh month of each year.

50. A Chinese term referring to rebels and outlaws. Here "white waves" indicates Hōnen and other priests of the Pure Land school, as well as the followers of other misleading schools. The "ocean of the Buddha" signifies Shakyamuni's teachings. The phrases "green groves" and "mountain of the Law" likewise refer to Hōnen and his followers and Shakyamuni's teachings, respectively.

51. Fu Hsi, Shen Nung, Yao, and Shun are legendary sage rulers of ancient China.

52. Expressions taken from early Chinese literature that indicate dramatic change.

53. "A friend in the orchid room" indicates a person of virtue. The implication is that the company of a virtuous person works as a good influence, just as one is imbued with fragrance on entering a room filled with orchids. It is said that mugwort supported by hemp plants grows upright.

54. The six kinds of relatives refer to a father, a mother, an elder brother, a younger brother, a wife, and a son or daughter.

55. According to the Nirvana Sutra, the place called the Avīchi hell, or the hell of incessant suffering, measures eighty-four thousand yojanas in total length and breadth. It is said that when a person falls into this hell he or she alone is sufficient to fill it up completely. The great size of the body symbolizes the magnitude of the pain one suffers in this hell.

The Postscript to "On Establishing the Correct Teaching for the Peace of the Land"

I COMPILED the above work in the first year of the Bunnō era (1260), with the cyclical sign kanoe-saru. That is, I began the work during the Shōka era (1257–1259) and completed it in the first year of Bunnō.

In the first year of the Shōka era, cyclical sign hinoto-mi, on the twenty-third day of the eighth month, at the time when the hour of the dog gives way to the hour of the boar (around 9:00 p.m.), there was a severe earthquake. Observing this event, I conceived the work. Later, in the first year of Bunnō, cyclical sign kanoe-saru, on the sixteenth day of the seventh month, I presented it to His Lordship, the lay priest of Saimyō-ji,[1] who is now deceased, by way of the lay priest Yadoya.[2] Still later, in the first year of the Bun'ei era (1264), cyclical sign kinoe-ne, on the fifth day of the seventh month, when a great comet appeared, I became even more certain of the origins of these disasters. Then, on the eighteenth day of the intercalary first month of the fifth year of Bun'ei, cyclical sign tsuchinoe-tatsu, nine years after the first year of Bunnō [when I submitted On Establishing the Correct Teaching for the Peace of the Land], an official letter came from the great kingdom of the Mongols that lies to the west, threatening to attack our country. Again, in the sixth year of the same era (1269), a second letter arrived. Thus the prediction that I made in my memorial [On Establishing the Correct Teaching] has already proved to be true. In view of this, we may suppose that the predictions I made will continue to come true in the future as well.

This work of mine has now been substantiated by fact. But this is not solely due to Nichiren's power. Rather it has come about as a response to the true words of the Lotus Sutra.

I copied this work on the eighth day of the twelfth month in the sixth year of Bun'ei (1269), cyclical sign tsuchinoto-mi.

Background

In 1269, Mongol emissaries again arrived at Dazaifu, the government outpost on the southern island of Kyushu, pressing for an answer to their earlier demands. Nichiren

Shonin is believed to have sent off another round of letters to high officials, which again failed to elicit a response. On the eighth day of the twelfth month of 1269, the Shonin copied On Establishing the Correct Teaching for the Peace of the Land and appended this postscript. In the postscript, he warns that the prophecies set forth in that document nine years earlier are now coming true.

Notes

1. The lay priest of Saimyō-ji indicates Hōjō Tokiyori (1227–1263), the fifth regent of the Kamakura shogunate. He became regent in 1246, but relinquished the regency to Hōjō Nagatoki and took holy orders under Dōryū, a naturalized Zen priest from China, in 1256. As a lay priest he lived at Saimyō-ji temple, which he had built, but he continued as the de facto ruler. He was called the lay priest of Saimyō-ji.

2. Yadoya Mitsunori, also known as the lay priest Yadoya, was a ranking official close to Hōjō Tokiyori.

The Izu Exile

I HAVE received the rice dumplings wrapped in bamboo leaves, sake, dried rice, peppers, paper, and other items from the messenger whom you took the trouble to send. He also conveyed your message that these offerings should be kept secret. I understand.

When, on the twelfth day of the fifth month, having been exiled, I arrived at that harbor I had never even heard of before, and when I was still suffering after leaving the boat, you kindly took me into your care. What karma has brought us together? Can it be that, because in the past you were a votary of the Lotus Sutra, now, in the Latter Day of the Law, you have been reborn as Funamori no Yasaburō and have taken pity on me? Though a man may do this, for your wife, as a married woman, to have given me food, brought me water to wash my hands and feet with, and treated me with great concern, I can only call as wondrous.

What caused you to inwardly believe in the Lotus Sutra and make offerings to me during my more than thirty-day stay there? I was hated and resented by the steward and the people of the district even more than I was in Kamakura. Those who saw me scowled, while those who merely heard my name were filled with spite. And yet, though I was there in the fifth month when rice was scarce, you secretly fed me. Have my parents been reborn in a place called Kawana, in Itō of Izu Province?

The fourth volume of the Lotus Sutra states, "[I will send . . .] men and women of pure strong mind of determination, to offer alms to the teachers of the Law."[1] The meaning of this sutra passage is that the heavenly gods and benevolent deities will assume various forms such as those of men and women, and present offerings to help the persons who practice the Lotus Sutra. There can be no doubt that this refers to you and your wife being born as a man and a woman, and making offerings to Nichiren, the teacher of the Law.

Since I wrote to you in detail earlier,[2] I will make this letter brief. But I would like to mention one thing in particular. When the steward of this district sent me a request to pray for his recovery from illness, I wondered if I should accept it. But since he showed some degree of strong mind of determination in me, I decided I would appeal to the Lotus Sutra. This time I saw no reason why the ten demon daughters should not join forces to aid me. I therefore addressed the Lotus Sutra,

Shakyamuni, Many Treasures, and the Buddhas of the ten directions, and also the Sun Goddess, Hachiman, and other deities, both major and minor. I was sure that they would consider my request and show some sign. Certainly they would never forsake me, but would respond as attentively as a person rubs a sore or scratches an itch. And as it turned out, the steward recovered. In gratitude he presented me with a statue of the Buddha that had appeared from the sea along with a catch of fish. He did so because his illness had finally ended, an illness that I am certain was inflicted by the ten demon daughters. This benefit too will surely become a benefit for you and your wife.

Living beings like ourselves have dwelt in the sea of the sufferings of birth and death since time without beginning. But they become votaries of the Lotus Sutra, and realize that their bodies and minds, which have existed since the beginningless past, are inherently endowed with the eternally unchanging nature; awaken to their mystic reality with their mystic wisdom; and attain the Buddha's body, which is as indestructible as a diamond. How then could they be different from that Buddha? Shakyamuni Buddha, the lord of teachings, who said numberless major world system dust particle kalpas ago, "I am the only person [who can rescue and protect others],"[3] refers to living beings like ourselves. This is the Lotus Sutra's teaching of three thousand realms in a single moment of life, and the action of "I am always here, preaching the Law."[4] Even though such an admirable Lotus Sutra and Shakyamuni Buddha exist, ordinary people are unaware of it. The passage in the "Life Span" chapter that reads, "I make it so that living beings in their befuddlement do not see me even when close by," refers to this. The disparity between delusion and enlightenment is like that between the four views in the grove of sal trees.[5] What is called the Buddha of three thousand realms in a single moment of life means that the entire realm of phenomena attains Buddhahood.

The demon who appeared before the boy Snow Mountains was Shakra in disguise. The dove that sought the protection of King Shibi was the god Vishvakarman. King Universal Brightness, who returned to the palace of King Spotted Feet [to be executed], was Shakyamuni Buddha, the lord of teachings. While the eyes of ordinary people are blind to this, the eyes of the Buddha see it. A sutra passage states that there are paths by which birds and fish come and go in both the sky and the sea. A wooden statue [of the Buddha] is itself a golden Buddha, and a golden Buddha is a wooden statue. Aniruddha's gold turned into a hare and then a corpse.[6] In the palm of Mahānāma's hand, even sand turned into gold.[7] These things are beyond ordinary understanding. An ordinary person is a Buddha, and a Buddha, an ordinary person. This is what is meant by three thousand realms in a single moment of life and by the phrase "I in fact attained Buddhahood."[8]

In that case, perhaps the World-Honored One of Great Enlightenment, the lord of teachings, has been reborn and has helped me as you and your wife. Though the distance between Itō and Kawana is short, our hearts are kept far apart. I write this letter for the sake of the future. Do not discuss it with others, but ponder it yourself. If people should learn anything at all of it, it will go hard with you. Keep it deep in your heart and never speak of it. With my deepest regards. Nam-Myoho-Renge-Kyo.

Nichiren

The twenty-seventh day of the sixth month in the first year of Kōchō (1261)

Sent to Funamori Yasaburō.

Background

In the eighth month of 1260, infuriated by Nichiren Shonin's refutation of the Pure Land school in his *On Establishing the Correct Teaching for the Peace of the Land,* a group of Nembutsu followers attacked his dwelling at Matsubagayatsu in Kamakura. The Shonin narrowly escaped and went to the home of his loyal disciple Toki Jōnin in Shimōsa Province. In the spring of 1261, however, he returned to Kamakura and resumed his propagation efforts.

On the twelfth day of the fifth month, 1261, without any official investigation, the government sentenced the Shonin to exile in the Izu Peninsula, which was a stronghold of the Pure Land school. The Shonin was taken to Kawana, a small fishing village on the northeastern coast of the Izu Peninsula. Here he was given shelter and food by Funamori Yasaburō, a fisherman, and his wife, and the couple became his steadfast followers. The steward of Itō District in Izu, Itō Sukemitsu, learning of the Shonin's presence a month after his arrival, had the Shonin summoned in order that he might offer prayers for Sukemitsu's recovery from a serious illness. Sukemitsu regained his health, and it is said that he, too, became the Shonin's follower.

Both Yasaburō and his wife were concerned about the Shonin's safety when he went to Itō to pray for the steward's health. Yasaburō sent a messenger to the Shonin at Itō with various offerings. *The Izu Exile* is the Shonin's reply. The Shonin's exile ended on the twenty-second day of the second month, 1263, and he returned toKamakura.

Notes

1. Lotus Sutra, chap. 10.

2. Little is known about the letter referred to here; only the letter *The Izu Exile* is extant today.

3. Lotus Sutra, chap. 3.

4. Ibid., chap. 16.

5. Shakyamuni passed away after expounding his last teaching, the Nirvana Sutra, in a grove of sal trees. The Sutra on Resolving Doubts about the Middle Day of the Law describes that grove of sal trees in four different ways: (1) as a grove composed of earth, trees, plants, and stone walls; (2) as a

place adorned with the seven kinds of treasures, including gold and silver; (3) as a place where all Buddhas practice Buddhism; and (4) as the eternal, enlightened land of the Buddha. The different views arise in accordance with the capacity and state of life of the people.

6. Aniruddha was one of Shakyamuni's ten major disciples, known as the foremost in divine insight. This story is found in *The Words and Phrases of the Lotus Sutra*. Long ago, a pratyekabuddha named Ridawas engaged in the practice of begging alms, but could obtain nothing. Seeing this, a poor man offered him millet. Later, when the poor man went in search of more millet, a hare jumped on his back and then turned into a corpse. Frightened, the man tried to shake it off, but in vain. As soon as he returned home, however, the corpse fell off and turned into gold. Hearing of this, wicked men came to rob him, but to them it looked merely like a corpse. In the eyes of the poor man, however, it was genuine gold, and he became wealthy. Ninety-one kalpas later, he was born as Aniruddha.

7. Mahānāma was one of the five monks who were ordered byShakyamuni's father, the king, to accompany Shakyamuni when he forsook the secular world and entered religious life. They followed and practiced asceticism with Shakyamuni, but left him

when he renounced this path. Shortly after Shakyamuni obtained enlightenment, however, he preached his first sermon to them at Deer Park, and they became his first disciples. According to the Increasing by One Āgama Sutra Mahānāma was said to possess occult powers. The story of "sand in his palm turning into gold" is found in Ts'ung-i's *Supplement to T'ien-t'ai's Three Major Works*.

8. Lotus Sutra, chap. 16. About this phrase, Nichiren Shonin states in *The Record of the Orally Transmitted Teachings* that "I" indicates all the people in each of the Ten Worlds, and that it means that the people of the Ten Worlds are all Buddhas eternally endowed with the three bodies.

The Universal Salty Taste

THERE are six kinds of flavors. The first is subtle, the second, salty, the third, pungent, the fourth, sour, the fifth, sweet, and the sixth, bitter. Even if one were to prepare a feast of a hundred flavors, if the single flavor of salt were missing, it would be no feast for a great king. Without salt, even the delicacies of land and sea are tasteless.

The ocean has eight mysterious qualities. First, it gradually becomes deeper. Second, being deep, its bottom is hard to fathom. Third, its salty taste is the same everywhere. Fourth, its ebb and flow follows certain rules. Fifth, it contains various treasure storehouses. Sixth, creatures of great size exist and dwell in it. Seventh, it refuses to house corpses. Eighth, it takes in all rivers and heavy rainfall without either increasing or decreasing.

[The Nirvana Sutra] compares "it gradually becomes deeper" to the Lotus Sutra leading everyone, from ordinary people who lack understanding to sages who possess it, to attain the Buddha way. The reason [the sutra uses the metaphor] "being deep, its bottom is hard to fathom" is that the realm of the Lotus Sutra can only be understood and shared between Buddhas, while those at the stage of near-perfect enlightenment or below are unable to master it. "Its salty taste is the same everywhere" compares all rivers, which contain no salt, to all sutras other than the Lotus, which offer no way to attain enlightenment. [The Nirvana Sutra] compares the water of all the rivers flowing into the sea and becoming salty to the people of different capacities instructed through the various provisional teachings who attain the Buddha way when they take strong mind of determination in the Lotus Sutra. It compares "its ebb and flow follows certain rules" to upholders of the Mystic Law who even though they were to lose their lives would attain the stage of non-regression. It compares "it contains various treasure storehouses" to the countless practices and good deeds of all the Buddhas and bodhisattvas, and the blessings of the various pāramitās being contained in the Mystic Law. The reason for "creatures of great size exist and dwell in it" is that, because the Buddhas and bodhisattvas possess great wisdom, they are called "creatures of great size," and that their great bodies, great aspiring minds, great distinguishing features, great evil-conquering force, great preaching, great authority, great transcendental powers, great compassion, and great pity all arise naturally from the Lotus Sutra. The reason for "it refuses to house corpses" is that with the Lotus Sutra one can free oneself for all eternity from slander and incorrigible disbelief. The reason for "without either increasing or p.40decreasing" is that the heart of the Lotus Sutra is the universality of the Buddha nature in all living beings.

The brine in a tub or jar of pickled vines ebbs and flows in accordance with the brine of the sea.1 One who upholds the Lotus Sutra and is subjected to imprisonment is like the salt in a tub or jar, while the Thus Come One Shakyamuni who freed himself from the burning house2 is like the salt of the sea. To condemn one who upholds the Lotus is to condemn the Thus Come One Shakyamuni. How astonished Brahmā, Shakra, and the four heavenly kings must be! If not now, when will the ten demon daughters' vow to split the head of one who persecutes a follower of the Lotus into seven pieces3 be carried out?

Ajātashatru, who had imprisoned King Bimbisāra, suddenly broke out in virulent sores in his present existence. How can one who has imprisoned an upholder of the Lotus not suffer from virulent sores in this existence?

Nichiren

Background

The date and recipient of this letter are unknown, as are the reasons for its writing. The statements "One who upholds the Lotus Sutra and is subjected to imprisonment" and "To condemn one who upholds the Lotus" indicate that Nichiren Shonin wrote this letter at a time when he or his disciples were undergoing persecution. Several views exist concerning the year of its writing. One is that it was written in 1261 when the Shonin was in exile in Izu; another, in 1271 when he was in exile on Sado Island; and a third, in 1279, during the worst period of the Atsuhara Persecution. Of these, 1261 seems most likely.

In this letter, the Shonin says that there are six kinds of flavors, of which salt is the most important. Without salt, any food will be bland. In employing this simile, the Shonin is indicating that none of the sutras assume their true significance unless they are based on the truth revealed in the Lotus Sutra. Then he cites the eight mystic qualities of the ocean enumerated in the Nirvana Sutra. But while the Nirvana Sutra actually applies these qualities to itself, the Shonin asserts that it is using them to praise the superiority of the Lotus Sutra.

In the final section, the Shonin compares the salt in a jar or tub of pickled vines to a follower of the Lotus Sutra, and the salt of the ocean, to Shakyamuni Buddha. The brine in a jar or tub ebbs and flows exactly as the ocean does, and by analogy, to imprison a votary of the Lotus Sutra is to imprison Shakyamuni Buddha.

Notes

1. In the pickling process, salt is added to a jar of vines to draw out their water. This salty water is said to increase and decrease in accord with the rise and fall of the ocean tides.

2. "Burning house" refers to the passage from the "Simile and Parable" chapter of the Lotus Sutra that reads, "There is no safety in the threefold world; it is like a burning house."

3. Lotus Sutra, chap. 26.

The Four Debts of Gratitude

CONCERNING my present exile,[1] there are two important matters that I must mention. One is that I feel immense joy. The reason is that this world is called the sahā world, sahā meaning endurance. This is why the Buddha is also called "One Who Can Endure." In the sahā world,[2] there are one billion Mount Sumerus, one billion suns and moons, and one billion groups of four continents. Among all these worlds, it was in the world at the center—with its Mount Sumeru, sun and moon, and four continents—that the Buddha made his advent. Japan is a tiny island country situated in a remote corner of that world, to the northeast of the country in which the Buddha appeared.

Since all the lands in the ten directions, with the exception of this sahā world, are pure lands, their people, being gentlehearted, neither abuse nor hate the worthies and sages. In contrast, this world is inhabited by people who were rejected from the pure lands in the ten directions. They have committed the ten evil acts or the five cardinal sins, slandered the worthies and sages, and have been unfilial to their fathers and mothers or disrespectful to the monks. For these offenses they fell into the three evil paths, and only after dwelling there for countless kalpas were they reborn in this world. Yet the residue of the evil karma formed in their previous existences has not yet been eradicated, and they still tend to perpetrate the ten evil acts or the five cardinal sins, to revile the worthies and sages, and to be undutiful to their fathers and mothers or irreverent toward the monks.

For these reasons, when the Thus Come One Shakyamuni made his advent in this world, some people offered him food into which they had mixed poison. Others tried to harm him by means of swords and staves, mad elephants, lions, fierce bulls, or savage dogs. Still others charged him with violating women, condemned him as a man of lowly status, or accused him of killing. Again, some, when they encountered him, covered their eyes to avoid seeing him, and others closed their doors and shuttered their windows. Still others reported to the kings and ministers that he held erroneous views and was given to slandering exalted personages. These incidents are described in the Great Collection Sutra, the Nirvana Sutra, and other scriptures. The Buddha was innocent of all such evil deeds. Yet this world is peculiar or deficient in that those with bad karma are born into it and inhabit it in great numbers. Moreover, the devil king of the sixth heaven, scheming to prevent the people of this world from leaving it p.42for the pure lands, seizes every opportunity to carry out his perverse acts.

It appears that his scheming is ultimately intended to prevent the Buddha from expounding the Lotus Sutra. The reason is that the nature of this devil king is to rejoice at those who create the karma of the three evil paths and to grieve at those who form the karma of the three good paths.3 Yet he does not lament so greatly over those who form the karma of the three good paths, but he sorrows indeed at those who aspire to the three vehicles. Again, he may not sorrow so much over those who seek to attain the three vehicles, but he grieves bitterly at those who form the karma to become Buddhas and avails himself of every opportunity to obstruct them. He knows that those who hear even a single sentence or phrase of the Lotus Sutra will attain Buddhahood without fail and, exceedingly distressed by this, contrives various plots and restrains and persecutes believers in an attempt to make them abandon their strong mind of determination.

Although the age in which the Buddha lived was certainly a defiled one, the five impurities had only just begun to manifest themselves; in addition, the devil stood in awe of the Buddha's powers. Yet, even in a time when the people's greed, anger, foolishness, and false views were still not rampant, a group of Brahmans of the Bamboo Staff school killed the Venerable Maudgalyayana, who was known as the foremost in transcendental powers; and King Ajātashatru, by releasing a mad elephant, threatened the life of the only one in all the threefold world who is worthy of honor.[4] Devadatta killed the nun Utpalavarnā, who had attained the state of Arhat; and the Venerable Kokālika spread evil rumors about Shariputra, who was renowned as the foremost in wisdom. How much worse things became in the world as the five impurities steadily increased! And now, in the latter age, hatred and jealousy toward those who believe even slightly in the Lotus Sutra will be all the more terrible. Thus the Lotus Sutra states, "Since hatred and jealousy toward this sutra abound even when the Thus Come One is in the world, how much more will this be so after his passing?"[5] When I read this passage for the first time, I did not think that the situation would be as bad as it predicts. Now I am struck by the unfailing accuracy of the Buddha's words, especially in light of my present circumstances.

I, Nichiren, do not observe the precepts with my body. Nor is my heart free from the three poisons. But since I believe in this [Lotus] sutra myself and also enable others to form a relationship with it, I had thought that perhaps society would treat me rather gently. Probably because the world has entered into the latter age, even monks who have wives and children have followers, as do priests who eat fish and fowl. I have neither wife nor children, nor do I eat fish or fowl. I have been blamed merely for trying to propagate the Lotus Sutra. Though I have neither wife nor child, I am known throughout the country as a monk who transgresses the code of conduct, and though I have never killed even a single ant or mole cricket, my bad reputation has spread throughout the realm. This may well resemble the situation of Shakyamuni Buddha, who was slandered by a multitude of non-Buddhists during his lifetime.

It seems that, solely because my strong mind of determination in the Lotus Sutra accords slightly more with its teachings than does the strong mind of determination of others, evil demons must have possessed their bodies and be causing them to feel hatred toward me. I am nothing but a lowly and ignorant monk without precepts. Yet, when I think that such a person should be mentioned in the Lotus Sutra, which was expounded more than two thousand years ago, and p.43that the Buddha prophesied that that person would encounter persecution, I cannot possibly express my joy.

It is already twenty-four or twenty-five years since I began studying Buddhism. Yet I have believed wholeheartedly in the Lotus Sutra only for the past six or seven years. Moreover, although I had strong mind of determination in the sutra, because I was negligent and because of my studies and the interruptions of mundane affairs, each day I would recite only a single scroll, a chapter, or the title. Now, however, for a period of more than 240 days—from the twelfth day of the fifth month of last year to the sixteenth day of the first month of this year—I think I have practiced the Lotus Sutra twenty-four hours each day and night. I say so because, having been exiled on the Lotus Sutra's account, I now read and practice it continuously, whether I am walking, standing, sitting, or lying down. For anyone born human, what greater joy could there be?

It is the way of ordinary people that, even though they spur themselves on to arouse the aspiration for enlightenment and wish for happiness in the next life, they exert themselves no more than one or two out of all the hours of the day, and this only after reminding themselves to do so. As for myself, I read the Lotus Sutra without having to remember to, and practice it even when I do not read its words aloud.

During the course of countless kalpas, while transmigrating through the six paths and the four forms of birth, I may at times have risen in revolt, committed theft, or broken into others' homes at night and, on account of these offenses, been convicted by the ruler and condemned to exile or death. This time, however, it is because I am so firmly resolved to propagate the Lotus Sutra that people with evil karma have brought false charges against me; hence my exile. Surely this will work in my favor in future lifetimes. In this latter age, there cannot be anyone else who upholds the Lotus Sutra twenty-four hours of the day and night without making a deliberate effort to do so.

There is one other thing for which I am most grateful. While transmigrating in the six paths for the duration of countless kalpas, I may have encountered a number of sovereigns and become their favorite minister or regent. If so, I must have been granted fiefs and accorded treasures and stipends. Never once, however, did I encounter a sovereign in whose country the Lotus Sutra had spread, so that I could hear its name, practice it and, on that very account, be slandered by other people and have the ruler send me into exile. The Lotus Sutra states, "As for this Lotus Sutra, throughout immeasurable numbers of lands one cannot even hear its name, much less be able to see it, accept and embrace, read and recite it."6 Thus those people who slandered me and the ruler [who had me banished] are the very persons to whom I owe the most profound debt of gratitude.

One who studies the teachings of Buddhism must not fail to repay the four debts of gratitude. According to the Contemplation on the Mind-Ground Sutra, the first of the four debts is that owed to all living beings. Were it not for them, one would find it impossible to make the vow to save innumerable living beings. Moreover, but for the evil people who persecute bodhisattvas, how could those bodhisattvas increase their merit?

The second of the four debts is that owed to one's father and mother. To be born into the six paths, one must have parents. If one is born into the family of a murderer, a thief, a violator of the rules of proper conduct, or a slanderer of the Law, then even though one may not commit these offenses oneself, one in effect forms the same karma as those p.44who do. As for my parents in this lifetime, however, they not only gave me birth but made me a believer in the Lotus Sutra. Thus I owe my present father and mother a debt far greater than I would had I been born into the family of Brahmā, Shakra, one of the four heavenly kings, or a wheel-turning king, and so inherited the threefold world or the four continents, and been revered by the four kinds of believers in the worlds of human and heavenly beings.

The third is the debt owed to one's sovereign. It is thanks to one's sovereign that one can warm one's body in the three kinds of heavenly light7 and sustain one's life with the five kinds of grain8 that grow on earth. Moreover, in this lifetime, I have taken strong mind of determination in the Lotus Sutra and encountered a ruler who will enable me to free myself in my present existence from the sufferings of birth and death. Thus, how can I dwell on the insignificant harm that he has done me and overlook my debt to him?

The fourth is the debt owed to the three treasures. When the Thus Come One Shakyamuni was engaged in bodhisattva practices for countless kalpas, he gathered all of the good fortune and virtue he had gained thereby, divided it into sixty-four parts, and took on their merit. Of these sixty-four, he reserved only one part for himself. The remaining sixty-three parts he left behind in this world, making a vow as follows: "There will be an age when the five impurities will become rampant, erroneous teachings will flourish, and slanderers will fill the land. At that time, because the innumerable benevolent guardian deities will be unable to taste the flavor of the Law, their majesty and strength will diminish. The sun and moon will lose their brightness, the heavenly dragons will not send down rain, and the earthly deities will decrease the fertility of the soil. The roots and stalks, branches and leaves, flowers and fruit will all lose their medicinal properties as well as the seven flavors.9 Even those who became kings because they had observed the ten good precepts in previous lifetimes will grow in greed, anger, and foolishness. The people will cease to be dutiful to their parents, and the six kinds of relatives10 will fall into disaccord. At such a time, my disciples will consist of unlearned people without precepts. For this reason, even though they shave their heads, they will be forsaken by the tutelary deities and left without any means of subsistence. It is in order to sustain these monks and nuns [that I now leave these sixty-three parts behind]."

Moreover, as for the benefits that the Buddha had attained as a result of his practices, he divided them into three parts, of which he himself made use of only two. For this reason, although he was to have lived in this world until the age of 120, he passed away after eighty years, bequeathing the remaining forty years of his life span to us.11

Even if we should gather all the water of the four great oceans to wet inkstones, burn all the trees and plants to make ink sticks, collect the hairs of all beasts for writing brushes, employ all the surfaces of the worlds in the ten directions for paper, and, with these, set down expressions of gratitude, how could we possibly repay our debt to the Buddha?

Concerning the debt owed to the Law, the Law is the teacher of all Buddhas. It is because of the Law that the Buddhas are worthy of respect. Therefore, those who wish to repay their debt to the Buddha must first repay the debt they owe to the Law.

As for the debt owed to the Buddhist Order, both the treasure of the Buddha and the treasure of the Law are invariably perpetuated by the Order. To illustrate, without firewood, there can be no fire, and if there is no earth, p.45trees and plants cannot grow. Likewise, even though Buddhism existed, without the members of the Order who studied it and passed it on, it would never have been transmitted throughout the two thousand years of the Former and Middle Days into the Latter Day of the Law. Accordingly, the Great Collection Sutra states: "Suppose that, in the last of the five five-hundred-year periods, there should be someone who harasses unlearned monks without precepts by accusing them of some offense. You should know that this person is extinguishing the great torch of Buddhism." Therefore, the debt we owe to the Order is difficult to recompense.

Thus it is imperative that one repay one's debt of gratitude to the three treasures. In ancient times, there were sages such as the boy Snow Mountains, Bodhisattva Ever Wailing, Bodhisattva Medicine King, and King

Universal Brightness, all of whom [offered their lives in order to make such repayment]. The first offered his body as food to a demon. The second sold his own blood and marrow. The third burned his arms, and the fourth was ready to part with his head. Ordinary people in this latter age, however, though receiving the benefits of the three treasures, completely neglect to repay them. How, then, can they attain the Buddha way? The Contemplation on the Mind-Ground, the Brahmā Net, and other sutras state that those who study Buddhism and receive the precepts of perfect and immediate enlightenment must repay the four debts of gratitude without fail. I am but an ignorant ordinary person made of flesh and blood; I have not rid myself of even a fraction of the three categories of illusion. Yet, on account of the Lotus Sutra, I have been reviled, slandered, attacked with swords and staves, and sent into exile. In light of these persecutions, I believe I may be likened to the great sages who burned their arms, crushed their marrow, or did not begrudge being beheaded. This is what I mean by immense joy.

The second of the two important matters is that I feel intense grief. The fourth volume of the Lotus Sutra states: "If there should be an evil person who, his mind destitute of goodness should for the space of a kalpa appear in the presence of the Buddha and constantly curse and revile the Buddha, that person's offense would still be rather light. But if there were a person who spoke only one evil word to curse or defame the lay persons or monks or nuns who read and recite the Lotus Sutra, then his offense would be very grave."12 When I read this and similar passages, my belief is aroused, sweat breaks out from my body, and tears fall from my eyes like rain. I grieve that, by being born in this country, I have caused so many of its people to create the worst karma possible in a lifetime. Those who beat and struck Bodhisattva Never Disparaging came to repent of it while they were alive; yet, even so, their offenses were so difficult to expiate that they fell into the Avīchi hell and remained there for a thousand kalpas. But those who have done me harm have not yet repented of it even in the slightest.

Describing the karmic retribution that such people must receive, the Great Collection Sutra states: "[The Buddha asked], 'If there should be a person who draws blood from the bodies of a thousand, ten thousand, or a million Buddhas, in your thinking, how is it? Will he have committed a grave offense or not?' The great king Brahmā replied: 'If a person causes the body of even a single Buddha to bleed, he will have committed an offense so serious that he will fall into the hell of incessant suffering. His offense will be unfathomably grave, and he will have to remain in the great Avīchi hell for so many kalpas that their number cannot be calculated even by means of counting sticks. Graver still is the offense a person would commit by causing the bodies of ten thousand or a million Buddhas to bleed. No one could possibly explain in full either that person's offense or its karmic retribution—no one, that is, except the Thus Come One himself.' The Buddha said, 'Great King Brahmā, suppose there should be a person who, for my sake, takes the tonsure and wears a surplice. Even though he has not at any time received the precepts and therefore observes none, if someone harasses him, abuses him, or strikes him with a staff, then that persecutor's offense will be even graver than that [of injuring ten thousand or a million Buddhas].'"

Nichiren

The sixteenth day of the first month in the second year of Kōchō (1262), cyclical sign mizunoe-inu

To Kudō Sakon-no-jō

Background

Nichiren Shonin wrote this letter while he was in exile in Itō on the Izu Peninsula. It was addressed to Kudō Sakon-no-jō Yoshitaka, known also as Kudō Yoshitaka, the lord of Amatsu in Awa Province.

Kudō Yoshitaka is said to have converted to Nichiren Shonin's teachings around 1256, about the same time Shijō Kingo and Ikegami Munenaka did, a few years after the Shonin first proclaimed his teachings. While the Shonin was in exile on Izu, Yoshitaka sent offerings to him and continued to maintain pure strong mind of determination. He was killed defending the Shonin at the time of the Komatsubara Persecution in the eleventh month of 1264. The Four Debts of Gratitude is the only letter still extant that the Shonin addressed to him.

In this letter, in light of the reason for his banishment, Nichiren Shonin expresses his conviction that he is a true practitioner of the Lotus Sutra. He mentions the "two important matters" that concern his Izu Exile. He states, "One is that I feel immense joy," and explains the reasons for his joy. The greater part of the letter consists of this explanation. Following this, he states, "The second of the two important matters is that I feel intense grief." Citing passages from the Lotus and Great Collection sutras that reveal the gravity of the offense of slandering the Law and its devotees, the Shonin explains that he grieves at the thought of the great karmic retribution his tormentors must undergo. This is the concluding part of the letter.

In the body of the letter, the Shonin gives two reasons for his "immense joy." One is that he has been able to prove himself to be the votary of the Lotus Sutra by fulfilling the Buddha's prediction made in the sutra that its votary in the Latter Day of the Law will meet with persecution. The other reason is that, by suffering banishment for the sutra's sake, he can repay the four debts of gratitude. He declares that the ruler who condemned him to exile is the very person to whom he is the most grateful; thanks to the ruler, he has been able to fulfill the words of the Lotus Sutra and so prove himself to be its true votary.

Then, the Shonin stresses the importance of repaying the four debts of gratitude set forth in the Contemplation on the Mind-Ground Sutra. p.47The four debts of gratitude are the debts owed to all living beings, to one's father and mother, to one's sovereign, and to the three treasures—the Buddha, the Law, and the Buddhist Order. Among these four debts of gratitude, the Shonin places special emphasis on the debt owed to the three treasures, without which one could not attain Buddhahood.

Notes

1. Reference is to the Shonin's exile to Itō on the Izu Peninsula, from the twelfth day of the fifth month, 1261, to the twenty-second day of the second month, 1263.

2. Here "the sahā world" indicates the major world system that surrounds our world.

3. The three good paths are those of asuras, human beings, and heavenly beings, in contrast to the three evil paths of hell, hungry spirits, and animals.

4. The story of Ajātashatru is included as one of the nine great persecutions suffered by Shakyamuni.

5. Lotus Sutra, chap. 10.

6. Ibid., chap. 14.

7. The light of the sun, moon, and stars.

8. Wheat, rice, beans, and two types of millet. Also a generic term for all grains.

9. Sweet, pungent, sour, bitter, salty, astringent, and subtle flavors.

10. The six kinds of relatives refer to a father, a mother, an elder brother, a younger brother, a wife, and a son or daughter. Another classification gives a father, a son or daughter, an elder brother, a younger brother, a husband, and a wife.

11. The source of this statement has not been traced; presumably it is based on a passage in the Great Collection Sutra.

12. Lotus Sutra, chap. 10

The Teaching, Capacity, Time, and Country

Written by Nichiren, the shramana of Japan

WITH regard to the first item, the teaching consists of all the sutras, rules of monastic discipline, and treatises expounded by the Thus Come One Shakyamuni, comprising 5,048 volumes contained in 480 scroll cases. The teachings of Buddhism, after circulating throughout India for a thousand years, were introduced to China 1,015 years after the Buddha's passing. During the 664-year period beginning with that year, the tenth of the Yung-p'ing era (c.e. 67), cyclical sign hinoto-u, in the reign of Emperor Ming of the Later Han, and ending with the eighteenth year of the K'ai-yüan era (c.e. 730), cyclical sign kanoe-uma, in the reign of Emperor Hsüan-tsung of the T'ang, all of the Buddhist teachings were introduced to China.

The contents of these sutras, rules of monastic discipline, and treatises can be divided into the categories of Hinayana and Mahayana teachings, provisional and true sutras, and exoteric and esoteric sutras, and one should carefully distinguish between them. Such designations did not originate with the later scholars and teachers of Buddhism; they derive from the preaching of the Buddha himself. Therefore, they should be employed without exception by all living beings in the worlds of the ten directions. Anyone who fails to do so should be regarded as non-Buddhist.

The custom of referring to the teachings of the Āgama sutras as Hinayana derives from the various Mahayana sutras of the Correct and Equal, Wisdom, and Lotus and Nirvana periods. In the Lotus Sutra the Buddha says that, if he had preached only the Hinayana teachings and withheld the Lotus Sutra, he would have been guilty of stinginess and greed. Moreover, the Nirvana Sutra states that those who accept only the Hinayana sutras and declare that the Buddha is characterized by impermanence will have their tongues fester in their mouths.

Second is the matter of capacity. One who attempts to propagate the teachings of Buddhism must understand the capacity and basic nature of the persons one is addressing. The Venerable Shāriputra attempted to instruct a blacksmith by teaching him to meditate on the vileness of the body, and to instruct a washerman by teaching him to conduct breath-counting meditation.1 Even though these disciples spent over ninety days in their respective meditations, they did not gain the slightest understanding of the Buddha's teachings. On the contrary, they took on erroneous views and ended by becoming icchantikas, or persons of incorrigible disbelief.

The Buddha, on the other hand, instructed the blacksmith in breath-counting meditation, and the washerman in the meditation on the vileness of the body, and as a result both obtained understanding in no time at all. If even Shāriputra, the foremost in wisdom among the disciples of the Buddha, failed to understand people's capacity, then how much more difficult must it be for ordinary teachers today, in the Latter Day of the Law, to have such an understanding! Ordinary teachers who lack an understanding of people's capacity should teach only the Lotus Sutra to those who are under their instruction.

Question: What about the passage in the Lotus Sutra that says, "Do not preach this sutra to persons who are without wisdom"?2

Answer: When I speak of understanding capacity, I am referring to preaching by a person of wisdom. Again, one should preach only the Lotus Sutra even to those who slander the Law, so that they may establish a so-called "poison-drum relationship" with it. In this respect, one should proceed as Bodhisattva Never Disparaging did.

However, if one is speaking to persons who one knows have the capacity to become wise, then one should first instruct them in the

Hinayana teachings, then instruct them in the provisional Mahayana teachings, and finally instruct them in the true Mahayana. But if speaking to those one knows to be ignorant persons of lesser capacity, then one should first instruct them in the true Mahayana teaching. In that way, whether they choose to believe in the teaching or to slander it, they will still receive the seeds of Buddhahood.

Third is the consideration of time. Anyone who hopes to spread the Buddhist teachings must make certain to understand the time. For example, if a farmer were to plant his fields in autumn and winter, then, even though the seed and the land and the farmer's efforts were the same as ever, this planting would not result in the slightest gain but rather would end in loss. If the farmer planted one small plot in that way, he would suffer a minor loss, and if he planted acres and acres, he would suffer a major loss. But if he plows and plants in the spring and summer, then, whether the fields are of superior, medium, or inferior quality, each will bring forth its corresponding share of crops.

The preaching of the Buddhist teachings is similar to this. If one propagates the teaching without understanding the time, one will reap no benefit but, on the contrary, will fall into the evil paths. When Shakyamuni Buddha made his appearance in this world, he was determined to preach the Lotus Sutra. But though the capacities of his listeners may have been right, the proper time had not yet come. Therefore, he spent a period of more than forty years without preaching the Lotus Sutra, explaining, as he says in the Lotus Sutra itself, that "the time to preach so had not yet come."3

The day after the Buddha's passing begins the thousand-year period known as the Former Day of the Law, when those who uphold the precepts are many while those who break them are few. The day after the end of the Former Day of the Law marks the beginning of the thousand-year period known as the Middle Day of the Law, when those who break the precepts are many while those without precepts are few. And the day after the ending of the Middle Day of the Law begins the ten-thousand-year period known as the Latter Day of the Law, when those who break the precepts are few while those without precepts are many.

During the Former Day of the Law, one should cast aside those who break the precepts, or who have no precepts p.50at all, giving alms only to those who uphold the precepts. During the Middle Day of the Law, one should cast aside those without precepts and give alms only to those who break them. And during the Latter Day of the Law, one should give alms to those without precepts, treating them in the same way as if they were the Buddha.

However, whether in the Former, the Middle, or the Latter Day of the Law, one should never in any of these three periods give alms to those who slander the Lotus Sutra, whether they keep the precepts, break the precepts, or do not receive them at all. If alms are given to those who slander the Lotus Sutra, then the land will invariably be visited by the three calamities and seven disasters, and the persons who give such alms will surely fall into the great citadel of the hell of incessant suffering.

When the votary of the Lotus Sutra denounces the provisional sutras, it is like a ruler, a parent, or a teacher disciplining a retainer, a son, or a disciple. But when practitioners of the provisional sutras denounce the Lotus Sutra, it is like retainers, sons, or disciples attempting to punish their ruler, parent, or teacher.

At present, it has been 210 or more years since we entered the Latter Day of the Law. One should consider very carefully whether now is a time best suited for the provisional sutras or Nembutsu teachings, or whether it is the time when the Lotus Sutra should spread.

Fourth is the consideration of the country. One must never fail to take into account the kind of country in which one is spreading the Buddhist teachings. There are cold countries, hot countries, poor countries, rich countries, central countries, and peripheral countries, large countries and small countries, countries wholly given over to thieving, countries wholly given over to the killing of living things, and countries known for their utter lack of filial piety. In addition, there are countries wholly devoted to the Hinayana teachings, countries wholly devoted to the Mahayana teachings, and countries in which both Hinayana and Mahayana are pursued. In the case of Japan, therefore, we must carefully consider whether it is a country suited exclusively to Hinayana, a country suited exclusively to Mahayana, or a country suited for the practice of both Hinayana and Mahayana.

Fifth is the sequence of propagation. In a country where the Buddhist teachings have never been introduced, there of course will be none who are familiar with Buddhism. But in a country where Buddhism has already been introduced, there will be those who believe in the Buddhist teachings. Therefore, one must first learn what kind of Buddhist doctrines have already spread in a particular country before attempting to propagate Buddhism there.

If the Hinayana and provisional Mahayana teachings have already spread, then one should by all means propagate the true Mahayana teaching. But if the true Mahayana teaching has already spread, then one must not propagate the Hinayana or provisional Mahayana teachings. One throws aside shards and rubble in order to pick up gold and gems, but one must not throw aside gold and gems in order to pick up shards and rubble.

If one takes the five principles outlined above into account when propagating the Buddhist teachings, then one can surely become a teacher to the entire nation of Japan. To understand that the Lotus Sutra is the king of sutras, the foremost among them all, is to have a correct understanding of the teaching.

Yet Fa-yün of Kuang-che-ssu temple and Hui-kuan of Tao-ch'ang-ssu temple claimed that the Nirvana Sutra is superior to the Lotus Sutra. p.51Ch'eng-kuan of Mount Ch'ing-liang and Kōbō of Mount Kōya claimed that the Flower Garland and Mahāvairochana sutras are superior to the Lotus Sutra. Chi-tsang of Chia-hsiang-ssu temple and the priest K'uei-chi of Tz'u-en-ssu temple claimed that the two sutras known as the Wisdom and the Profound Secrets are superior to the Lotus Sutra. One man alone, the Great Teacher Chih-che of Mount T'ien-t'ai, not only asserted that the Lotus Sutra is superior to all the other sutras, but urged that anyone claiming there is a sutra superior to the Lotus should be admonished; he said that, if such persons persist in their false claim, their tongues will surely fester in their mouths during the present existence, and after death they will fall into the Avīchi hell. One who is able to distinguish right from wrong among all these different opinions may be said to have a correct understanding of the teaching.

Of all the thousand or ten thousand scholars of the present age, surely each and every one is confused as to this point. If so, then there must be very few who have a correct understanding of the teaching. If there are none with a correct understanding of the teaching, there will be none who read the Lotus Sutra. If there are none who read the Lotus Sutra, there will be none who can act as a teacher to the nation. If there is no one to act as a teacher to the nation, then everyone within the nation will be confused as to the distinctions within the body of sutras, such as those between the Hinayana and the Mahayana, the provisional and the true, and the exoteric and the esoteric sutras. Not a single person will be able to escape the sufferings of birth and death, and in the end they will all become slanderers of the Law. Those who, because of slandering the Law, fall into the Avīchi hell, will be more numerous than the dust particles of the land, while those who, by embracing the Law, are freed from the sufferings of birth and death, will number less than the specks of dirt that can be placed on a fingernail. What a fearful thing it is!

During the four hundred or more years since the time of Emperor Kammu, all the people in Japan have had the capacity to attain enlightenment solely through the Lotus Sutra. They are like those persons with capacities suited to the pure and perfect teaching who for a period of eight years listened to the preaching of the Lotus Sutra on Eagle Peak. (Confirmation of this may be found in the records of the Great Teacher T'ien-t'ai, Prince Shōtoku, the Reverend Ganjin, the Great Teacher Kompon [Dengyō], the Reverend Annen, and Eshin.)4 To understand this is to have an understanding of the people's capacity.

Yet the Buddhist scholars of our time say that the people of Japan all have capacities fit only for the recitation of Amida Buddha's name, the Nembutsu. They are like Shāriputra in the episode I mentioned earlier who, because he was misled as to the capacity of the persons under his instruction, in the end turned them into icchantikas.

In Japan at present, some 2,210 years after the passing of the Thus Come One

Shakyamuni, in the last of the five five-hundred-year periods after his passing, the hour has come for the widespread propagation of Myoho-Renge-Kyo. To understand this is to have an understanding of the time.

Yet there are Buddhist scholars in Japan today who cast aside the Lotus Sutra and instead devote themselves exclusively to practicing the invocation of Amida Buddha's name. There are others who teach the Hinayana precepts and speak contemptuously of the priests [who were ordained with the Mahayana precepts] on Mount Hiei, as well as those who present what they describe as a separate transmission p.52outside the sutras, disparaging the correct doctrine of the Lotus Sutra. Such persons may surely be said to misunderstand the time. They are like the monk Superior Intent who slandered Bodhisattva Root of Joy, or the Scholar Gunaprabha who behaved with contempt toward Bodhisattva Maitreya,5 thus inviting the terrible sufferings of the Avīchi hell.

Japan is a country related exclusively to the Lotus Sutra, just as the country of Shrāvastī in India was related solely to the Mahayana teachings. In India there were countries that were wholly devoted to Hinayana, those that were wholly devoted to Mahayana, and those that were devoted to both Hinayana and

Mahayana teachings. Japan is a country that is exclusively suited to Mahayana, and among those teachings it should be dedicated solely to the Lotus Sutra. (The above statement is attested to in The Treatise on the Stages of Yoga Practice, the writings of Seng-chao, and the records of Prince Shōtoku, the Great Teacher Dengyō, and Annen.)6 To understand this is to understand the country.

Yet there are Buddhist scholars in our present age who address the people of Japan and instruct them only in the precepts of the Hinayana, or who attempt to make them all into followers of the Nembutsu. This is like "placing impure food in a jeweled vessel." (This simile of the jeweled vessel is taken from An Essay on the Protection of the Nation by the Great Teacher Dengyō.)

In Japan during the 240 or more years from the time when Buddhism was first introduced from the Korean kingdom of Paekche in the reign of Emperor Kimmei to the reign of Emperor Kammu, only the Hinayana and provisional Mahayana teachings were propagated throughout the country. Though the Lotus Sutra existed in Japan, its significance had not yet been made clear. This was similar to the situation years before in China, where the Lotus Sutra had existed for more than 300 years before its significance was clarified.

In the time of Emperor Kammu, the Great Teacher Dengyō refuted the Hinayana and provisional Mahayana teachings, and made clear the true significance of the Lotus Sutra. From that time on, opposing opinions ceased to prevail, and everyone single-mindedly put strong mind of determination in the Lotus Sutra. Even those scholars of the earlier six schools [of Nara] who studied Hinayana and Mahayana teachings such as the Flower Garland, Wisdom, Profound Secrets, and Āgama sutras regarded the Lotus Sutra as the ultimate authority. Needless to say, this was even more so with scholars of the Tendai and True Word schools, and of course with lay believers who had no special knowledge of the subject. In its relation to the Lotus Sutra, the country was like the K'un-lun Mountains where there is not a single worthless stone, or the mountain island of P'eng-lai where no poisons are known.

However, during the fifty or more years since the Kennin era (1201–1204), the priests Dainichi and Budda7 have spread the teachings of the Zen school, casting aside all the various sutras and postulating a doctrine that is transmitted outside the scriptures. And Hōnen and Ryūkan have established the Pure Land school, contradicting the teachings of the true Mahayana and setting up the provisional doctrines. These men are in effect casting aside gems and instead gathering stones, abandoning the solid earth and trying to climb up into the air. They know nothing about the order in which the various doctrines should be propagated. The Buddha warned of such persons when he said that it was better to encounter a mad elephant than an evil friend.8

In the "Encouraging Devotion" chapter of the Lotus Sutra, it is p.53recorded that, in the last five-hundred-year period, or two thousand or so years after the Buddha's passing, there will be three types of enemies of the Lotus Sutra. Our present age corresponds to this last five-hundred-year period. And as I, Nichiren, ponder the truth of the Buddha's words, I realize that these three types of enemies are indeed real. If I allow them to remain hidden, then I will not be the votary of the Lotus Sutra. Yet if I cause them to appear, then I am almost certain to lose my life.

The fourth volume of the Lotus Sutra states, "Since hatred and jealousy toward this sutra abound even when the Thus Come One is in the world, how much more will this be so after his passing?"9 The fifth volume says, "It will face much hostility in the world and be difficult to believe."10 The same volume also reads, "We care nothing for our bodies or lives but are anxious only for the unsurpassed way."11 And the sixth volume reads, "Not hesitating even if it costs them their lives."12

The ninth volume of the Nirvana Sutra states: "For example, it is like a royal envoy skilled in discussion and clever with expedient means who, when sent on a mission to another land, would rather, even though it costs him his life, in the end conceal none of the words of his ruler. Wise persons too do this. In the midst of ordinary people and without begrudging their lives, those who are wise should without fail proclaim the Thus Come One's prize teaching from the correct and equal sutras of the great vehicle." The Great Teacher Chang-an, commenting on this passage, says: "'[A royal envoy . . . would rather], even though it costs him his life, in the end conceal none of the words of his ruler' means that one's body is insignificant while the Law is supreme. One should give one's life in order to propagate the Law."13

When I examine these passages, I know that, if I do not call forth these three enemies of the Lotus Sutra, then I will not be the votary of the Lotus Sutra. Only by making them appear can I be the votary. And yet if I do so, I am almost certain to lose my life. I will be like the Venerable Āryasimha or Bodhisattva Āryadeva.

Nichiren

The tenth day of the second month

Background

In the seventh month of 1260, Nichiren Shonin submitted his treatise On Establishing the Correct Teaching for the Peace of the Land to the former regent Hōjō Tokiyori, who, though retired from office, was still the most influential member of the ruling Hōjō clan.

Infuriated at the Shonin's criticism of the Pure Land school set forth in this treatise, a group of Pure Land believers attacked his dwelling at Matsubagayatsu, Kamakura, in an attempt to do away with him. The Shonin narrowly escaped to Toki Jōnin's residence in the nearby province of Shimōsa. When he reappeared in Kamakura in the spring of 1261 and resumed his propagation activities, the government arrested him and, without investigation, ordered him exiled to Itō on the Izu Peninsula. He remained in Izu from the twelfth day of the fifth month until he was pardoned and returned to Kamakura on the twenty-second day of the second month, 1263. This work is p.54dated simply "the tenth day of the second month," but it is generally assumed that it was written in the second year of Kōchō (1262) while he was in exile in Izu.

The Shonin wrote this letter, reconfirming the correctness of his teaching in light of the five principles for propagation: the teaching, the people's capacity, the time, the country, and the sequence of propagation. He also reaffirms his own mission in view of the Lotus Sutra's predictions that its votary in the Latter Day of the Law will undergo persecutions at the hands of the three powerful enemies.

Buddhist scholars of the past had set forth various criteria that one must understand and take into account in propagating Buddhism. Nichiren Shonin organized these criteria into an integral system, establishing the five principles for propagation as a standard for the comparative evaluation of the various Buddhist teachings. In this letter he explains these five guides, demonstrating in terms of each why the Lotus Sutra is the supreme teaching. Although this letter refers only to the Lotus Sutra, in light of the Shonin's other writings we may understand this to mean the sutra's essence, Nam-Myoho-Renge-Kyo, and the practice and spirit it encompasses.

Notes

1. This story is found in the Nirvana Sutra. Mentioned are the five meditations to stop the mind's disturbances and eliminate delusion. They are: meditation on the vileness of the body, meditation on compassion, meditation on dependent origination, meditation on the correct discernment of the phenomenal world, and breath-counting meditation. Meditation on the vileness of the body is concentrating on the impurity of the body to sever one's attachment to it. Breath-counting meditation is a method of calming the mind by counting the breaths.

2. Lotus Sutra, chap. 3.

3. Ibid., chap. 2.

4. This passage is given as a note in the text. The "records" may refer to the descriptions in The Words and Phrases of the Lotus Sutra by T'ien-t'ai; The Biography of Prince Shōtoku; The Life of the Great Priest of T'ang China Who Journeyed to the East; An Essay on the Protection of the Nation and The Outstanding Principles of the Lotus Sutra by Dengyō; An Extensive Commentary on the Universally Bestowed Bodhisattva Precepts by Annen; and The Essentials of the One Vehicle Teaching by Eshin.

5. The monk Superior Intent lived in the Latter Day of the Buddha Lion Sound King. He slandered Bodhisattva Root of Joy who taught the doctrine of the true aspect of reality, and was therefore said to have fallen into hell. The Scholar Gunaprabha first studied the Mahayana, but converted to the Hinayana after reading The Great Commentary on the Abhidharma. According to The Record of the Western Regions, he ascended to the Tushita heaven in order to resolve his doubts concerning the Hinayana and the Mahayana. There he met Bodhisattva Maitreya, but did not respect him because Maitreya was not an ordained monk. Thus he failed to learn from Maitreya because of his arrogance.

6. The Treatise on the Stages of Yoga Practice is a work attributed to Maitreya or Asanga. The "writings of Seng-chao" refers to The Afterword of the Lotus Sutra Translation. Seng-chao (384–414) was one of Kumārajīva's major disciples. The records of Shōtoku, Dengyō, and Annen probably indicate the same sources cited in n. 4.

7. The priest Budda is generally believed to refer to Butchi-bō Kakuan, a disciple of Dainichi (n.d.) who spread the Zen teachings in Japan before Eisai (1141–1215), the founder of the Rinzai school of Zen Buddhism. Dainichi, also called Nōnin,

named his school the Japanese Bodhidharma school.

8. Nirvana Sutra.

9. Lotus Sutra, chap. 10.

10. Ibid., chap. 14.

11. Ibid., chap. 13.

12. Ibid., chap. 16.

13. The Annotations on the Nirvana Sutra.

Questions and Answers about Embracing the Lotus Sutra

QUESTION: I have had the rare opportunity to be born a human being and the good fortune to encounter Buddhism. But it is said that there are shallow teachings and there are profound teachings, and that some people rank high in capacity while others rank low. Just what teachings should I practice to attain Buddhahood as quickly as possible? I beg you to instruct me on this point.

Answer: Each family has its respected elders, and each province, its persons of noble station. But although people all look up to their particular lord and pay honor to their own parents, could anyone stand higher than the ruler of the nation?

In the same way, confrontations between the Mahayana and the Hinayana or between the provisional and true teachings are comparable to disputes among rival houses; but among all the sacred teachings expounded by the Buddha in the course of his lifetime, the Lotus Sutra alone holds the position of absolute superiority. It is the guidepost that points the way to the immediate attainment of perfect wisdom, the carriage that takes us at once to the place of enlightenment.

Question: As I understand it, a teacher is someone who has grasped the central meaning of the sutras and treatises and who writes commentaries explaining them. If that is so, then it is only natural that the teachers of the various schools should each formulate doctrines according to their own understanding, and on that basis write their commentaries, establish principles, and dedicate themselves to the attainment of enlightenment. How could such efforts be in vain? To insist that the Lotus Sutra alone holds the position of absolute superiority is to adopt too narrow a view, I believe.

Answer: If you think that to proclaim the absolute superiority of the Lotus Sutra is to take too narrow a view, then one would have to conclude that no one in the world was more narrow-minded than Shakyamuni Buddha. I am afraid you are greatly mistaken in this matter. Let me quote from one of the sutras and from the commentary of one school, and see if I can resolve your confusion.

The Immeasurable Meanings Sutra says: "[Because people's natures and desires are not alike], I preached the Law in various different ways. Preaching the Law in various different ways, I made use of the power of expedient means. But in these more than forty years, I have not yet revealed the truth."

Hearing this pronouncement, Great Adornment and the others of the eighty thousand bodhisattvas replied in p.56unison, voicing their understanding that "[as for those living beings who are unable to hear this sutra . . .] though immeasurable, boundless, inconceivable asamkhya kalpas may pass, they will in the end fail to gain unsurpassed enlightenment."

The point of this passage is to make clear that, no matter how much one may aspire to the Buddha way by calling upon the name of Amida Buddha, or by embracing the teachings of the Zen school—relying on the sutras of the Flower Garland, Āgama, Correct and Equal, and Wisdom periods preached by the Buddha during the previous forty years and more—one will never succeed in attaining supreme enlightenment, even though a countless, limitless, inconceivable number of asamkhya kalpas should pass.

And this is not the only passage of this type. The "Expedient Means" chapter of the Lotus Sutra states, "The World-Honored One has long expounded his doctrines and now must reveal the truth." It also says, "[In the Buddha lands of the ten directions] there is only the Law of the one vehicle, there are not two, there are not three." These passages mean that only this [Lotus] sutra represents the truth.

Again, in the second volume it says, "I am the only person who can rescue and protect others."1 And it speaks of "desiring only to accept and embrace the sutra of the great vehicle and not accepting a single verse of the other sutras."2 These passages mean that only Shakyamuni Buddha can save and protect all living beings, and that one should wish to accept and uphold only the Lotus Sutra, and never even a verse from any other sutra.3

It also says, "If a person fails to have strong mind of determination but instead slanders this sutra, immediately he will destroy all the seeds for becoming a Buddha in this world. . . . When his life comes to an end he will enter the Avīchi hell."4 This passage means that, if one does not believe in the Lotus Sutra but instead turns against it, one will immediately destroy the seeds for attaining Buddhahood in this world. After death, one will fall into the hell of incessant suffering.

Examining these passages, T'ien-t'ai concluded that it was statements such as these that had prompted the words, "Is this not a devil pretending to be the Buddha?"5 If we merely rely upon the commentaries of various teachers and do not follow the statements of the Buddha himself, then how can we call our beliefs Buddhism? To do so would be absurd beyond description!

Therefore, the Great Teacher Chishō stated that, if one claims that there is no division of Mahayana and Hinayana among the sutras and no distinction of partial and perfect among revelations of the truth, and therefore accepts all the words of the various teachers, and then the preachings of the Buddha will have been to no purpose.6

T'ien-t'ai asserted, "That which has a profound doctrine and accords with the sutras is to be written down and made available. But put no strong mind of determination in anything that in word or meaning fails to do so."7 He also said, "All assertions that lack scriptural proof are to be branded as false."8 How would you interpret such statements?

Question: What you have just said may apply to the commentaries of the teachers. But what about the sutras preached before the Lotus Sutra that state, "This is the foremost sutra" or "This is the king of sutras"? If one were to go by what you have said, then one would have to reject these pronouncements, which are the words of the Buddha himself. Is this not so?

Answer: Although these earlier sutras may include such statements as "this is the foremost sutra" or "this is the king of sutras," they are all nevertheless provisional teachings. One p.57should not rely on such pronouncements. The Buddha himself commented on this point when he said, "Rely on sutras that are complete and final and not on those that are not complete and final."9 And the Great Teacher Miao-lo stated: "Though other sutras may call themselves the king among sutras, there is none that announces itself as foremost among all the sutras preached in the past, now being preached, or to be preached in the future.10 Thus one should understand them according to the principle of 'combining, excluding, corresponding, and including.'"11 This passage of commentary is saying in essence that even if there should be a sutra that calls itself the king of sutras, if it does not also declare itself superior to those preached before it and those to be preached after, then one should know that it is a sutra belonging to the expedient teachings.

It is the way of the sutras preached before the Lotus Sutra to say nothing concerning the sutras that would be preached in the future. Only in the case of the Lotus Sutra, because it is the final and ultimate statement of the Buddha's teachings, do we find a clear pronouncement that this sutra alone holds the place of absolute superiority "among the sutras I have preached, now preach, and will preach."

Hence one commentary states, "Only in the Lotus Sutra did the Buddha explain the meaning of his earlier teachings and clarify the true meaning of this present teaching."12 Thus we may see that, in the Lotus Sutra, the Thus Come One gave definite form both to his true intention and to the methods to be used in teaching and converting living beings.

It is for this reason that T'ien-t'ai stated: "After the Thus Come One attained enlightenment, for forty years and more he did not reveal the truth. With the Lotus Sutra, he for the first time revealed the truth."13 In other words, for more than forty years after the Thus Come One went out into the world, he did not reveal the true teaching. In the Lotus Sutra, he for the first time revealed the true way that leads to the attainment of Buddhahood.

Question: I understand what you say about the Lotus Sutra being foremost among all the sutras that the Buddha "has preached, now preaches, and will preach." But there is a certain teacher who says that the statement "In these more than forty years, I have not yet revealed the truth" is meant to apply only to the voice-hearers, who were able to achieve Buddhahood through the Lotus Sutra. It does not apply to the bodhisattvas, who had already gained the benefit of enlightenment through the sutras preached prior to the Lotus Sutra. What is your opinion on this matter?

Answer: You are referring to the view that the Lotus Sutra was preached for the benefit of those of the two vehicles and not for bodhisattvas, and that the words "I have not yet revealed the truth" therefore apply only to the two vehicles. This was the opinion put forth by the Great Teacher Tokuitsu, a priest of the Dharma Characteristics school. It has been repudiated by the Great Teacher Dengyō, who wrote: "There is at present a certain feeder on lowly food who has composed several volumes of spurious writings, slandering the Law and slandering persons. How can he possibly escape falling into hell!"14 As a result of these words of censure directed at him, Tokuitsu's tongue split into eight pieces and he died.

Be that as it may, the assertion that the statement "I have not yet revealed the truth" was made for the sake of the people of the two vehicles is in itself completely reasonable. The reason is that, from the very beginning, the fundamental purpose of the Thus Come p.58One's preaching was to open the way to enlightenment for the people of the two vehicles. And the methods of instruction used throughout his teaching life, as well as the skillful means exhibited in his three cycles of preaching, were chiefly employed for them.

In the Flower Garland Sutra, beings dwelling in hell are deemed able to become Buddhas, but voice-hearers and cause-awakened ones are condemned as incapable of doing so. In the Correct and Equal sutras, it is stated that, just as lotus flowers cannot grow on the peak of a high mountain, so the people of the two vehicles have scorched the seeds of Buddhahood [and hence can never attain it]. And in the Wisdom sutras, we read that persons who have committed the five cardinal sins can attain Buddhahood, but that those of the two vehicles are rejected as unable to do so. The Thus Come One now declared as his true intention that these pitiful, abandoned persons could indeed attain Buddhahood, using this as a standard to demonstrate the superiority of the Lotus Sutra.

Therefore, T'ien-t'ai stated: "Neither the Flower Garland Sutra nor the Larger Wisdom Sutra could cure [the plight of these persons of the two vehicles]. The Lotus Sutra alone was able to produce the roots of goodness in those who have nothing more to learn,15 and to make it possible for them to attain the Buddha way. Therefore, the sutra is called myō, or wonderful. Again, the icchantikas, or persons of incorrigible disbelief, nevertheless have minds, and so it is still possible for them to attain Buddhahood. But persons of the two vehicles have annihilated consciousness, and therefore cannot arouse the mind that aspires to enlightenment. And yet the Lotus Sutra can cure them, which is why it is called myō, or wonderful."16

There is no need for me to explain in detail the import of this passage. One should understand once and for all that even the medicine of the teachings offered by the Flower Garland, Correct and Equal, and Larger Wisdom sutras cannot cure the grave illness that afflicts persons of the two vehicles. Moreover, in the sutras preached before the Lotus Sutra, even guilty persons who are condemned to inhabit the three evil paths are regarded as bodhisattvas and therefore able to attain Buddhahood, but no such recognition is accorded to the persons of the two vehicles.

With regard to this point, the Great Teacher Miao-lo stated: "In the various sutras, it is sometimes taught that beings in all other paths are led to the true [path of Buddhahood], but there is absolutely no such hope offered to the two vehicles. Therefore, [in the Lotus Sutra] beings in the six paths are grouped with bodhisattvas [as being assured of Buddhahood], and the power of the sutra is set forth with respect to those of the two vehicles for whom Buddhahood is the most difficult to achieve."17 Indeed, T'ien-t'ai established that the attainment of Buddhahood by persons of the two vehicles is proof that all living beings without exception can become Buddhas.

Could one think it difficult for an asura to cross the great ocean? Could one possibly think it easy for a little child to overthrow a strong man? In like manner, the sutras preached before the Lotus Sutra explain that persons who have the seeds of the Buddha nature may attain Buddhahood, but nowhere is it stated that those whose seeds are hopelessly scorched can ever do so. It is only the good medicine of the Lotus Sutra that can readily cure this grave affliction.

Now, if you wish to attain Buddhahood, you have only to lower the banner of your arrogance, cast aside the staff of your anger, and devote yourself exclusively to the one vehicle of the p.59Lotus Sutra. Worldly fame and profit are mere baubles of your present existence, and arrogance and prejudice are ties that will fetter you in the next one. Ah, you should be ashamed of them! And you should fear them, too!

Question: Since, by means of a single instance, one may surmise the nature of all, on hearing your brief remarks about the Lotus Sutra, I feel that my ears and eyes have been clearly opened for the first time. But how can one understand the Lotus Sutra, so as to quickly reach the shore of enlightenment?

I have heard it said that only one for whom the sun of wisdom shines unclouded in the great sky of the three thousand realms in a single moment of life, and for whom the water of wisdom in the broad pond of the threefold contemplation in a single mind is clear and never muddied, has the capacity to carry out the practice of this sutra. But I have never exerted myself to study the various schools of the southern capital of Nara, and so I know nothing of the doctrines of The Treatise on the Stages of Yoga Practice and The Treatise on the Consciousness-Only Doctrine; and my eyes are equally unopened with respect to the teachings of the northern peak of Hiei, and so I am quite confused about the significance of the works Great Concentration and Insight and The Profound Meaning of the Lotus Sutra. With regard to the Tendai and Dharma Characteristics schools, I am like a person with a pot over his head who is standing with his face to a wall. It would seem, therefore, that my capacity is not suited to the Lotus Sutra. What am I to do?

Answer: It is the way of scholars these days to assert that only those who possess superior wisdom and strenuously exert themselves in the practice of meditation have the capacity to benefit from the Lotus Sutra, and to discourage persons who lack wisdom from even trying. But this is in fact an utterly ignorant and erroneous view. The Lotus Sutra is the teaching that enables all living beings to attain the Buddha way. Therefore, the persons of superior faculties and superior capacity should naturally devote themselves to contemplation and to meditating on the Law. But, for persons of inferior faculties and inferior capacity, the important thing is simply to have a heart of strong mind of determination. Hence the sutra states: "If there are good men or good women who . . . believe and revere it with pure hearts and harbor no doubts or perplexities, they will never fall into hell or the realm of hungry spirits or of beasts, but will be born in the presence of the Buddhas of the ten directions."18 One should have complete strong mind of determination in the Lotus Sutra and look forward to being born in the presence of the Buddhas in one's next life.

To illustrate, suppose that a person is standing at the foot of a tall embankment and is unable to ascend. And suppose that there is someone on top of the embankment who lowers a rope and says, "If you take hold of this rope, I will pull you up to the top of the embankment." If the person at the bottom begins to doubt that the other has the strength to pull him up, or wonders if the rope is not too weak and therefore refuses to put forth his hand and grasp it, then how is he ever to get to the top of the embankment? But if he follows the instructions, puts out his hand, and takes hold of the rope, then he can climb up.

If one doubts the strength of the Buddha when he says, "I am the only person who can rescue and protect others"; if one is suspicious of the rope held out by the Lotus Sutra when its teachings declare that one can "gain entrance through strong mind of determination alone";19 if one fails to chant the Mystic Law which guarantees that "such a person assuredly and without doubt [will attain the p.60Buddha way],"20 then the Buddha's power cannot reach one, and it will be impossible to scale the embankment of enlightenment.

Lack of strong mind of determination is the basic failing that causes a person to fall into hell. Therefore, the sutra states, "If with regard to this sutra one should harbor doubt and fail to believe, one will fall at once into the evil paths."21

When one has had the rare good fortune to be born a human being, and the further good fortune to encounter the teachings of Buddhism, how can one waste this opportunity? If one is going to take strong mind of determination at all, then among all the various teachings of the Mahayana and the Hinayana, provisional and true doctrines, one should believe in the one vehicle, the true purpose for which the Buddhas come into the world and the direct path to attaining enlightenment for all living beings.

If the sutra that one embraces is superior to all other sutras, then the person who can uphold its teachings must likewise surpass other people. That is why the Lotus Sutra states, "A person who can accept and uphold this sutra is likewise foremost among all living beings."22 There is no question about these golden words of the great sage. And yet people fail to understand this principle or to examine the matter, but instead seek worldly reputation or give way to suspicion and prejudice, thus forming the basis for falling into hell.

All I wish is that you will embrace this sutra and cast your name upon the sea of the vows made by the Buddhas of the ten directions, that you entrust your honor to the heaven that is the compassion of the bodhisattvas of the three existences. One who thus embraces the Lotus Sutra will cause the heavenly gods, dragons, and the others of the eight kinds of nonhuman beings, as well as all the great bodhisattvas, to become one's followers. Not only that, but that person's physical body, still in the process of forming causes for achieving Buddhahood, will acquire the Buddha eye of one who has perfected that course; and this ordinary flesh that exists in the realm of the conditioned will put on the holy garments of the unconditioned. Then one need never fear the three paths23 or tremble before the eight difficulties.24 One will ascend to the peak of the mountain of the seven expedients and sweep away the clouds of the nine worlds. Flowers will bloom in the garden of immaculate earth, and the moon will shine brightly in the sky of the Dharma nature. One can rely on the passage that promises, "Such a person assuredly and without doubt will attain the Buddha way," and there is no question about the Buddha's pronouncement that "I am the only person who can rescue and protect others."

The blessings gained by arousing even a single moment of strong mind of determination in and understanding of the Lotus Sutra surpass those of practicing the five prāmitās;25 and the benefit enjoyed by the fiftieth person who rejoices on hearing the Lotus Sutra is greater than that acquired by giving alms for eighty years.26 The doctrine of the immediate attainment of enlightenment far outshines the doctrines of other scriptures; and the pronouncements concerning the revelation of the Buddha's original enlightenment and his immeasurable life span are never found in any other teachings.

Thus it was that the eight-year-old dragon girl was able to come out of the vast sea and in an instant give proof of the power of this sutra, and Superior Practices, a bodhisattva of the essential teaching, emerged from beneath the great earth and thereby demonstrated the unfathomably long life span of the Buddha. This is the king of sutras, defying description in words, the p.61wonderful Law that is beyond the mind's power to comprehend.

To ignore the supremacy of the Lotus Sutra and assert that other sutras stand on a par with it is to commit the worst possible slander of the Law, a major offense of the utmost gravity. No analogy could suffice to illustrate it. The Buddhas, for all their powers of magical transformation, could never finish describing its consequences, and the bodhisattvas, with all the wisdom at their command, could not fathom its immensity. Thus, the "Simile and Parable" chapter of the Lotus Sutra says, "If I were to describe the punishments [that fall on persons who slander this sutra], I could exhaust a kalpa and never come to the end." This passage means that not even a whole kalpa would be time enough to explain the full gravity of the offense of a person who acts even once against the Lotus Sutra.

For this reason, a person who commits this offense will never be able to hear the preaching of the Buddhas of the three existences, and will be cut off from the doctrines of the Thus Come Ones, who are as numerous as the sands of the Ganges. Such a person will move from darkness into greater darkness. How could he escape the pains and sufferings of the great citadel of the Avīchi hell? Could a thoughtful person fail to dread the prospect of lengthy kalpas of misery?

Thus the sutra states, "If this person . . . on seeing those who read, recite, copy, and uphold this sutra, should despise, hate, envy, or bear grudges against them . . . When his life comes to an end he will enter the Avīchi hell." This passage means that a person who despises, looks down on, hates, envies, or holds a grudge against those who read and embrace the Lotus Sutra will fall into the great citadel of the Avīchi hell after he dies.27 Who could help but fear these golden words of the great sage? And who could doubt the clear-cut pronouncement of the Buddha when he said, "Honestly discarding expedient means, [I will preach only the unsurpassed way]"?28

However, people all turn their backs on these sutra passages, and the world as a whole is completely confused with regard to the principles of Buddhism. Why do you persist in following the teachings of evil friends? T'ien-t'ai said that to accept and put strong mind of determination in the doctrines of evil teachers is the same as drinking poison.29 You should deeply consider this and beware!

Taking a careful look at the world today, we see that, although people declare that the Law is worthy of respect, they all express hatred for the person who upholds it. You yourself seem to be very much confused as to the source from which the Law springs. Just as all the different kinds of plants and trees come forth from the earth, so all the various teachings of the Buddha are spread by persons. As T'ien-t'ai said: "Even during the Buddha's lifetime, the Law was revealed by people. How, then, in the latter age, can one say that the Law is worthy of respect, but that the person who upholds it is to be despised?"30

Hence, if the Law that one embraces is supreme, then the person who embraces it must accordingly be foremost among all others. And if that is so, then to speak ill of that person is to speak ill of the Law, just as to show contempt for the child is to show contempt for the parents.

You should realize from this that the people of today speak words that in no way match what is in their hearts. It is as though they were to beat their parents with a copy of The Classic of Filial Piety. When they know that, unseen by others, the Buddhas and bodhisattvas are observing them, how can they fail to be ashamed of such actions! The pains of hell are frightful indeed. Beware of them! Beware of them!

p.62When you look at those of superior capacity, do not disparage yourself. The

Buddha's true intention was that no one, even those of inferior capacity, be denied enlightenment. Conversely, when you compare yourself with persons of inferior capacity, do not be arrogant and over-proud. Even persons of superior capacity may be excluded from enlightenment if they do not devote themselves wholeheartedly.

One may think fondly of one's native village, but, paying no visit and with no particular reason to go, one in time gives up the idea of returning. Or one may pine for a particular person, but, with no hope of winning that person's love and having exchanged no vows, one abandons the thought of waiting. So in like manner we neglect to journey to the pure land of Eagle Peak, though it surpasses in grandeur the palaces of nobles and high ministers, and moreover is quite easy to reach. We fail to behold the gentle and benign figure of the Buddha, who has declared, "I am a father to you,"31 though we ought surely to present ourselves before him. Should we not grieve at this, until our sleeves are drenched with tears and our heart consumed by regret?

The color of the clouds in the sky as twilight falls, the waning light of the moon when dawn is breaking—these things make us ponder. In the same way, whenever events remind us of life's uncertainty, we should fix our thoughts on the existence to come. When we view the blossoms of spring or the snow on a winter morning, we should think of it, and even on evenings when winds bluster and gathering clouds tumble across the sky, we should not forget it even for an instant.

Life lasts no longer than the time the exhaling of one breath awaits the drawing of another. At what time, what moment, should we ever allow ourselves to forget the compassionate vow of the Buddha, who declared, "At all times I think to myself: [How can I cause living beings to gain entry into the unsurpassed way and quickly acquire the body of a Buddha]?"32 On what day or month should we permit ourselves to be without the sutra that says, "[If there are those who hear the Law], then not a one will fail to attain Buddhahood"?33

How long can we expect to live on as we have, from yesterday to today or from last year to this year? We may look back over our past and count the years we have accumulated, but when we look ahead into the future, who can for certain number himself among the living for another day or even for an hour? Yet, though one may know that the moment of one's death is already at hand, one clings to arrogance and prejudice, to worldly fame and profit, and fails to devote oneself to chanting the Mystic Law. Such an attitude is futile beyond description! Even though the Lotus Sutra is called the teaching that enables all living beings to attain the Buddha way, how could a person such as this actually attain it? It is said that even the moonlight will not deign to shine on the sleeve of an unfeeling person.

Moreover, as life does not go beyond the moment, the Buddha expounded the blessings that come from a single moment of rejoicing [on hearing the Lotus Sutra]. If two or three moments were required, this could no longer be called the original vow of the Buddha endowed with great impartial wisdom, the single vehicle of the teaching that directly reveals the truth and leads all living beings to attain Buddhahood.

As for the time of its propagation, the Lotus Sutra spreads during the latter age, when the Buddha's Law is about to perish. As for what capacity of persons it is suited to, it can save even those who commit the five cardinal sins, or who slander the correct p.63teaching. Therefore, you must be guided by the intent of [the Lotus Sutra, which is] the immediate attainment of enlightenment, and never give yourself up to the mistaken views that stem from doubts or attachments.

How long does a lifetime last? If one stops to consider, it is like a single night's lodging at a wayside inn. Should one forget that fact and seek some measure of worldly fame and profit? Though you may gain them, they will be mere prosperity in a dream, a delight scarcely to be prized. You would do better simply to leave such matters to the karma formed in your previous existences.

Once you awaken to the uncertainty and transience of this world, you will find endless examples confronting your eyes and filling your ears. Vanished like clouds or rain, the people of past ages have left nothing but their names. Fading away like dew, drifting far off like smoke, our friends of today too disappear from sight. Should you suppose that you alone can somehow remain forever like the clouds over Mount Mikasa?[34]

The spring blossoms depart with the wind; maple leaves turn red in autumn showers. All are proof that no living thing can stay for long in this world. Therefore, the Lotus Sutra counsels us, "Nothing in this world is lasting or firm but all are like bubbles, foam, heat shimmer."[35]

"[At all times I think to myself]: How can I cause living beings to gain entry into the unsurpassed way?" These words express the Buddha's deepest wish to enable both those who accept the Lotus Sutra and those who oppose it to attain Buddhahood. Because this is his ultimate purpose, those who embrace the Lotus Sutra for even a short while are acting in accordance with his will. And if they act in accordance with the Buddha's will, they will be repaying the debt of gratitude they owe to the Buddha. The words of the sutra, which are as full of compassion as a mother's love, will then find solace, and the cares of the Buddha, who said, "I am the only person who can rescue and protect others," will likewise be eased. Not only will Shakyamuni Buddha rejoice, but because the Lotus Sutra is the ultimate purpose for which all Buddhas appear in the world, the Buddhas of the ten directions and the three existences will likewise rejoice. As Shakyamuni said, "[If one can uphold it even for a short while] I will surely rejoice and so will the other Buddhas."36 Not only will the Buddhas rejoice, but the gods also will join in their delight. Thus, when the Great Teacher Dengyō lectured on the Lotus Sutra, Great Bodhisattva Hachiman presented him with a purple surplice,37 and when the Honorable Kūya38 recited the Lotus Sutra, the great deity of Matsuo Shrine was able to gain protection from the cold wind.

For this reason, when praying that "the seven disasters will instantly vanish, and the seven blessings will instantly appear,"39 this sutra is the most effective of all. That is because it promises that its votaries "will enjoy peace and security in their present existence."40 And when offering prayers to avert the disasters of foreign invasion and internal revolt, nothing can surpass this wonderful sutra, because it makes certain that persons who embrace it will "suffer no decline or harm within the area of a hundred yojanas."41

Nonetheless, the way that prayers are offered in our present age is the exact opposite of what it ought to be. Prayers today are based upon the provisional teachings, which were intended for propagation in previous ages, rather than upon the secret Law of the highest truth, which is intended for propagation in the latter age. To proceed in this way is like trying to make use of last year's calendar, or to employ a crow p.64for the kind of fishing that only a cormorant can do.

This situation has come about solely because the error-bound teachers of the provisional teachings are accorded high honor, while the teacher enlightened to the true doctrine has not been duly recognized. How sad to think that this rough gem, such as was presented by Pien Ho42 to the kings Wen and Wu, should find no place of acceptance! How joyful, though, that I have obtained in this life the priceless gem concealed in the topknot of the wheel-turning king,43 for which Shakyamuni Buddha appeared in this world!

What I am saying here has been fully attested to by the Buddhas of the ten directions and is no mere idle talk. Therefore, knowing that the Lotus Sutra says, "It will face much hostility in the world and be difficult to believe,"44 how can you retain even a trace of disbelief; and when it says, "Such a person assuredly and without doubt will attain the Buddha way," how can you refuse to become a Buddha?

Since the remotest past up until now, you have merely suffered in vain the pains of countless existences. Why do you not, if only this once, try planting the wonderful seeds that lead to eternal and unchanging Buddhahood? Though at present you may taste only a tiny fraction of the everlasting joys that await you in the future, surely you should not spend your time thoughtlessly coveting worldly fame and profit, which are as fleeting as a bolt of lightning or the morning dew. As the Thus Come One teaches, "There is no safety in the threefold world; it is like a burning house."45 And in the words of a bodhisattva, "All things are like a phantom, like a magically conjured image."46

Everywhere other than the Capital of Tranquil Light is a realm of suffering. Once you leave the haven of inherent enlightenment, what is there to bring you joy? I pray that you will embrace the Mystic Law, which guarantees that people "will enjoy peace and security in their present existence and good circumstances in future existences."47 This is the only glory that you need seek in your present lifetime, and is the action that will draw you toward Buddhahood in your next existence. Single-mindedly chant Nam-Myoho-Renge-Kyo and urge others to do the same; that will remain as the only memory of your present life in this human world. Nam-Myoho-Renge-Kyo, Nam-Myoho-Renge-Kyo.

Nichiren

Background

Although there are different opinions concerning the date of this letter, it is generally accepted that Nichiren Shonin wrote it in the third month of the third year of Kōchō (1263), shortly after he had been pardoned and had returned to Kamakura following two years of exile on the Izu Peninsula. The Shonin was then forty-two years old.

As the title indicates, this work discusses the significance of embracing the Lotus Sutra and is written in the form of five questions and answers. In the first section, the questioner asks: Which teaching should one practice in order to attain Buddhahood quickly? In answer, the Shonin declares that the Lotus Sutra enables all people to achieve Buddhahood without p.65exception and is therefore the highest of all the sutras.

In the second section, the questioner objects to such exclusive emphasis on the Lotus Sutra as narrow-minded. The Shonin replies that his assertion of the sutra's supremacy among all the Buddhist teachings is based on the Buddha's own words as they appear in the sutras themselves, and not on the arbitrary theories or commentaries of later scholars and teachers. When the questioner points out that other sutras also identify themselves as "the foremost sutra" or "the king of sutras," the Shonin explains that such statements are relative. Only the Lotus declares itself to be supreme among all the sutras preached in the past, now being preached, or to be preached in the future. Next, the Shonin says that Shakyamuni Buddha did not reveal the truth during the first forty years and more of his preaching, and that only the Lotus Sutra is the true way that leads to Buddhahood.

The questioner then asks about an interpretation put forth by the Dharma Characteristics school, which claims that the Lotus Sutra is a provisional teaching, expounded solely for the purpose of leading to Buddhahood the people of the two vehicles, voice-hearers and cause-awakened ones, and not for the sake of the bodhisattvas, who had already gained benefit through the pre-Lotus Sutra teachings. The Shonin acknowledges that the Lotus Sutra was indeed expounded chiefly for the people of the two vehicles, whose capacity for supreme enlightenment had been denied in the earlier Mahayana sutras. However, he continues, this does not mean that the Lotus Sutra is a provisional teaching, or that it benefits only the people of the two vehicles. Rather, by singling out those of the two vehicles, for whom Buddhahood is especially difficult to attain, and asserting that even these people can become Buddhas through the power of the Lotus Sutra, Shakyamuni made clear that this sutra is the one vehicle that opens the way to Buddhahood for all people.

In the last section, the questioner, now convinced, asks how one should embrace the Lotus Sutra in order to reach enlightenment quickly. Nichiren Shonin replies that one need not master the principle of three thousand realms in a single moment of life, or perfect the threefold contemplation in a single mind, as the Tendai scholars asserted. Rather, the essential thing is simply to have a heart of strong mind of determination in the sutra. Strong mind of determination, he explains, is the fundamental cause for attaining enlightenment, and to slander the Lotus Sutra and its votary is an act that invites indescribable misery.

A concluding passage of great poetic beauty stresses the fleeting nature of human existence. To be born as a human and, moreover, to encounter the supreme teaching of Buddhism are rare opportunities. Rather than wasting one's brief yet precious life in the pursuit of worldly fame and profit, the Shonin says, one should dedicate oneself to strong mind of determination in the Lotus Sutra and so attain the everlasting joy of enlightenment. He declares that to chant Nam-Myoho-Renge-Kyo oneself and to enable others to do the same are the most important tasks in this present existence.

Notes

1. Lotus Sutra, chap. 3.

2. Ibid.

3. In the Japanese text, the two passages from the Lotus Sutra are written in Chinese original form, followed by the Shonin's interpretation.

4. Lotus Sutra, chap. 3.

5. Ibid.

A Collection of Orally Transmitted Teachings.

7. The Profound Meaning of the Lotus Sutra.

8. Ibid.

9. Nirvana Sutra.

10. A summary of a passage in the "Teacher of the Law" chapter of the Lotus Sutra.

11. The Annotations on "The Words and Phrases of the Lotus Sutra." T'ien-t'ai's principle of "combining, excluding, corresponding, and including" clarifies the relationship between the four teachings of doctrine and the first four of the five periods, and shows that the Lotus Sutra is the only true, perfect teaching.

12. The Annotations on "The Profound Meaning of the Lotus Sutra."

13. Profound Meaning.

14. A rephrasing of a passage in The Outstanding Principles of the Lotus Sutra. By referring to Tokuitsu as a "feeder on lowly food," Dengyō implies that his opponent is content with the four inferior flavors (the provisional teachings of the Flower Garland, Āgama, Correct and Equal, and Wisdom periods), refusing to taste the finest delicacy of ghee, to which the Lotus Sutra is likened.

15. "Those who have nothing more to learn" refers to the people who have reached the state of Arhat, the highest stage of Hinayana enlightenment.

16. Great Concentration and Insight.

17. On "The Profound Meaning."

18. Lotus Sutra, chap. 12.

19. Ibid., chap. 3.

20. Ibid., chap. 21.

21. Ibid., chap. 15.

22. Ibid., chap. 23.

23. The three paths refer here to the path of fire, the path of blood, and the path of swords. Roads that the dead are said to travel. The term is used synonymously with the three evil paths of hell, hungry spirits, and animals.

24. Eight places, states, or circumstances wherein one is unable to see the Buddha or to listen to the Buddha's teaching. They are the realms of hell, hungry spirits, and animals; the heaven of long life, a division within the fourth meditation heaven in the world of form; Uttarakuru, the continent north of Mount Sumeru whose people experience many pleasures; obstruction of the sense organs; prejudice or false views arising from attachment to secular

knowledge; and the period before the Buddha's birth or after his death.

25. The five pāramitās refer to the first five of the six pāramitās or practices. According to the "Distinctions in Benefits" chapter of the Lotus Sutra, to arouse even a single moment of belief and understanding on hearing the Lotus Sutra produces benefit surpassing that of practicing the five pāramitās for eight hundred thousand million nayutas of kalpas.

26. This refers to the following passage in chapter 18 of the Lotus Sutra: "Suppose there is a great dispenser of charity who bestows goods on immeasurable multitudes, doing this for a full eighty years, responding to each person's desires. . . . But the fiftieth person who hears one verse [of the Lotus Sutra] and responds with joy gains blessings that are far greater, beyond description by simile or parable." See also continual propagation to the fiftieth person in Glossary.

27. Here, because the Shonin wrote the above sutra passage in Chinese, he then explains its meaning.

28. Lotus Sutra, chap. 2.

29. The Words and Phrases of the Lotus Sutra.

30. Probably a quote not from T'ien-t'ai but from Miao-lo, in On "The Words and

Phrases." The wording here differs slightly from Miao-lo's.

31. Lotus Sutra, chap. 3.

32. Ibid., chap. 16.

33. Ibid., chap. 2.

34. A mountain located in Nara. A place of great scenic beauty, it often appears in traditional Japanese poetry.

35. Lotus Sutra, chap. 18.

36. Ibid., chap. 11.

37. According to The Biography of the Great Teacher Dengyō, in 814 Dengyō visited Usa Hachiman Shrine in Kyushu, where he lectured on the Lotus Sutra. The deity, much moved, is said to have personally presented Dengyō with a purple robe.

38. Kūya (903–972) was a Nembutsu priest who spread the Pure Land teachings among the common people, traveling from one province to another. He chanted the name of Amida Buddha while dancing in the streets. According to The Biographies of Eminent Priests of Japan, when Kūya stayed at Unrin-in temple in Kyoto, he saw an elderly man, shivering with cold, who announced himself to be the deity of p.67Matsuo Shrine. Though the man had heard the Wisdom sutras, he said, he had not yet been able to hear the Lotus Sutra; so he was still shivering in the

wind of greed and delusion. Kūya recited the Lotus Sutra for him, whereupon the deity was relieved of his suffering.

39. These words appear in the Benevolent Kings Sutra. The "seven disasters" are: (1) extraordinary changes of the sun and moon, (2) extraordinary changes of the stars and planets, (3) fires, (4) unseasonable floods, (5) storms, (6) drought, and (7) war, including enemy attacks from without and rebellion from within. The "seven blessings" means averting or eradicating the seven disasters.

40. Lotus Sutra, chap. 5.

41. Ibid., chap. 26.

42. Pien Ho was a native of the state of Ch'u in China during the Spring and Autumn period (770–403 b.c.e.). According to Han Fei Tzu, Pien Ho found a precious stone at Mount Ch'u and presented it to King Li. When the king had it appraised, it was identified as a mere stone. So the king had Pien Ho's left leg cut off at the knee. After the king's death, Pien Ho again presented the precious stone, this time to King Wu, only to have his right leg cut off at the knee on a second charge of deception. Later, after King Wen had ascended the throne, Pien Ho wept for three days at the foot of Mount Ch'u, holding the precious stone and shedding tears of blood at the kings' ignorance. Hearing of this, King Wen asked for Pien Ho's stone and had it

polished. It was then recognized as being genuine and, in consequence, is said to have been widely treasured by the populace.

43. This story appears in chapter 14 of the Lotus Sutra. The "priceless gem" indicates the one Buddha vehicle.

44. Lotus Sutra, chap. 14.

45. Ibid., chap. 3.

46. Probably a reference to a similar passage in Nāgārjuna's Treatise on the Great Perfection of Wisdom, discussing the non-substantiality of all phenomena.

47. Lotus Sutra, chap. 5.

The Recitation of the "Expedient Means" and "Life Span" Chapters

IN the letter you sent by messenger, you say that you used to recite one chapter of the Lotus Sutra every day, completing the entire sutra in the space of twenty-eight days, but that now you read the "Medicine King" chapter1 once a day. You ask if you should simply read each chapter in turn, as you were originally doing.

As for the Lotus Sutra, one may recite the entire sutra of twenty-eight chapters in eight volumes every day; or one may recite only one volume, or one chapter, or one verse, or one phrase, or one word; or one may simply chant the Daimoku, Nam-Myoho-Renge-Kyo, only once a day, or chant it only once in the course of a lifetime; or hear someone else chant it only once in a lifetime and rejoice in the hearing, or rejoice in hearing the voice of someone else rejoice in the hearing, and so on in this manner to the fiftieth hearer.2 And if one were to be at the end, even if one's strong mind of determination were weak and one's sense of rejoicing diluted like the frailty of a child of two or three, or the inability of a cow or horse to distinguish before from after, the blessings one would gain would be a hundred, thousand, ten thousand, million times greater than those gained by persons of keen faculties and superior wisdom who study other sutras, persons such as Shāriputra, Maudgalyāyana, Manjushrī, and Maitreya, who had committed to memory the entire texts of the various sutras.

We find this mentioned in both the Lotus Sutra and the sixty volumes of commentary3 by T'ien-t'ai and Miao-lo. Thus the sutra states [concerning these blessings], "Even the Buddha wisdom could never finish calculating their extent."4 Not even the wisdom of the Buddha can fathom the blessings such a person will obtain. The Buddha wisdom is so marvelous that it knows even the number of raindrops that fall in this major world system during a period, for instance, of seven days or twice seven days. And yet we read that the blessings acquired by one who recites no more than a single word of the Lotus Sutra are the one thing it cannot fathom. How, then, could ordinary people like ourselves, who have committed grave offenses, possibly understand these blessings?

However, it is now some twenty-two hundred years since the Thus Come One's passing. For many years, the five impurities have flourished, and good deeds in any connection are rare. Though a person may do good, in the course of doing a single good deed he accumulates ten evil ones, so that in the end, for the sake of a small good, he commits great evil. And yet, in his heart, he prides himself on having p.69practiced great good—such are the times we live in.

Moreover, you were born in the remote land of Japan, a tiny island country in the east separated by two hundred thousand ri of mountains and seas from the country of the Thus Come One's birth. And you are a woman, burdened by the five obstacles and bound by the three obediences. How indescribably wonderful, therefore, that in spite of these hindrances you have been able to take strong mind of determination in the Lotus Sutra!

Even the wise or the learned, such as those who have pored over all the sacred teachings propounded by the Buddha in the course of his lifetime, and who have mastered both the exoteric and esoteric doctrines, are these days abandoning the Lotus Sutra and instead reciting the Nembutsu. What good karma you must have formed in the past, then, to have been born a person able to recite even so much as a verse or a phrase of the Lotus Sutra!

When I read over your letter, I felt as though my eyes were beholding something rarer than the udumbara flower, something even scarcer than the one-eyed turtle encountering a floating log with a hollow in it that fits him exactly.5 Moved to heartfelt admiration, I thought that I would like to add just one word or one expression of my own rejoicing, endeavoring in this way to enhance your merit. I fear, however, that, as clouds darken the moon or as dust defiles a mirror, my brief and clumsy attempts at description will only serve to cloak and obscure the incomparably wonderful blessings you will receive, and the thought pains me. Yet, in response to your question, I could scarcely remain silent. Please understand that I am merely joining my one drop to the rivers and the oceans, or adding my torch to the sun and the moon, hoping in this way to increase even slightly the volume of the water or the brilliance of the light.

First of all, when it comes to the Lotus Sutra, you should understand that, whether one recites all eight volumes, or only one volume, one chapter, one verse, one phrase, or simply the Daimoku, or title, the blessings are the same. It is like the water of the great ocean, a single drop of which contains water from all the countless streams and rivers, or like the wish-granting jewel, which, though only a single jewel, can shower all kinds of treasures upon the wisher. And the same is true of a hundred, a thousand, ten thousand, or a million such drops of water or such jewels. A single character of the Lotus Sutra is like such a drop of water or such a jewel, and the hundred million characters6 are like a hundred million such drops or jewels.

On the other hand, a single character of the other sutras, or the name of any of the various Buddhas, is like one drop of the water of a particular stream or river, or like only one stone from a particular mountain or a particular sea. One such drop does not contain the water of countless other streams and rivers, and one such stone does not possess the virtues that inhere in innumerable other kinds of stones.

Therefore, when it comes to the Lotus Sutra, it is praiseworthy to recite any chapter you have placed your trust in, whichever chapter that may be.

Generally speaking, among all the sacred teachings of the Thus Come One, none has ever been known to contain falsehoods. Yet when we consider the Buddhist teachings more deeply, we find that even among the Thus Come One's golden words there exist various categories such as Mahayana and Hinayana, provisional and true teachings, and exoteric and esoteric doctrines. These distinctions arise from the sutras themselves, and accordingly, we find that they are roughly p.70outlined in the commentaries of the various scholars and teachers.

To state the essence of the matter, among the doctrines propounded by Shakyamuni

Buddha in the fifty or more years of his teaching life, those put forward in the first forty or more years are of a questionable nature. We can say so because the Buddha himself clearly stated in the Immeasurable Meanings Sutra, "In these more than forty years, I have not yet revealed the truth." And in the Lotus Sutra, the Buddha himself proclaims concerning its every word and phrase, "Honestly discarding expedient means, I will preach only the unsurpassed way."7

Moreover, Many Treasures Buddha sprang up from the earth to add his testimony, declaring, "The Lotus Sutra of the Wonderful Law . . . all that you [Shakyamuni Buddha] have expounded is the truth!"8 And the Buddhas of the ten directions all gathered at the assembly where the Lotus Sutra was being preached and extended their tongues to give further support to the assertion that not a single word of the Lotus Sutra is false. It was as though a great king, his consort, and his most venerable subjects had all with one accord given their word.

Suppose that a man or a woman who has recited even a single word of the Lotus Sutra were to be dragged down by the unfathomably heavy karma of the ten evil acts, the five cardinal sins, or the four major offenses, and fall into the evil paths. Even if the sun and moon should never again emerge from the east, even if the great earth itself should turn over, even if the tides of the great ocean should cease to ebb and flow, even if broken stones are made whole, and even if the waters of the streams and rivers cease to flow into the ocean, no woman who believes in the Lotus Sutra could ever be dragged down by worldly faults and fall into the evil paths.

If a woman who believes in the Lotus Sutra should ever fall into the evil paths as a result of jealousy or ill temper or because of excessive greed, then the Thus Come One Shakyamuni, the Buddha Many Treasures, and the Buddhas of the ten directions would immediately be guilty of breaking the vow they have upheld over the span of countless kalpas never to tell a lie. Their offense would be even greater than the wild falsehoods and deceptions of Devadatta or the outrageous lies told by Kokālika. But how could such a thing ever happen? Thus a person who embraces the Lotus Sutra is absolutely assured of its blessings.

On the other hand, even if one does not commit a single evil deed throughout one's entire lifetime, and observes the five precepts, the eight precepts, the ten precepts, the ten good precepts, the two hundred and fifty precepts, the five hundred precepts, or countless numbers of precepts; even if one learns all the other sutras by heart, makes offerings to all the other Buddhas and bodhisattvas, and accumulates immeasurable merit, if one but fails to put one's strong mind of determination in the Lotus Sutra; or if one has strong mind of determination in it, but considers that it ranks on the same level as the other sutras and the teachings of the other Buddhas; or if one recognizes its superiority, but constantly engages in other religious disciplines, practicing the Lotus Sutra only from time to time; or if one associates on friendly terms with priests of the Nembutsu, who do not believe in the Lotus Sutra but slander it; or if one thinks that those who insist the Lotus Sutra does not suit the people's capacity in the latter age are guilty of no fault, then all the merit of the countless good acts one has performed throughout one's life will suddenly vanish. Moreover, the blessings resulting from one's practice of the Lotus Sutra will for some time be obscured, and one will fall into the great citadel of the Avīchi hell as p.71 surely as rain falls from the sky or rocks tumble down from the peaks into the valleys.

Even if one has committed the ten evil acts or the five cardinal sins, so long as one does not turn one's back on the Lotus Sutra, one will without doubt be reborn in the pure land and attain Buddhahood. On the other hand, we read in the sutra that, even if one observes the precepts, embraces all the other sutras, and believes in the various Buddhas and bodhisattvas, if one fails to take strong mind of determination in the Lotus Sutra, one is certain to fall into the evil paths.

Limited though my ability may be, when I observe the situation in the world these days, it seems to me that the great majority of both lay believers and members of the clergy are guilty of slandering the correct teaching.

But to return to your question. As I said before, though no chapter of the Lotus Sutra is negligible, among the entire twenty-eight chapters, the "Expedient Means" chapter and the "Life Span" chapter are particularly outstanding. The remaining chapters are all in a sense the branches and leaves of these two chapters. Therefore, for your regular recitation, I recommend that you practice reading the prose sections of the "Expedient Means" and "Life Span" chapters. In addition, it might be well if you wrote out separate copies of these sections. The remaining twenty-six chapters are like the shadow that follows one's body or the value inherent in a jewel. If you recite the "Life Span" and "Expedient Means" chapters, then the remaining chapters will naturally be included even though you do not recite them. It is true that the "Medicine King" and "Devadatta" chapters[9] deal specifically with women's attainment of Buddhahood or rebirth in the pure land. But the "Devadatta" chapter is a branch and leaf of the "Expedient Means" chapter, and the "Medicine King" chapter is a branch and leaf of the "Expedient Means" and the "Life Span" chapters.10 Therefore, you should regularly recite these two chapters, the "Expedient Means" and "Life Span" chapters. As for the remaining chapters, you may turn to them from time to time when you have a moment of leisure.

Also in your letter, you say that three times each day you bow in reverence to the seven characters of the title,11 and that each day you repeat the words Namu-ichijō-myōten12 ten thousand times. At times of menstruation, however, you refrain from reading the sutra. You ask if it is unseemly to bow in reverence to the seven characters or to recite Namu-ichijō-myōten without facing [the Lotus Sutra], or if you should refrain from doing even that during your menstrual period. You also ask how many days following the end of your period you should wait before resuming recitation of the sutra.

This is a matter that concerns all women and about which they always inquire. In past times, too, we find many persons addressing themselves to this question concerning women. But because the sacred teachings put forward by the Buddha in the course of his lifetime do not touch upon this point, no one has been able to offer any clear scriptural proof upon which to base an answer. In my own study of the sacred teachings, though I find clear prohibitions on certain days of the month against the impurity of things like meat or wine, the five spicy foods, or sexual acts, for instance, I have never come across any passage in the sutras or treatises that speaks of avoidances connected with menstruation.

While the Buddha was in the world, many women in their prime became nuns and devoted themselves to the Buddha's teachings, but they were never shunned on account of their menstrual period. Judging from this, I would say that menstruation does not represent p.72any kind of impurity coming from an external source. It is simply a characteristic of the female sex, a phenomenon related to the perpetuation of the seed of birth and death. Or in another sense, it might be regarded as a kind of chronically recurring illness. In the case of feces and urine, though these are substances produced by the body, so long as one observes cleanly habits, there are no special prohibitions to be observed concerning them. Surely the same must be true of menstruation. That is why, I think, we hear of no particular rules for avoidance pertaining to the subject in India or China.

Japan, however, is a land of the gods. And it is the way of this country that, although the Buddhas and bodhisattvas have manifested themselves here in the form of gods,13 strangely enough, in many cases they do not conform to the sutras and treatises. Nevertheless, if one goes against them, one will incur actual punishment.

When we scrutinize the sutras and treatises with care, we find that there is a teaching about a precept known as following the customs of the region14 that corresponds to this. The meaning of this precept is that, so long as no seriously offensive act is involved, then even if one were to depart to some slight degree from the teachings of Buddhism, it would be better to avoid going against the manners and customs of the country. This is a precept expounded by the Buddha. It appears that some wise men who are unaware of this point, express extreme views, saying such things as, because the gods are demon-like beings they are unworthy of reverence, and that this has offended many lay supporters.

If so, since the gods of Japan have in most cases desired that prohibitions be observed during the period of menstruation, perhaps people born in this country should seriously observe such prohibitions.

However, I do not think that such prohibitions should interfere with a woman's daily religious devotions. I would guess that it is persons who never had any strong mind of determination in the Lotus Sutra to begin with who tell you otherwise. They are trying to think of some way to make you stop reciting the sutra, but they do not feel that they can come right out and advise you to cast the sutra aside. So they use the pretext of bodily impurity to try to distance you from it. They intimidate you by telling you that, if you continue your regular devotions during a period of impurity, you will be treating the sutra with disrespect. In this way they mean to trick you into incurring an offense.

I hope you will keep in mind all that I have said regarding this matter. On this basis, even if your menstrual period should last as long as seven days, if you feel so inclined, dispense with the reading of the sutra and simply recite Nam-Myoho-Renge-Kyo. Also, when making your devotions, you need not bow facing the sutra.

On the other hand, if suddenly you should feel, for example, the approach of death, then even if you are eating fish or fowl,15 if you are able to read the sutra, you should do so, and likewise chant Nam-Myoho-Renge-Kyo. Needless to say, the same principle applies during your period of menstruation.

Though reciting the words Namu-ichijō-myōten amounts to the same thing, it would be better if you just chanted Nam-Myoho-Renge-Kyo, as Bodhisattva Vasubandhu and the Great Teacher T'ien-t'ai did.16 There are specific reasons why I say this.

Respectfully,

Nichiren

The seventeenth day of the fourth month in the first year of Bun'ei (1264), cyclical sign kinoe-ne

To the wife of Daigaku Saburō

Background

Nichiren Shonin wrote this letter in 1264, while living in Kamakura, to the wife of Hiki Daigaku Saburō Yoshimoto. Yoshimoto had studied Confucianism in Kyoto where he had served under the Retired Emperor Juntoku. He later went to Kamakura where he was employed by the military government as a Confucian scholar. He is said to have become the Shonin's follower around 1260. Tradition has it that he resolved to embrace the Shonin's teaching upon reading a draft of On Establishing the Correct Teaching for the

Peace of the Land. Both Yoshimoto and his wife were strong believers.

The present letter was written in response to inquiries by Yoshimoto's wife about the formalities to be observed in her daily practice of Buddhism and about the recitation of the sutra and the Daimoku during her menstrual period. Thus this letter is also referred to by the title Letter on Menstruation.

Judging from this letter, it appears that the Shonin had early on established the formula of reciting the "Expedient Means" and "Life Span" chapters of the Lotus Sutra as the daily practice supporting the chanting of the Daimoku. Yoshimoto's wife had at first been following the practice prevalent in her day, that is, continuously reading through the entire sutra, a chapter a day. She had then begun to read only the "Medicine King" chapter. The Shonin praises her efforts and suggests reading the "Expedient Means" and "Life Span" chapters and reciting Nam-Myoho-Renge-Kyo instead of Namu-ichijō-myōten.

Both the question in connection with menstruation and the Shonin's explanation are best understood in the historical context of Kamakura-era Japan. Shinto (literally, the way of the gods), the indigenous Japanese religion, strongly emphasized the observance of ritual purity and had established numerous avoidances, or taboos, to this end. Death, illness, wounds, childbirth, menstruation, and so forth were all regarded as sources of impurity, and a person who experienced any of these, directly or indirectly, was required to undergo ritual purification before engaging in any form of worship. Women were accordingly prohibited from taking part in religious ceremonies during their menstrual period. These taboos were deeply rooted in the popular consciousness and were observed long after the introduction of Buddhism, ultimately becoming mixed with Buddhist practices to the point that few people were aware of their non-Buddhist origin. For example, it was partly out of concern for avoiding such "impurity" that women were often prohibited from entering the grounds of Buddhist monasteries.

In response to the question from Yoshimoto's wife, the Shonin first states that no sutra mentions taboos concerning menstruation. Furthermore, he explains, from a Buddhist perspective no reason exists to consider the menses impure; it is simply a natural function of the body.

However, the Shonin continues, the custom of observing such prohibitions and taboos has been firmly established in Japanese society, and one should not categorically reject social customs and observances simply because they are unrelated to Buddhism. In this connection, he refers to the Buddhist principle of respecting the customs of the region. According to this principle, even if one must depart in terms of minor details from the Buddhist teaching, one should avoid needlessly violating the rules of society. Such flexibility is characteristic of Buddhism, which concerns itself with enabling people to awaken to the fundamental truth of p.74all things, not with governing the details of their lives. Thus, as it has spread, Buddhism has adapted its peripheral aspects to the time and the place, embracing local customs while maintaining its essential message intact.

Nevertheless, though minor details in the practice of Buddhism may be adapted to fit the society, basic principles should not be compromised. The Shonin therefore advises Yoshimoto's wife that honoring the social conventions—in this case, the observance of prohibitions concerning menstruation—does not mean that she should blindly obey them to the extent that they interfere with her daily Buddhist practice.

Notes

1. The "Medicine King" chapter is the twenty-third chapter of the Lotus Sutra. It contains a passage stating that after her death a woman

who practices the Lotus Sutra will go directly to the pure land; thus, it was particularly appealing to women.

2. The Shonin refers here to the principle of continual propagation to the fiftieth person, described in the "Responding with Joy" chapter of the Lotus Sutra. Suppose, the sutra says, a person was to hear the Lotus Sutra and rejoice, then preach it to a second person, who also rejoices and in turn preaches it to a third, and so on, until the fiftieth person hears the sutra. The benefit received by that person on hearing the sutra and rejoicing, even at fifty removes, would be immeasurable.

3. Sixty volumes of commentary: T'ien-t'ai's three major works—The Profound Meaning of the Lotus Sutra, The Words and Phrases of the Lotus Sutra, and Great Concentration and Insight—each consisting of ten volumes, and Miao-lo's three commentaries on those works, each also consisting of ten volumes.

4. Lotus Sutra, chap. 23.

5. These are both Buddhist metaphors for something of very rare occurrence; they are mentioned frequently by the Shonin. The udumbara is a legendary plant said to bloom once every three thousand years to herald the advent of a wheel-turning king or a Buddha. The one-eyed turtle is mentioned in the "King Wonderful Adornment" chapter of the Lotus

Sutra. For the one-eyed turtle, see also Glossary.

6. This is a figurative expression; the Lotus Sutra actually consists of 69,384 characters.

7. Lotus Sutra, chap. 2.

8. Ibid., chap. 11.

9. The "Devadatta" chapter tells the story of the dragon king's daughter, who attained supreme enlightenment in a single moment through the power of the Lotus Sutra. She was considered to represent women's potential for Buddhahood.

10. This statement derives from the Buddhist tradition of analyzing sutras or portions thereof so that they fall into "three divisions" (preparation, revelation, and transmission). In the theoretical teaching, or the first fourteen chapters of the Lotus Sutra, the "Expedient Means" chapter is characterized as revelation and the "Devadatta" chapter as transmission; hence the Shonin says that the "Devadatta" chapter is a "branch and leaf" of the "Expedient Means" chapter. When the entire sutra is considered in terms of the three divisions, both the "Expedient Means" and "Life Span" chapters are characterized as revelation, and the "Medicine King" chapter as transmission; hence the "Medicine King" chapter is a "branch and leaf" of both the "Expedient Means" and "Life Span" chapters.

11. The seven characters consist of the five characters of Myoho-Renge-Kyo and the two for volume numbers.

12. Namu-ichijō-myōten means "devotion to the wonderful sutra of the one vehicle." It was an expression of devotion to the Lotus Sutra that was chanted as an invocation.

13. The Shonin is referring to the widespread belief that the indigenous Japanese deities were local manifestations or incarnations of Buddhas and bodhisattvas. This concept, which took firm hold around the tenth century, reflected a tendency toward the synthesis of Buddhist and Shinto elements.

14. The precept of adapting to local customs. It is mentioned in passages in The Fivefold Rules of Discipline and in the preface to The Essentials of "The Fourfold Rules of Discipline." The precept states that, in matters p.75that the Buddha himself did not expressly either permit or forbid, one may act in accordance with local custom, provided that the fundamental principles of Buddhism are not violated.

15. Eating the flesh of either fish or fowl was also considered a source of impurity.

16. The Treatise on the Lotus Sutra, attributed to Vasubandhu, contains a salutation in praise of the three treasures of the Lotus Sutra that the Shonin may have

interpreted as an expression of devotion to the Mystic Law. The Method of Repentance through the Lotus Meditation, a Chinese text usually attributed either to T'ien-t'ai or to his teacher Nan-yüeh, also contains in several places the phrase "Nam-Myoho-Renge-Kyo."

Encouragement to a Sick Person

I HAVE heard that you are suffering from illness. Is this true? The impermanence of this world is such that even the healthy cannot remain forever, let alone those who are ill. Thoughtful persons should therefore prepare their minds for the life to come. Yet one cannot prepare one's mind for the next life by one's own efforts alone. Only on the basis of the teachings of Shakyamuni Buddha, the original teacher of all living beings, can one do so.

The Buddha's teachings, however, are various, perhaps because people's minds also differ greatly. In any event, Shakyamuni Buddha taught for no more than fifty years. Among the teachings he expounded during the first forty and more years, we find the Flower Garland Sutra, which says, "The mind, the Buddha, and all living beings—these three things are without distinction"; the Āgama sutras, which set forth the principles of suffering, emptiness, impermanence, and non-self; the Great Collection Sutra, which asserts the interpenetration of the defiled aspect and the pure aspect;1 the Larger Wisdom Sutra, which teaches mutual identification and non-duality; and the Two-Volumed, Meditation, and Amida sutras, which emphasize rebirth in the Land of Perfect Bliss. All of these teachings were expounded specifically for the purpose of saving all living beings in the Former, Middle, and Latter Days of the Law.

Nevertheless, for some reason of his own, the Buddha declared in the Immeasurable Meanings Sutra, "[Preaching the Law in various different ways], I made use of the power of expedient means. But in these more than forty years, I have not yet revealed the truth." Like a parent who has second thoughts about the transfer deed he wrote out earlier, Shakyamuni looked back with regret upon all the sutras he had expounded during the previous forty and more years, including those that taught rebirth in the Land of Perfect Bliss, and declared that "though immeasurable, boundless, inconceivable asamkhya kalpas may pass, they will in the end fail to gain unsurpassed enlightenment [through these sutras]."2 He reiterated this in the "Expedient Means" chapter of the Lotus Sutra, saying, "Honestly discarding expedient means, I will preach only the unsurpassed way." By "discarding expedient means," he meant that one should discard the Nembutsu and other teachings preached during those more than forty years.

Having thus undoubtedly regretted and reversed his previous teachings, he made clear his true intention, saying, "The World-

Honored One has long expounded his doctrines and now must reveal the truth,"3 and "For long he p.77remained silent regarding the essential, in no hurry to speak of it at once."4 Thereupon Many Treasures Buddha sprang forth from beneath the earth and added his testimony that what Shakyamuni had said is true, and the Buddhas of the ten directions assembled in the eight directions5 and reached with their long broad tongues to the palace of the great heavenly king Brahmā in testament. All the beings of the two worlds and the eight groups, who were gathered at the two places and the three assemblies, without a single exception witnessed this.

In light of the above sutra passages, setting aside evil people and non-Buddhists who do not believe in Buddhism, with regard to those who, though Buddhist believers, have devout strong mind of determination in provisional teachings preached before the Lotus Sutra such as the Nembutsu, and devote themselves to reciting it ten, a hundred, a thousand, ten thousand, or as many as sixty thousand times a day without chanting Nam-Myoho-Renge-Kyo even once in the course of ten or twenty years, are they not like a person who, clinging to the transfer deed already nullified by his parent, refuses to accept its revised version? They may appear to others as well as to themselves to have strong mind of determination in the Buddha's teachings, but if we go by what the Buddha actually taught, they are unfilial people.

This is why the second volume of the Lotus Sutra states: "But now this threefold world is all my domain, and the living beings in it are all my children. Now this place is beset by many pains and trials. I am the only person who can rescue and protect others, but though I teach and instruct them, they do not believe or accept my teachings."6

This passage means that to us living beings the Thus Come One Shakyamuni is our parent, our teacher, and our sovereign. Although Amida, Medicine Master, and other Buddhas are sovereigns to us living beings, they are neither parents nor teachers. Shakyamuni is the only Buddha endowed with all three virtues and to whom we owe a profound debt of gratitude. There are parents and parents, yet none of them can equal Shakyamuni Buddha. There are all manner of teachers and sovereigns, but none as admirable as he is. Could those who disobey the teaching of this parent, teacher, and sovereign possibly not be abandoned by the heavenly gods and the earthly deities? They are the most unfilial of all children. It is for this reason that the Buddha said, "Though I teach and instruct them, they do not believe or accept my teachings." Even if they follow the sutras preached before the Lotus and practice them for a hundred, a thousand, ten thousand, or a million kalpas, if they do not believe in the Lotus Sutra and chant Nam-Myoho-Renge-Kyo even once, they will be unfilial. They will therefore be abandoned by the sacred ones7 of the three existences and the ten directions, and hated by both the heavenly gods and the earthly deities. (This is the first of the five guides for propagation.)

Even those people who commit the five cardinal sins, the ten evil acts, or innumerable other wrongdoings may attain the way if only their faculties are keen. Devadatta and Angulimāla represent such people. And even those of dull faculties may attain the way, provided they are free of misdeeds. Chūdapanthaka is an example. The faculties of ordinary people like ourselves are even duller than those of Chūdapanthaka. We are unable to discern the colors and shapes of things, as if we had a sheep's eyes. In the vast depths of our greed, anger, and foolishness, we commit the ten evil acts every day, and though we may not commit the five cardinal sins, we also perpetrate offenses similar to these daily.

Moreover, every single person is p.78guilty of slander of the Law, an offense exceeding even the ten evil acts or the five cardinal sins. Although few people slander the Lotus Sutra with actual words of abuse, there are none who accept it. Some appear to accept the sutra, but their strong mind of determination in it is not as deep as their strong mind of determination in the Nembutsu or other teachings. And even those with profound strong mind of determination do not reproach the enemies of the Lotus Sutra. However great the good causes one may make, or even if one reads and copies the entirety of the Lotus Sutra a thousand or ten thousand times, or attains the way of perceiving three thousand realms in a single moment of life, if one fails to denounce the enemies of the Lotus Sutra, it will be impossible to attain the way. To illustrate, it is like the case of someone in the service of the imperial court. Even though he may have served for a decade or two, if he knows someone to be an enemy of the emperor but neither reports him to the throne nor shows personal animosity toward him, all the merit of his past services will be thereby negated, and he will instead be charged with an offense. You must understand that the people of this age are slanderers of the Law. (This is the second.)

The thousand years beginning from the day after the Buddha's passing are called the Former Day of the Law, a period when there were many who upheld the precepts, and people attained the way. The thousand years of the Former Day were followed by the Middle Day of the Law, which also lasted a thousand years. During this period, many people broke the precepts, and few attained the way. The thousand-year Middle Day is followed by the ten thousand years of the Latter Day of the Law. During this period, people neither uphold the precepts nor break them; only those without precepts fill the country. Moreover, it is called a defiled age, an age rife with disorder. In an uncorrupted age, called a pure age, wrong is discarded while right is observed, just as crooked timber is planed according to the mark left by a thread stretched straight. During the Former and Middle Days of the Law, the five impurities began to appear, and in the Latter Day, they are rampant. They give rise to the great waves of a gale, which not only beat against the shore, but strike each other. The impurity of thought has been such that, as the Former and Middle Days of the Law gradually passed, people transmitted insignificant erroneous teachings while destroying the unfathomable correct teaching. It therefore appears that more people have fallen into the evil paths because of errors with respect to Buddhism than because of secular misdeeds.

Now the two thousand years of the Former and Middle Days of the Law have passed, and it has been more than two hundred years since the Latter Day began. Now is the time when, because the impurity of thought prevails, more people fall into the evil paths with the intention of creating good causes than they do by committing evil. As for evil acts, even ignorant people, if they recognize them for what they are, may refrain from committing them. This is like extinguishing a fire with water. But people think that good deeds are all equal in their goodness; thus they adhere to lesser good and do not realize that, in doing so, they bring about major evil. Therefore, even when they see sacred structures related to Dengyō, Jikaku, and others that are neglected and in disrepair, they leave them as they are for the simple reason that they are not halls dedicated to the Nembutsu. Instead, they build Nembutsu halls beside those sacred structures, confiscate the lands that have been donated to them, and offer them to the halls they have erected. According to a passage of the Sutra on Resolving Doubts p.79about the Middle Day of the Law, such deeds will bring few benefits. You should understand from the above that even if one performs a good deed, should it be an act of lesser good that destroys great good, it will cause one to fall into the evil paths.

The present age coincides with the beginning of the Latter Day of the Law. Gone completely are those people with the capacity to attain enlightenment through either the Hinayana or the provisional Mahayana sutras. There now remain only those whose capacity is suited solely to the true Mahayana sutra. A small boat cannot carry a large rock. Those who are evil or ignorant are like a large rock, while the Hinayana and provisional Mahayana sutras as well as the Nembutsu are like a small boat. If one tries to cure virulent sores with hot-spring baths, because the ailment is so serious, such mild treatment will be of no avail. For us in this defiled world of the latter age, embracing the Nembutsu and other teachings is like working rice paddies in winter; it does not suit the time. (This is the third.)

One should also have a correct understanding of the country. People's minds differ according to their land. For example, a mandarin orange tree south of the Yangtze River becomes a triple-leaved orange tree when it is transplanted to the north of the Huai River.8 Even plants and trees, which have no mind, change with their location. How much more, then, must beings with minds differ according to the place!

A work by the Tripitaka Master Hsüan-tsang called The Record of the Western Regions describes many countries in India. In accordance with the customs of the country, there are ones whose inhabitants are undutiful to their parents, and ones where people observe filial piety. In some countries, anger and resentment prevail, while in others, ignorance and foolishness are rampant. There are countries devoted solely to Hinayana, others devoted solely to Mahayana, and still others where both Mahayana and Hinayana are pursued. There are countries wholly given over to the killing of living creatures, countries wholly given over to thieving, countries where rice abounds, and countries that produce much millet. The variety of countries is great.

Then what teaching should the country of Japan learn if its people are to free themselves from the sufferings of birth and death? As for this question, the Lotus Sutra states, "After the Thus Come One has entered extinction, I will cause it [the Lotus Sutra] to be widely propagated throughout Jambudvīpa and will see that it never comes to an end."9 This passage means that the Lotus is the sutra related to the people of Jambudvīpa, the continent of the south. Bodhisattva Maitreya said, "There is a small country in the eastern quarter whose people are related solely to the Mahayana."10 According to this passage from his treatise, within Jambudvīpa there is a small country in the eastern quarter where the capacity of the people is especially suited to the Mahayana sutra. Seng-chao wrote, "This text is destined for a small country in the northeast."11 This indicates that the Lotus Sutra has a connection with a country in the northeast. The Reverend Annen stated, "All in my country of Japan believe in the Mahayana."12 Eshin said in his Essentials of the One Vehicle Teaching, "Throughout Japan, all people share the same capacity to attain Buddhahood through the perfect teaching."

Thus according to the opinions of the Thus Come One Shakyamuni, Bodhisattva Maitreya, the Tripitaka Master Shūryasoma, the Tripitaka Master Kumārajīva, the Dharma Teacher Seng-chao, the Reverend Annen, and the sage of former times Eshin, people p.80in the country of Japan have a capacity suited solely to the Lotus Sutra. Those who put into practice even a phrase or a verse of this sutra are certain to attain the way, for it is the teaching related to them. This may be likened to iron particles drawn to a magnet or dewdrops collecting on a mirror.13 Other good practices such as the Nembutsu are unrelated to our country. They are like a magnet that cannot attract iron, or a mirror that is unable to gather dew. For this reason, Annen stated in his commentary, "If it is not the true vehicle, one is doubtless deceiving both oneself and others."14 This passage means that one who instructs the people of Japan in a teaching other than the Lotus Sutra is deceiving not only oneself but others, too. One therefore must always consider the country when propagating the Buddhist teachings. One should not assume that a teaching suited to one country must inevitably be suited to another as well. (This is the fourth.)

Furthermore, in a country where Buddhism has already spread, one must also take into account the sequence of propagation. It is the rule in propagating Buddhism that one must always learn the nature of the teachings that have already spread. To illustrate, when giving medicine to a sick person, one should know what kind of medicine was administered before. Otherwise, different kinds of medicine may conflict and work against one another, killing the patient. Likewise, different teachings of Buddhism may conflict and interfere with one another, destroying the practitioner. In a country where non-Buddhist teachings have already spread, one should use Buddhism to refute them. For example, the Buddha appeared in India and defeated the non-Buddhists; Kāshyapa Mātanga and Chu Fa-lan went to China and called the Taoists to task; Prince Jōgū was born in the country of Japan and put Moriya to the sword.15

The same principle applies in the realm of Buddhism itself. In a country where the Hinayana has spread, one must refute it by means of the Mahayana sutras, just as Bodhisattva Asanga refuted the Hinayana teachings upheld by Vasubandhu. In a country where provisional Mahayana has been propagated, one must refute it with the true Mahayana, just as the Great Teacher T'ien-t'ai Chih-che defeated the three schools of the south and the seven schools of the north in China. As for the country of Japan, it has now been more than four hundred years since the two schools of Tendai and True Word were propagated. During this period, it has been determined that all four categories of Buddhists—priests, nuns, laymen, and laywomen—have capacities suited to the Lotus Sutra. All people, whether good or evil, wise or ignorant, are endowed with the benefit of the fiftieth hearer. They are like the K'un-lun Mountains, where no worthless stone is to be found, or the mountain island of P'eng-lai, where no harmful potion is known.

Within the past fifty or so years, however, a man of flagrant slander named Hōnen has appeared. He deceived all the people by showing them a stone that resembled a gem and persuading them to discard the gem they already possessed in favor of it. This is what the fifth volume of Great Concentration and Insight means when it says, "They revere shards and rubble, looking on them as bright gems." All the people are clutching ordinary rocks in their hands, convinced that they are precious gems. That is to say, they have discarded the Lotus Sutra to chant the name of Amida Buddha. But when I point this out, they become furious and revile the votary of the Lotus Sutra, thereby increasing all the more their karma to fall into the hell of incessant suffering. (This is the fifth.)

But you, heeding my assertion, p.81discarded the Nembutsu and embraced the Lotus Sutra. Nevertheless, no doubt you may have reverted to being a follower of the Nembutsu. Remember that to discard the Lotus Sutra and become a believer in the Nembutsu is to be like a rock hurtling down from a mountain peak into the valley below, or like rain falling from the sky to the ground. There is no doubt that such a person will fall into the great Avīchi hell. Those related to the sons of the Buddha Great Universal Wisdom Excellence had to spend major world system dust particle kalpas there, and those who received the seeds of Buddhahood in the even more remote past had to spend numberless major world system dust particle kalpas there. This was because they met with companions of great evil and discarded the Lotus Sutra, falling back to provisional teachings such as the Nembutsu. As the members of your family seem to be Nembutsu adherents, they certainly must be urging it upon you. That is understandable, since they themselves believe in it. You should regard them, however, as people deluded by the followers of the diabolical Hōnen. Arouse strong strong mind of determination, and do not heed what they say. It is the way of the great devil to assume the form of a venerable monk or to take possession of one's father, mother, or brother in order to obstruct happiness in one's next life. Whatever they may say, however cleverly they may try to deceive you into discarding the Lotus Sutra, do not assent to it.

Stop and consider. If the passages of proof offered to support the claim that the Nembutsu does in truth lead to rebirth in the Pure Land were reliable, then in the past twelve years during which I have been asserting that Nembutsu believers will fall into the hell of incessant suffering, would they have consistently failed to reproach me, though I spoke out everywhere possible? They are indeed feeble! Teachings such as those left behind by Hōnen and Shan-tao have been known to me since I was seventeen or eighteen. And the arguments that people put forth these days are no improvement.

Consequently, since their teachings are no match for mine, they resort to sheer force of numbers in trying to fight against me. Nembutsu believers number in the thousands or ten thousands, and their supporters are many. I, Nichiren, am alone, without a single ally. It is amazing that I should have survived until now. This year, too, on the eleventh day of the eleventh month, between the hours of the monkey and the cock (around 5:00 p.m.)

on the highway called Matsubara in Tōjō in the province of Awa, I was ambushed by several hundred Nembutsu believers and others.16 I was alone except for about ten men accompanying me, only three or four of whom were capable of offering any resistance at all. Arrows fell on us like rain, and swords descended like lightning. One of my disciples was slain in a matter of a moment, and two others were gravely wounded. I myself sustained cuts and blows, and it seemed that I was doomed. Yet, for some reason, my attackers failed to kill me; thus I have survived until now.

This has only strengthened my strong mind of determination in the Lotus Sutra. The fourth volume of the sutra says, "Since hatred and jealousy toward this sutra abound even when the Thus Come One is in the world, how much more will this be so after his passing?"17 The fifth volume states, "It [the Lotus Sutra] will face much hostility in the world and be difficult to believe."18 In Japan there are many who read and study the Lotus Sutra. There are also many who are beaten in punishment for attempting to seduce other men's wives or for theft or other offenses. Yet not one person has ever suffered injury on account of the Lotus Sutra. Therefore, the p.82upholders of the sutra in Japan are not yet worthy of these sutra passages. I alone have read the sutra with my entire being. This is the meaning of the passage that says, "We care nothing for our bodies or lives but are anxious only for the unsurpassed way."19 I am therefore the foremost votary of the Lotus Sutra in Japan.

Should you depart from this life before I do, you must report to Brahmā, Shakra, the four heavenly kings, and King Yama. Declare yourself to be a disciple of the priest Nichiren, the foremost votary of the Lotus Sutra in Japan. Then they cannot possibly treat you discourteously. But if you should be of two minds, alternately chanting the Nembutsu and reciting the Lotus Sutra, and fear what others may say about you, then even though you identify yourself as Nichiren's disciple, they will never accept your word. Do not resent me later. Yet since the Lotus Sutra answers one's prayers regarding matters of this life as well, you may still survive your illness. In that case, I will by all means meet with you as soon as possible and talk with you directly. Words cannot all be set down in a letter, and a letter never adequately conveys one's thoughts, so I will stop for now.

With my deep respect,

Nichiren

The thirteenth day of the twelfth month in the first year of Bun'ei (1264)

To Nanjō Shichirō

Background

Nichiren Shonin wrote this letter in the twelfth month of 1264, when he was forty-three. Its recipient was Nanjō Hyōe Shichirō, who was the steward of Ueno Village in Fuji District of Suruga Province. He was also called Ueno and was the father of Nanjō Tokimitsu. Sometime between 1260 and 1261, or between 1263 and 1264, while on an official tour of duty in Kamakura, he met the Shonin and was converted to his teaching. However, it appears from this letter that he still retained a lingering attachment to his earlier belief in the Nembutsu and hesitated to commit himself exclusively to the Lotus Sutra.

About one month had passed since Tōjō Kagenobu, the steward of Tōjō Village in Awa Province, had attempted to kill the Shonin at Komatsubara. The Shonin had first incurred the enmity of the steward, a confirmed Nembutsu believer, when he proclaimed his teaching in 1253. Enraged, Tōjō had ordered him arrested. The Shonin had barely managed to escape, and since then he had not been able to return to Awa, his native province. In 1264, however, the year after he had been pardoned from his sentence of exile to Izu and had returned to Kamakura, the Shonin learned that his mother was seriously ill and went to Awa despite the danger to himself. After praying successfully for her recovery, he remained there and resumed his propagation efforts. On his way to visit a believer named Kudō Yoshitaka, he and his group were attacked by Tōjō Kagenobu and his men at Komatsubara. This incident is known as the Komatsubara Persecution.

Shortly after this incident, the Shonin learned that Nanjō Hyōe Shichirō was suffering from a severe illness p.83and wrote this letter to strengthen his strong mind of determination.

In his letter, the Shonin sets forth the criteria known as the five guides for propagation—the teaching, the people's capacity, the time, the country, and the sequence of propagation—factors that one must correctly understand and consider in propagating Buddhism. The Shonin may have formulated the concept of the five guides while in exile on Izu, for they are explained in detail in The Teaching, Capacity, Time, and Country, which he wrote during that period. Elaborating on these five criteria in the present letter, he emphasizes the supremacy of the Lotus Sutra over all other teachings and encourages Nanjō Shichirō to completely discard his lingering attachment to his former belief in the Nembutsu and to arouse single-minded strong mind of determination in the Mystic Law.

Then the Shonin briefly describes the Komatsubara Persecution, which had taken place a month earlier, pointing out that he alone has suffered persecution for the sake of the Lotus Sutra exactly as the sutra itself predicts. He therefore declares himself to be the foremost votary of the Lotus Sutra in Japan.

Notes

1. In his Diamond Scalpel, Miao-lo defines the essence of the Great Collection Sutra as "the interpenetration of the defiled aspect and the pure aspect" and the essence of the Wisdom sutras as "mutual identification and nonduality." Both statements can be interpreted to mean that because all phenomena have emptiness, or non-substantiality, as their true nature, they are without fixed substance, and thus there is no fundamental separation between delusion and enlightenment, or between ordinary people and the Buddha.

2. In the Immeasurable Meanings Sutra these words are spoken by Bodhisattva Great Adornment.

3. Lotus Sutra, chap. 2.

4. Ibid., chap. 5.

5. North, south, east, west, northwest, northeast, southeast, and southwest. This means that all the Buddhas assembled at the ceremony of the Lotus Sutra were on the same horizontal plane.

6. Lotus Sutra, chap. 3. This passage shows the Buddha's three virtues of sovereign, teacher, and parent. "Now this threefold world is all my domain" shows the virtue of sovereign; "The living beings in it are all my children," the virtue of parent; and "Now this place is beset by many pains and trials. I am the only person who can rescue and protect others," the virtue of teacher.

7. The sacred ones refer to Buddhas and bodhisattvas.

8. This phenomenon is referred to in such Chinese classics as The Records of Yen Tzu. It means that a person changes according to his or her circumstances. The Huai River flows eastward from the southern part of Honan Province north of the Yellow River into Lake Hungtse.

9. Lotus Sutra, chap. 28. These words are spoken by Bodhisattva Universal Worthy in a vow he makes before Shakyamuni Buddha.

10. This passage is quoted in Annen's Extensive Commentary on the Universally Bestowed Bodhisattva Precepts as a citation from The Treatise on the Stages of Yoga Practice. No such passage is found in the extant version of that text, but a different version may have been in circulation at that time, or the passage may have been omitted for some reason in the course of transcription.

11. The Afterword to the Lotus Sutra Translation. This passage quotes the words of Shūryasoma when he bequeathed the Lotus Sutra to Kumārajīva.

12. On the Universally Bestowed Bodhisattva Precepts.

13. Vapor condenses on a mirror placed outdoors at night. It was believed that the mirror drew this water from the moon.

14. On the Universally Bestowed Bodhisattva Precepts.

15. Mononobe no Moriya (d. 587), a high official of the Yamato court, is said to have ordered that all the temples and monasteries built by the Soga clan be burned. p.84He and his family were defeated and killed by an army led by Soga no Umako, not by Prince

Jōgū, better known as Prince Shōtoku. But Nichiren Shonin mentions his name here because Jōgū supported the pro-Buddhist Soga.

16. This refers to the Komatsubara Persecution, which occurred about a month before this letter was written.

17. Lotus Sutra, chap. 10.

18. Ibid., chap. 14.

19. Ibid., chap. 13.

Opening the Eyes of Wooden and Painted Images

Background

THE Buddha possesses thirty-two features. All of them represent the physical aspect. Thirty-one of them, from the lowest, the markings of the thousand-spoked wheel on the sole of each foot, up to the unseen crown of his head,[1] belong to the category of visible and non-coextensive physical attributes.[2] They can therefore be depicted in tangible form, such as pictures or statues. The remaining feature, the pure and far-reaching voice, belongs to the category of invisible and coextensive physical attributes.[3] It therefore cannot be captured either in a painting or in a wooden image.

Since the Buddha's passing, two kinds of images, wooden and painted, have been made of him. They possess thirty-one features but lack the pure and far-reaching voice. Therefore, they are not equal to the Buddha. They are also devoid of the spiritual aspect. The Buddha in the flesh is as different from a wooden or painted image as the heavens are from the earth, or clouds from mud. Why, then, does The Epilogue to the Mahāparinirvāna Sutra state that both the living Buddha and a wooden or painted image made of him after his passing bestow equal benefit? Indeed, the Jeweled Necklace Sutra absolutely declares that a wooden or painted image is inferior to the living Buddha.

When one places a sutra in front of a wooden or painted image of the Buddha, the image becomes endowed with all thirty-two features. Yet even though it has the thirty-two features, without the spiritual aspect it is in no way equal to a Buddha, for even some human and heavenly beings possess the thirty-two features. When the Five Precepts Sutra is placed before a wooden or painted image having thirty-one features, the image becomes equal to a wheel-turning king. When the discourse on the ten good precepts is placed before it, the image becomes equal to the lord Shakra. When the discourse on emancipation from the world of desire is placed before it, the image becomes equal to the king Brahmā. But in none of these cases does it in any way become equal to a Buddha.

When an Āgama sutra is placed in front of a wooden or painted image, the image becomes equal to a voice-hearer. When one of the common teachings on wisdom,4 which were preached at the various assemblies held during the Correct and Equal and the Wisdom periods, is placed before it, the image becomes equal to a cause-awakened one. When one of the specific or perfect teachings preached during the Flower Garland, Correct and Equal, or Wisdom period is placed before it, the image becomes equal to a p.86bodhisattva. Yet in none of these cases, either, does it in any way become equal to a Buddha. Buddha Eye's5 mudra and Mahāvairochana's mantra described in the Mahāvairochana, Diamond Crown, and Susiddhikara sutras are useless, for although their names represent the Buddha eye and the great sun, in reality they do not possess these qualities. Similarly, even the Buddha who appears in the Flower Garland Sutra is not the Buddha of the perfect teaching, though his name [Vairochana] suggests that he is.6

When the Lotus Sutra is placed before an image possessing thirty-one features, the image never fails to become the Buddha of the pure and perfect teaching. It is for this reason that the Universal Worthy Sutra, referring to the Buddha of the Lotus Sutra, explains, "A Buddha's three types of bodies are born from this correct and equal sutra." The correct and equal sutra in this phrase does not mean the sutras of the Correct and Equal period; it indicates the Lotus Sutra. The Universal Worthy Sutra also states, "This great vehicle sutra is the eye of the Buddhas. It is through this sutra that the Buddhas are able to acquire the five types of vision."7

The written words of the Lotus Sutra express in visible and non-coextensive form the Buddha's pure and far-reaching voice, which is itself invisible and coextensive, and so possess the two physical aspects of color and form. The Buddha's pure and far-reaching voice, which once vanished, has reappeared in the visible form of written words to benefit the people.

A person gives utterance to speech on two occasions: On one occasion, it is to tell other people what one does not oneself believe in an effort to deceive them. That person's voice in this case "accords with others' minds." On the other, it is to voice what one truly has in mind. Thus one's thoughts are expressed in one's voice. The mind represents the spiritual aspect, and the voice, the physical aspect. The spiritual aspect manifests itself in the physical. A person can know another's mind by listening to the voice. This is because the physical aspect reveals the spiritual aspect. The physical and spiritual, which are one in essence, manifest themselves as two distinct aspects; thus the Buddha's mind found expression as the written words of the Lotus Sutra. These written words are the Buddha's mind in a different form. Therefore, those who read the Lotus Sutra must not regard it as consisting of mere written words, for those words are in themselves the Buddha's mind.

For this reason, T'ien-t'ai in his commentary states: "When the Buddha begins preaching after repeated entreaties from his listeners, he expounds the heart of his teaching. The heart of his teaching is the Buddha's mind, and the Buddha's mind is itself the Buddha's wisdom. The Buddha's wisdom is extremely profound. Therefore, the Buddha refuses three times to proceed with his preaching, and his listeners entreat him four times to continue to preach. The preaching of the Lotus Sutra was accompanied by such difficulties. Compared to the Lotus Sutra, the preaching of the other sutras was an easy matter."8 In this commentary, T'ien-t'ai uses the term "Buddha's mind" to indicate that the sutra, itself a physical entity, actually embodies the Buddha's spiritual aspect.

Because the Lotus Sutra manifests the Buddha's spiritual aspect, when one embodies that spiritual aspect in a wooden or painted image possessing thirty-one features, the image in its entirety becomes the living Buddha. This is what is meant by the enlightenment of plants.

It is for this reason that T'ien-t'ai states, "All things having color or fragrance are manifestations of the Middle p.87Way."9 Commenting on this, Miao-lo adds: "However, although people may admit that all things having color or fragrance are manifestations of the Middle Way, they are nevertheless shocked and harbor doubts when they hear for the first time the doctrine that insentient beings possess the Buddha nature."10 Ch'eng-kuan of the Flower Garland school stole T'ien-t'ai's doctrine of three thousand realms in a single moment of life, using it to interpret the Flower Garland Sutra. Then he wrote: "Both the Lotus and Flower Garland sutras reveal the doctrine of three thousand realms in a single moment of life. The Flower Garland Sutra, however, is the teaching of enlightenment for people of the sudden teaching, because it was preached earlier, while the Lotus Sutra is the teaching of enlightenment for people of the gradual teaching, because it was preached later. The Flower Garland Sutra is the root, because it preceded all the other sutras. The Lotus Sutra consists of nothing but branches and leaves."11 He puffed himself up like a mountain, thinking that he alone had mastered the true teaching. In reality, however, he did not know about the enlightenment of plants, the heart of the doctrine of three thousand realms in a single moment of life. Miao-lo ridiculed the ignorance Ch'eng-kuan showed in the above-quoted statement.

Our contemporary scholars of the Tendai school think that they alone have mastered the doctrine of three thousand realms in a single moment of life. Yet they equate the Lotus Sutra with the Flower Garland Sutra or with the Mahāvairochana Sutra. Their arguments do not go beyond even Ch'eng-kuan's views but remain on the same level as those of Shan-wu-wei and Pu-k'ung. In the final analysis, when the eye-opening ceremony12 for a newly made wooden or painted image is conducted by True Word priests, the image becomes not a true Buddha but a Buddha of the provisional teachings. It does not even become a Buddha of the provisional teachings. Even though it may resemble the Buddha in appearance, in reality it remains the same insentient plant from which it originated. Moreover, it does not even remain an insentient plant; it becomes a devil or a demon. This is because the erroneous doctrine of the True Word priests, expressed in mudras and mantras, becomes the mind of the wooden or painted image. This is like those instances in which the mind causes a person to alter and turn into a rock, as happened with Ulūka or Kapila.

Unless one who has grasped the essence of the Lotus Sutra conducts the eye-opening ceremony for a wooden or painted image, it will be as if a masterless house were to be occupied by a thief, or as if, upon death, a demon were to take possession of one's body. When, in present-day Japan, eye-opening ceremonies for the Buddha images are conducted according to the True Word rite, demons occupy them and deprive people of their lives, for a demon is also known as a robber of life. Moreover, devils enter those images and deprive people of benefits; another name for a devil is a robber of benefit. Because the people worship demons, they will bring the country to ruin in their present lifetime, and because they revere devils, they will fall into the hell of incessant suffering in the next.

When the spirit departs from the body after death, a demon may enter in its place and destroy one's descendants. This is what is meant by a hungry demon that devours even itself. However, if a wise person extols the Lotus Sutra and inspirits the dead person's remains, then, although the deceased's body remains human, that person's mind will become the Dharma body. This accords with the doctrine that one can in one's present form attain the p.88stage where one perceives the non-birth and non-extinction of the phenomenal world. A wise person who has mastered the perfect teaching of the sutras of the Flower Garland, Correct and Equal, or Wisdom period can bring a dead person's remains into the stage of realizing the non-birth and non-extinction of all phenomena. This is what the Nirvana Sutra means when it states, "Although his body remains human, his mind will become equal to that of the Buddha." Chunda set an example of attaining in his present body the realization of the non-birth and non-extinction of all phenomena.

If a wise person enlightened to the Lotus Sutra conducts a service for a deceased person, the deceased's body, just as it is, will become the Dharma body. This is what the phrase "in one's present form" means. Then the wise person will retrieve the departed spirit, bring it back into the remains of the deceased, and transform it into the Buddha's mind. This is what the phrase "attaining Buddhahood" indicates. The words "in one's present form" represent the physical aspect, and "attaining Buddhahood," the spiritual. The deceased person's physical and spiritual aspects will be transformed into the mystic reality and mystic wisdom of beginningless time. This is attaining Buddhahood in one's present form.

Thus the Lotus Sutra states, "This reality [of all phenomena] consists of the appearance (the body of the dead person), nature (the mind), entity (the true entity of body and mind) . . ."13 It also reads, "He profoundly understands the signs of guilt and good fortune / and illuminates the ten directions everywhere. / His subtle, wonderful pure Dharma body / is endowed with the thirty-two features."14 In this last quotation, the first two lines indicate the realization of the non-birth and non-extinction of all phenomena, and the latter two, the attainment of Buddhahood in one's present form. The model of the latter is the dragon king's daughter, while that of the former is Chunda.

Back to Top

Background

This letter is thought to have been written in the first year of Bun'ei (1264), while Nichiren Shonin was living in Kamakura. But the recipient of the letter is not named. In this letter, the Shonin deals with the concept of the enlightenment of insentient beings, first in terms of Buddha images and then in terms of the deceased.

The letter begins with reference to the thirty-two features that the Buddha is said to possess. They represent the Buddha's capacity, virtues, abilities, and so forth. Of the thirty-two features, thirty-one can be depicted in pictures or statues; only the Buddha's pure and far-reaching voice cannot.

Next, Nichiren Shonin compares a wooden or painted image to the living Buddha. Wooden and painted images of the Buddha are inferior to the living Buddha because they lack not only the feature of the pure and far-reaching voice but also the Buddha's mind, that is, his spiritual aspect. The pure and far-reaching voice is the manifestation of the

Buddha's mind. The Buddha's compassion to save the people manifests itself in his voice, that is, in his teachings. Thus, when a sutra is placed before a Buddha image (that is, used to "open the eyes" of the image or consecrate it), it is the same as if it possessed the pure and far-reaching p.89voice. This is because a sutra embodies the Buddha's teachings conveyed by his voice.

However, the Shonin goes on to explain that the kind of sutra used to consecrate an image will determine the nature of the spiritual aspect that the image manifests. He concludes that, since the Lotus Sutra embodies the Buddha's true spiritual aspect, when the Lotus Sutra is used to "open the eyes" of a Buddha image, that image will become equal to the living Buddha. This accords with the principle of the attainment of Buddhahood by plants, "plants" here representing all insentient life.

This concept of the enlightenment of plants in turn derives from the doctrine of three thousand realms in a single moment of life, which teaches that all life—insentient and sentient—possesses the Buddha nature.

Subsequently the Shonin sharply attacks the use of True Word rituals to open the eyes of Buddha images. He points out that using distorted teachings such as those of the True Word to consecrate images will cause demons or devils to occupy them—that is, it will bring forth not the Buddhahood but the diabolical nature inherent in the insentient life of the image, causing suffering for individual believers and disaster for the land in which they live.

In the final section, the Shonin touches on the subject of prayers for the deceased. The idea of the spirit departing from the dead person's body and a demon taking its place actually stems from popular folk belief. The Shonin employs it to make readily understandable to his contemporaries the concept that the religious conduct of the living has an influence on the lives of those who have passed away. In this context, he explains two levels of enlightenment: the realization of the non-birth and non-extinction of all phenomena and the attainment of Buddhahood in one's present form. Both can of course be achieved while one is alive, but since the subject of this letter is the enlightenment of insentient beings, the Shonin explains both in terms of the deceased—death being life's insentient phase—as represented by the dead person's remains. In the text, "a wise person [who simply] extols the Lotus Sutra" is anyone but "a wise person enlightened to the Lotus Sutra" that specifically indicates Nichiren Shonin. The Shonin embodied his perfect enlightenment to the Law of Nam-Myoho-Renge-Kyo in the form of the Gohonzon.

Back to Top

Notes

1. A Buddha is said to possess the markings of a wheel of the Law on the sole of each foot. The "unseen crown of his head" is also often cited as a protuberant knot of flesh resembling a topknot on the crown of the Buddha's head. The top of the Buddha's head is said to be invisible, indicating his inconceivably great wisdom, the boundlessness of his enlightened life, and so forth.

2. The category of visible and non-coextensive physical attributes is the first of the three categories of physical attributes enumerated in The Heart of the Abhidharma. "Non-coextensive" here means that the physical attributes in this category cannot simultaneously occupy the same space. The second category is that of invisible and non-coextensive physical attributes, and the third, invisible and coextensive physical attributes. Mention of this third category immediately follows in the text.

3. According to The Dharma Analysis Treasury, all sounds and voices including the Buddha's pure and far-reaching voice fall under the category of invisible and non-coextensive physical attributes. However, the Shonin assigns the Buddha's pure and far-reaching voice to the category of invisible and coextensive physical attributes, probably to emphasize that it embodies the Buddha's teaching.

4. "The common teachings on wisdom" p.90 refers to the teachings on wisdom which were expounded in common for both voice-hearers and cause-awakened ones of the two vehicles and for novice bodhisattvas. Wisdom here means the wisdom that illuminates all phenomena and their essential truth. In terms of the four teachings of doctrine set forth by T'ien-t'ai, the common teachings on wisdom correspond to the connecting teaching.

5. Buddha Eye is one of the Buddhas who appear in the esoteric teachings. Also called Buddha Mother, this Buddha is said to give birth to all other Buddhas.

6. The Buddha of the perfect teaching refers to the Buddha expounded in the Lotus Sutra. Vairochana, the Buddha of the Flower Garland Sutra, means "coming from or belonging to the sun."

7. The Universal Worthy Sutra actually reads, "This correct and eqaul sutra is the eye of the Buddhas." "This great vehicle sutra" also means the Lotus Sutra.

8. The Profound Meaning of the Lotus Sutra.

9. Great Concentration and Insight.

10. The Annotations on "Great Concentration and Insight."

11. This assertion appears in Ch'eng-kuan's Meaning of the Flower Garland Sutra Based on An Earlier Commentary, though the wording differs slightly. Ch'eng-kuan asserted that, although both the Lotus Sutra and the Flower Garland Sutra lead to enlightenment, the Buddha taught the former as the conclusion of a gradual process of instruction, but expounded the latter to people of superior capacity directly from his own enlightenment without giving any prior instruction. For this reason, he declared the Flower Garland Sutra superior to the Lotus Sutra.

12. Ceremony for consecrating a newly made Buddha image. By means of this ceremony, it is said, the image is endowed with the Buddha's spiritual property, thus making it an object of devotion.

13. Lotus Sutra, chap. 2.

14. Ibid., chap. 12.

The Essence of the "Medicine King" Chapter

CONCERNING the general meaning of this chapter called the "Medicine King": the "Medicine King" chapter is in the seventh volume and is the twenty-third of the twenty-eight chapters that make up the Lotus Sutra.

The first volume of the sutra contains two chapters, the "Introduction" chapter and the "Expedient Means" chapter. The "Introduction" chapter serves as a prologue to the entire twenty-eight chapters.

The eight chapters beginning with "Expedient Means" and continuing through "Prophecies" are concerned primarily with clarifying how persons of the two vehicles can attain Buddhahood, and secondarily with clarifying how bodhisattvas and ordinary people can attain Buddhahood.

The following five chapters, the "Teacher of the Law," "Treasure Tower," "Devadatta," "Encouraging Devotion," and "Peaceful Practices" chapters, explain how the teachings set forth in the preceding eight chapters are to be carried out by ordinary people in the latter age.

The ensuing "Emerging from the Earth" chapter serves as an introduction to the "Life

Span" chapter. The subsequent twelve chapters, numbering from the "Distinctions in Benefits" chapter on, serve primarily to explain how the doctrines set forth in the "Life Span" chapter are to be carried out by ordinary people in the latter age, and secondarily to explain how those set forth in the eight chapters from "Expedient Means" on are to be carried out.

The "Medicine King" chapter, therefore, is a chapter that explains how one ought to carry out the teachings both of the eight chapters beginning with "Expedient Means" and of the "Life Span" chapter.

This chapter, the "Medicine King," contains ten analogies, the first of which is the analogy of the great ocean. I will begin by explaining this analogy in outline form. In the southern continent of Jambudvīpa, there are 2,500 rivers; in the western continent of Godaniya, there are 5,000 rivers. In all the four continents, there are a total of 25,900 rivers. Some of these rivers are forty *ri* in length, some a hundred *ri*, some only one *ri*, one *chō*, or one fathom. However, concerning the matter of depth, not one of these rivers can match the great ocean.

Among all the sutras, such as the Flower Garland Sutra, the Āgama sutras, the Correct and Equal sutras, the Wisdom, Profound Secrets, Amida, Nirvana, Mahāvairochana,

Diamond Crown, Susiddhikara, and Secret Solemnity sutras, all the sutras preached by the Thus Come One Shakyamuni, all the sutras preached by the Thus Come One Mahāvairochana, all the sutras preached by the Thus Come One Amida, all the sutras preached by the Thus Come One Medicine Master, and all the sutras preached by the various Buddhas of the three existences of past, present, and future—among all these sutras, the Lotus Sutra stands foremost. Thus these other sutras are analogous to the large rivers, middle-sized rivers, and small rivers, while the Lotus Sutra is likened to the great ocean.

The ocean possesses ten virtues, in which it surpasses the rivers. First, the ocean gradually becomes deeper, which is not true of rivers. Second, the ocean refuses to house corpses, which is not true of rivers. Third, the ocean obliterates the names of the various rivers that flow into it, while rivers retain their names. Fourth, the ocean's taste is the same everywhere, while this is not true of rivers. Fifth, the ocean contains various treasures that are not found in rivers. Sixth, the ocean is extremely deep, which is not true of rivers. Seventh, the ocean is boundless in breadth, which rivers are not. Eighth, the ocean houses creatures of great size, which is not true of rivers. Ninth, the ocean has tides that ebb and flow, but rivers do not, and tenth, the ocean absorbs the waters of torrential rains or huge rivers without ever overflowing, but this is not true of rivers.

The Lotus Sutra likewise has ten virtues, while the other sutras have ten faults. In the case of this sutra, the benefits gained from it increase in depth and bounty, and they continue down to the fiftieth person who hears of it. In the case of the other sutras, however, there is no benefit to be gained even by the first person who hears them, much less by the second, third, or fourth person, and so on down to the fiftieth person.

Though rivers may be deep, their depth cannot match even the shallow places of the ocean. And though the various other sutras may claim that because of a single character, a single phrase, or the ten meditations[1] they encompass evil people who have committed the ten evil acts or the five cardinal sins, such benefits cannot match those gained by the fiftieth person who hears a single character or a single phrase of the Lotus Sutra and responds with joy.

In the case of the Lotus Sutra, just as the ocean refuses to house corpses, those who slander the Law by turning against the Lotus Sutra will be cast out by the sutra, even though in other respects they may be people of extreme goodness. And how much more so will this be true in the case of evil persons who, in addition to their other evil acts, slander the Law! Though one may speak slanderously of the other sutras, if one does not turn against the Lotus Sutra, one is certain to attain the Buddha way. But though one may put strong mind of determination in all the other sutras, if one turns against the Lotus Sutra, one will invariably fall into the great citadel of the Avīchi hell.

I move now to the eighth virtue of the ocean, the fact that it can house creatures of great size. And we find that in the ocean there are huge fish such as the makara.[2] The place called the hell of incessant suffering measures eighty thousand yojanas in total length and breadth. But when a person falls into the hell of incessant suffering by committing the five cardinal sins, this person alone is sufficient to fill it up completely.[3] Thus we know that the inhabitants of this hell, persons who have committed the five cardinal sins, are beings of very great size.

In the other sutras, which we have likened to small rivers or large rivers, no makara fish are to be found. However, in the great ocean that is the Lotus Sutra, they do exist. And in like p.93 manner, the other sutras do not in fact state that persons who commit the five cardinal sins are capable of attaining the Buddha way. Or even if the sutras do state this, in fact the true principle has yet to be revealed in them.

Therefore, the Great Teacher T'ien-t'ai Chih-che, who had memorized all the sacred teachings of the Buddha's lifetime, says in his commentary on the Lotus Sutra: "The other sutras only predict Buddhahood for bodhisattvas, but not for persons of the two vehicles. They only predict it for the good, but not for the evil; . . . This sutra predicts Buddhahood for all."[4] But I will not go into details on this matter.

Second is the analogy of mountains. The sutra says that, among the Ten Treasure Mountains and all the other mountains, Mount Sumeru is foremost. The Ten Treasure Mountains are: first, the Snow Mountains; second, Mount Fragrant; third, Mount Khadira; fourth, the Mountain of Immortals and Sages; fifth, Mount Yugamdhara; sixth, Horse Ear Mountain; seventh, Mount Nimindhara; eighth, Mount Chakravada; ninth, the Mountain of Past Wisdom; and tenth, Mount Sumeru.

The first nine of these ten mountains are analogous to the various other sutras, which are like ordinary mountains. Each of these mountains contains treasures. But Mount Sumeru contains a multitude of treasures, treasures superior to those of the other mountains. For example, it is like

Jambunada gold,[5] to which ordinary gold cannot compare.

The Flower Garland Sutra has its teaching that "the phenomenal world is created by the mind alone"; the Wisdom sutras have their eighteen kinds of non-substantiality; the Mahāvairochana Sutra has its fivefold meditation for attaining Buddhahood, and the Meditation Sutra has its doctrine of rebirth in the Pure Land. But the Lotus Sutra's teaching of the attainment of Buddhahood in one's present form surpasses all of these.

Mount Sumeru is golden in color. Every creature that comes to this mountain, whether ox or horse, human or heavenly being, bird or any other being, inevitably loses its original color and takes on the golden color of the mountain. This is not true of any of the other mountains. In the same manner, the various other sutras, when placed beside the Lotus Sutra, lose their original color. They are like black objects that, when exposed to the light of the sun or the moon, lose their color. So the teachings concerning rebirth in another land or the attainment of Buddhahood that color these other sutras inevitably lose their meaning when exposed to the light of the Lotus Sutra.

Third is the analogy of the moon. Among the various stars, some can light an area of no more than half a *ri,* some an area of no more than one *ri,* some an area of no more than eight *ri* or sixteen *ri.* But the moon can light an area of over eight hundred *ri.* Thus, although the various stars have their light, it cannot equal that of the moon.

Even if we were to assemble a hundred, a thousand, ten thousand, or a million stars, as well as all the stars from the world of the four continents, from a major world system, and from all the worlds of the ten directions, their light would not equal the light of a single moon. How then could the light of only one star equal the light of the moon?

Similarly, though we gather together all the various sutras, such as the Flower Garland Sutra, the Āgama sutras, the Correct and Equal sutras, the Wisdom, Nirvana, Mahāvairochana, and Meditation sutras, they could never equal even a single character of the Lotus Sutra.

Within the minds of all human beings, there exist the three categories of illusions of thought and desire, of illusions innumerable as particles of dust and sand, and of illusions about the true nature of existence, as well as karma created by the ten evil acts or the five cardinal sins—all of which are like a dark night. The Flower Garland and the other various sutras are like stars in this dark night, while the Lotus Sutra is like the moon. For those who have strong mind of determination in the Lotus Sutra, but whose strong mind of determination is not deep, it is as though a half moon were lighting the darkness. But for those who have profound strong mind of determination, it is as though a full moon were illuminating the night.

On a night when there is no moon, but only the light of the stars, strong men or robust individuals may walk abroad, but elderly people and women will find it impossible to do so. But when there is a full moon, even women and the elderly may walk about anywhere they please, proceeding to a banquet or going to meet others. Similarly, in the various sutras it is said that bodhisattvas and ordinary persons of great capacity can attain enlightenment. But for persons of the two vehicles, ordinary people, women, and evil men, or people in the latter age who are elderly and lazy and do not observe the precepts, no assurance is given that they can ever attain rebirth in the pure land or achieve Buddhahood. This is not so of the Lotus Sutra, however. There even persons of the two vehicles, women, and evil men are assured of becoming Buddhas, to say nothing of bodhisattvas and ordinary persons of great capacity.

Again, the moon shines more brightly around dawn than it does in the early evening, and is more luminous in autumn and winter than in spring and summer. In a similar fashion, the Lotus Sutra is even more effective in bringing benefit to living beings in the Latter Day of the Law than it is during the two thousand years that make up the Former and Middle Days of the Law.

Question: What passages of proof can you offer?

Answer: The truth is plain to see. In addition, this chapter later states as follows: "After I have passed into extinction, in the last five-hundred-year period you must spread it [the Lotus Sutra] abroad widely throughout Jambudvīpa and never allow it to be cut off."[6] This passage from the sutra, which states that it must be widely spread throughout Jambudvīpa, the southern continent, when two thousand years have passed, expresses the same meaning as the third analogy of the moon. The Great Teacher Kompon, also known as the Great Teacher Dengyō, was referring to this idea when he stated in his commentary: "The Former and Middle Days are almost over, and the Latter Day is near at hand. Now indeed is the time when the one vehicle of the Lotus Sutra will prove how perfectly it fits the capacities of all people."[7]

The benefits conferred by the Lotus Sutra surpass those of the various other sutras even during the thousand years of the Former Day of the Law and the thousand years of the Middle Day of the Law. But when the spring and summer of the two thousand years of the Former and Middle Days are over, and the autumn and winter of the Latter Day of the Law have come, then the light of this moon will shine more brightly than ever.

Fourth is the analogy of the sun. When the moon appears in the sky where the stars are shining, although its light surpasses that of the stars, the stars do not actually lose their light. But when the sun appears, not only do the stars lose their light, but the moon, too, is deprived of its light and loses its glow.

The sutras preached before the Lotus Sutra are like the stars, the theoretical teaching of the Lotus Sutra is like the moon, and the "Life Span" chapter is like the sun. When the "Life Span" chapter makes its appearance, then the moon of the theoretical teaching cannot equal it, to say nothing of the stars that are the previous sutras.

During the night, the time of the stars and the moon, people do not pursue their occupations. But when dawn comes, they invariably go about their various tasks. Similarly, while the earlier sutras or the theoretical teaching of the Lotus Sutra prevail, it will be difficult for people to free themselves from the sufferings of birth and death. But once the "Life Span" chapter of the essential teaching makes its appearance, then people are certain to free themselves from the sufferings of birth and death.

I will omit a discussion of the other six of the ten analogies.

In addition to these ten, there are many other analogies in this chapter. Among them is that of a traveler who finds a ship when he wishes to make a crossing. The meaning of this analogy is that, in the sea of the sufferings of birth and death, the sutras preached before the Lotus Sutra are like rafts or small boats. Although they can carry people from one shore in the realm of birth and death to another shore in that same realm, they are incapable of carrying them across the sea of birth and death to the distant shore of Perfect Bliss.[8]

These sutras are like the small boats of our world that can go from Tsukushi to the Bando region, or from Kamakura to Enoshima,[9] but cannot go as far as China. A China ship, on the other hand, is fully capable of going all the way from Japan to China without difficulty.

Again, there is the analogy that reads, "like the poor finding riches." The lands represented by the sutras preached before the Lotus Sutra are impoverished lands, and their inhabitants are like hungry spirits. The Lotus Sutra, on the other hand, is a veritable mountain of riches, and its inhabitants are wealthy.

Question: When you say that the lands of the sutras preached before the Lotus Sutra are impoverished lands, what passage of scripture are you referring to?

Answer: The "Bestowal of Prophecy" chapter [of the Lotus Sutra] states, "Suppose that someone coming from a land of famine should suddenly encounter a great king's feast."

Concerning rebirth in the pure land and the attainment of Buddhahood by women, a passage from the sutra has this to say: "If in the last five-hundred-year period after the Thus Come One has entered extinction there is a woman who hears this sutra and carries out its practices as the sutra directs, when her life here on earth comes to an end, she will immediately go to the World of Peace and Delight where the Buddha Amida dwells surrounded by the assembly of great bodhisattvas and there will be born seated on a jeweled seat in the center of a lotus blossom."[10]

Question: Why do this sutra and this chapter in the sutra make a particular point of discussing rebirth in the pure land by women?

Answer: The Buddha's intentions are difficult to fathom, and the significance of this matter is difficult to determine. But if I were to venture a guess, I would say that it is because women are looked upon as the root of various errors and the source of the downfall of the nation. Therefore, in both Buddhist and non-Buddhist scriptures, there are many prohibitions laid down with regard to women. Among these, for example, are the three obediences set forth in the non-Buddhist scriptures. The "three obediences" means to obey three times and refers to the fact that, when a woman is young, she must obey her parents; when she p.96 marries, she must obey her husband; and in old age, she must obey her son. She is thus confronted with these three obstacles and cannot conduct herself freely in the world.

If we turn to the Buddhist scriptures, we find that they speak of the five obstacles. Of these five obstacles that confront women, the first is the fact that, in the course of being reborn again and again in the six paths, they cannot, like men, ever be reborn as the great heavenly king Brahmā. Second, they can never be reborn as the heavenly king Shakra. Third, they cannot be reborn as a devil king. Fourth, they cannot be reborn as a wheel-turning king. And fifth, they must remain forever within the six paths, unable to emerge from the threefold world and become a Buddha. (This passage is found in the Meditation Outshining the Sun and Moon Sutra.)[11] The Silver-Colored Woman Sutra has this to say: "Even if the eyes of the Buddhas of the three existences were to fall to the ground, no woman in any of the realms of existence could ever attain Buddhahood."

Ordinary human beings though they are, worthy rulers and sages do not tell falsehoods. Thus Fan Yü-ch'i presented his head to Ching K'o, and Prince Chi-cha hung his sword on the grave of the lord of Hsü. They did these things so as not to go against their promises or be guilty of uttering falsehoods. And if such men do not utter falsehoods, how much more is this true of voice-hearers, bodhisattvas, or Buddhas!

In the past, when the Buddha was still an ordinary man and was practicing the teachings of the Hinayana sutras, he undertook to observe the five precepts. And among these five, the fourth is that one must never lie. He firmly observed this precept. Thereafter, even though it meant losing his property or his life, he never violated it.

When he was practicing the teachings of the Mahayana sutras, he observed the ten major precepts, and among these ten major precepts, the fourth is that one must never lie. He strong mind of determination fully observed this precept without once violating it throughout countless kalpas, until in the end, through the power acquired by observing this precept, he was able to attain the body of a Buddha. And among the thirty-two features that distinguish the body of a Buddha, he was able to obtain that of a long and broad tongue.

This tongue of the Buddha's is so thin and broad and long that it can be extended to cover his face or reach up to his hairline, or even to reach to the Brahmā heaven. On this tongue are five figures that are like embossed designs, and the tongue is the color of copper. Underneath it are two jewels that emit amrita.

This tongue was obtained by virtue of the fact that the Buddha observed the precept against lying. And with this tongue he stated that, though the eyes of all the Buddhas of the three existences might fall to earth, no woman in any of the realms of existence could become a Buddha. Thus we may suppose that no woman in any world whatsoever can ever hope to become a Buddha. And if so, then we must assume that, when one is born with the body of a woman, even if one were to rise to the position of one of the three generations of emperor's consorts,[12] it would not help one, and even if one were to perform meritorious acts and practice the teachings of Buddhism, it would do one no good.

Nevertheless, this "Medicine King" chapter of the Lotus Sutra allows the attainment of rebirth in the pure land by women. This is very strange indeed! Is the other sutra lying? Or is this sutra lying? No matter how we look at it, we must suppose that one of them is lying. And if one of them is lying, then the same Buddha is saying two different things, which is very hard to believe.

However, in the Immeasurable Meanings Sutra, the Buddha says, "In these more than forty years, I have not yet revealed the truth." And in the Nirvana Sutra he says, "Though the Thus Come One does not speak untruths, if I knew that by speaking falsely [I could help living beings gain the benefits of the Law, then for their sake I would go along with what is best and speak such words as an expedient means]."

In view of these passages, it would appear that the Buddha was speaking falsely when he declared that women could not attain rebirth in the pure land and achieve Buddhahood. And if we consider the passages in the Lotus Sutra that state, "The World-Honored One has long expounded his doctrines and now must reveal the truth,"[13] and "The Lotus Sutra of the Wonderful Law . . . all that you [Shakyamuni] have expounded is the truth,"[14] then we must conclude that the passage in the Lotus Sutra that declares that women can most assuredly attain rebirth in the pure land and achieve Buddhahood is a true statement and an expression of his observance of the precept against lying.

There are times when a worthy man of the secular world, because his son is behaving strangely or is guilty of some error, will declare that he is no longer his son. To prove the truth of the assertion, the man may even write out a vow or swear an oath. But when the time of his death approaches, he will forgive his son. Though he does these things, we do not deny that he is a worthy man or accuse him of speaking falsely. And the Buddha, too, at times acts in this same manner.

During the more than forty years when the earlier sutras were being preached, the Buddha acknowledged that bodhisattvas could attain the way, that ordinary persons could do so, and that good persons and men could do so, but he would not admit that persons of the two vehicles, women, or evil men could do so. There were times, however, when he did seem to admit the possibility. Therefore, the truth of this matter remained undetermined. But when he had completed his first forty-two years of preaching, and he was ready to enter the eight-year period when he would preach the Lotus Sutra on Mount Gridhrakūta at Rājagriha in the kingdom of Magadha, he first of all preached the Immeasurable Meanings Sutra. And in that sutra he stated, "In these more than forty years, [I have not yet revealed the truth]."

Nichiren

Background

This letter is thought to have been written in the second year of Bun'ei (1265), though different views exist regarding its date. The addressee is also uncertain, but because the attainment of Buddhahood by women is discussed in the latter part, it seems quite likely that it was directed to a woman believer, who may have been the mother of Nanjō Tokimitsu, the steward of Ueno Village in the Fuji area.

Nichiren Shonin begins by outlining the general structure of the Lotus Sutra and by clarifying the specific role played by the

"Medicine King" chapter of the sutra. He then explains the first four of the ten following analogies set forth in this chapter: the analogies of the great ocean, mountains, the moon, the sun, the wheel-turning king, the god Shakra, the god Brahmā, persons at the four stages of Hinayana enlightenment and pratyekabuddhas, bodhisattvas, and the Buddha. In this way he illustrates the supremacy of the Lotus Sutra over all other sutras and the benefits of belief in the Lotus Sutra.

In mentioning the analogy of the great ocean, the Shonin refers to the ocean's ten virtues and to the description found in the "Responding with Joy" chapter of the Lotus Sutra concerning the great benefit conferred upon the fiftieth person who rejoices on hearing this sutra.

In this manner, through the four analogies of the ocean, mountains, the moon, and the sun, the Shonin touches upon various principles of Buddhism, asserting that the benefit of the Lotus Sutra is immeasurable, and that it is the only scripture enabling all beings to attain Buddhahood in their present form. He points out that, among all the twenty-eight chapters of the Lotus Sutra, only the "Life Span" can free human beings from the sufferings of birth and death.

Next, the Shonin explains two additional analogies from the "Medicine King" chapter: the analogy of a ship that carries people across the sea of the sufferings of birth and death, and that of the poor finding riches. Thus, the Shonin likens the Lotus Sutra respectively to a great ship and to a mountain of riches.

Toward the end of this letter, the Shonin writes of the three obediences and the five obstacles. In secular and Buddhist thought, these were limitations traditionally believed to bind women. In the sutras preached prior to the Lotus Sutra, women are presented as being incapable of attaining Buddhahood. But the Shonin, citing passages from the Immeasurable Meanings, Lotus, and Nirvana sutras, declares that women are indeed able to attain Buddhahood.

Notes

1. "The ten meditations" here probably refers to the meditation that thePure Land school teaches on the basis of the Buddha Infinite Life Sutra and the Meditation on the Buddha Infinite Life Sutra. It consists of chanting the name of Amida Buddha ten

times and is said to lead to rebirth in the Pure Land of Amida Buddha.

2. The makara (Skt) is a huge legendary fish with eighteen heads and thirty-six eyes, described in *The Monastic Rules of the Sarvastivada School.*

3. The great size of the body symbolizes the magnitude of the suffering one undergoes in this hell.

4. *The Words and Phrases of the Lotus Sutra.*

5. Gold sifted from the sediment of the river running through the forest of jambu trees in Jambudvīpa.

6. Lotus Sutra, chap. 23.

7. *An Essay on the Protection of the Nation.*

8. Perfect Bliss is the name of the land of Amida Buddha. The Shonin uses the term here to indicate enlightenment.

9. Tsukushi is an ancient name of Kyushu, and Bando is another name for Kanto. Enoshima is a small island located west of Kamakura.

10. Lotus Sutra, chap. 23. The "World of Peace and Delight" is another name for the Pure Land of Perfect Bliss.

11. Probably the Meditation Outshining Sunlight Sutra.

12. The three generations of emperor's consorts mean the present emperor's consort, his father's consort, and his grandfather's consort.

13. Lotus Sutra, chap. 2.

14. Ibid., chap. 11.

Conversation between a Sage and an Unenlightened Man

Part One

HAVING received life, one cannot escape death. Yet though everyone, from the noblest, the emperor, on down to the lowliest commoner, recognizes this as a fact, not even one person in a thousand or ten thousand truly takes the matter seriously or grieves over it. Suddenly confronted with evidence of the impermanence of life, we may be frightened at the thought that we have remained so distant from Buddhism and lament that we have been too engrossed in secular affairs.1 Yet we assume that those who have preceded us in death are wretched, and that we who remain alive are superior. Busy with that task yesterday and this affair today, we are helplessly bound by the five desires of our worldly nature. Unaware that time passes as quickly as a white colt glimpsed through a crack in the wall,2 ignorant as sheep being led to the slaughter, held hopeless prisoners by our concern for food and clothing, we fall heedlessly into the snares of fame and profit and in the end make our way back to that familiar village in the three evil paths, where we are reborn time after time in the realm of the six paths. What person of feeling could fail to grieve at such a state of affairs, or could fail to be moved to sorrow!

Alas! Neither young nor old know what fate awaits them—such is the way of our sahā world. All those who meet are destined to part again—such is the rule in this floating world we live in. Although none of this had just struck me for the first time, [I was appalled at] seeing all those who took early leave of this world in the beginning of the Shōka era.3 Some of them left little children behind them, while others were forced to abandon their aged parents. How sad their hearts must have been when, though still in the prime of life, they were obliged to set off on their journey to the Yellow Springs. It was painful for those who departed, and painful for those left behind.

The king of Ch'u's passion for the goddess remained as a wisp of morning cloud,4 and Liu's grief at remembering his meeting with the immortal visitor was consoled by the sight of his descendants of the seventh generation.5 But how can a person like myself win release from sorrow? I find myself recalling the poet of old who hoped that because he was a humble-hearted dweller in the mountains he might be free of such sadness.6 Now, gathering together my thoughts as the men of Naniwa gather seaweed to extract salt, I give them form with my writing brush as a memento for people in later ages.

p.100How sad, how lamentable it is! From the beginningless past, we have been drunk on the wine of ignorance, reborn again and again in the six paths of existence and the four forms of birth. Sometimes we gasp amid the flames of the hell of burning heat or the hell of great burning heat;7 sometimes we are frozen in the ice of the hell of the crimson lotus or the hell of the great crimson lotus.8 Sometimes we must endure the hunger and thirst that torment those in the realm of hungry spirits, for five hundred lifetimes not so much as hearing the word "food" or "drink." Sometimes we suffer being wounded and killed in the realm of animals, the wounding and killing that occur when the small are swallowed up by the large, or the short engulfed by the long. Sometimes we face the contention and strife of the realm of asuras; sometimes we are born as human beings and undergo the eight sufferings of birth, aging, sickness, death, the pain of parting from loved ones, the pain of encountering those whom we hate, the pain of failing to obtain what we desire, and the pain that arises from the five components of body and mind.9 And sometimes we are born in the realm of heaven and experience the five signs of decay.

And so we go round and round like a cartwheel in this threefold world. Even among people once related as father and child, parents reborn do not know that they were parents, or children that they were children; and though husband and wife re-encounter each other, they do not know that they have already met. We go astray as though we had the eyes of sheep; we are as ignorant as though we had the eyes of wolves. We do not know our past relationship with the mother who gave us birth, and we are unaware of when we ourselves will succumb to death.

And yet we have obtained birth in the human world, something difficult to achieve, and have encountered the sacred teachings of the Thus Come One, which are rarely to be met. We are like the one-eyed turtle finding a floating log with a hole in it that fits him exactly. How regrettable it would be, then, if we did not take this opportunity to sever the bonds of birth and death, making no attempt to free ourselves from the cage of the threefold world!10

Then a wise man appeared and addressed the unenlightened man, saying: "You are quite right to lament as you do. But those who understand the impermanence of this world in this way and turn their hearts to goodness are rarer than the ch'i-lin's horns, while those who fail to understand and instead give themselves to evil thoughts are more numerous than the hairs on a cow. If you wish to arouse the aspiration for enlightenment and to quickly free yourself from the sufferings of birth and death, then I know of the finest doctrine that there is for such a purpose. If you wish, I will explain it to you so that you may know of it."

The unenlightened man rose from his seat, pressed his palms together, and said: "For some time now I have been studying the classics of secular literature and giving all my attention to matters of poetry, so I have no detailed knowledge of the Buddhist teachings. I hope that you will be kind enough to explain them to me, sir."

At that time the wise man said: "You must listen with the ears of Ling Lun,11 borrow the eyes of Li Chu,12 and still your mind, and I will explain things to you. The sacred teachings of Buddhism number no less than eighty thousand, but the most important teaching, the father and mother of all the schools, is that concerning the precepts and rules of conduct. In India, the bodhisattvas Vasubandhu and p.101Ashvaghosha and, in China, the priests Hui-k'uang and Tao-hsüan placed great emphasis on these. And in our own country, during the reign of the forty-fifth sovereign, Emperor Shōmu, the Reverend Chien-chen [Ganjin] brought to Japan the teachings of the Precepts school, along with those of the T'ien-t'ai school, and established an ordination platform for administering the precepts at Tōdai-ji temple. From that time down to the present, the precepts have been revered over many long years, and the honor paid to them increases daily.

"In particular, there is the Honorable Ryōkan of Gokuraku-ji. Everyone, from the supreme ruler on down to the common people, looks up to him as a living Thus Come One, and on observing his conduct, we find that it is indeed in keeping with such a reputation. He directed charitable activities at the port of Iijima, collected rice at the Mutsura Barrier,13 and used the funds to build roads in the various provinces. He set up barriers along the seven highways,14 collected a toll from everyone who passed by, and used the money to build bridges across a number of rivers. In such acts of compassion, he is equal to the Thus Come One, and his virtuous deeds surpass those of the sages of the past. If you wish to quickly free yourself from the sufferings of birth and death, then you should observe the five precepts and the two hundred and fifty precepts, deepen your compassion for others, refrain from killing any living thing, and, like the Honorable Ryōkan, engage in building roads and bridges. This is the finest of all teachings. Are you prepared to embrace it?"

The unenlightened man pressed his palms together more fervently than ever and said: "Indeed, I want very much to embrace it. Please explain it to me thoroughly. You speak of the five precepts and the two hundred and fifty precepts, but I do not know what they are. Please describe them to me in detail."

The wise man said: "Your ignorance is abysmal! Even a child knows what the five precepts and the two hundred and fifty precepts are. However, I will explain them for you. The five precepts comprise, first, the prohibition against taking life; second, the prohibition against stealing; third, the prohibition against lying; fourth, the prohibition against unlawful sexual intercourse; and fifth, the prohibition against drinking intoxicants. The two hundred and fifty precepts are numerous, and so I will not go into them here."

At this the unenlightened man bowed low and with the deepest respect said, "From this day forward, I will devote myself to this doctrine with all my heart."

This man had an old acquaintance, a lay Buddhist believer living in retirement, who paid him a visit to cheer him up. At first the visitor spoke about the affairs of the past, likening them to a dream that is endless and hazy, and then he talked of the future, pointing out how vast and dark it is, how difficult to predict. After he had sought in this way to divert his listener and explain his own views, he said: "Most of us who live in this world of ours find we cannot help thinking about the life to come. May I ask what kind of Buddhist doctrine you have embraced in order to free yourself from the sufferings of birth and death, or to pray for the welfare of those who have gone on to another life?"

The unenlightened man replied: "The other day an eminent priest called on me and instructed me in the five precepts and the two hundred and fifty precepts. In truth I am deeply impressed with his teachings and find them most admirable. Although I know I can never equal the Honorable Ryōkan, I have determined to do all I can to repair roads that are in poor p.102condition and to build bridges over rivers that are too deep for wading."

Then the lay believer gave him words of advice, saying: "Your concern for the way would seem to be admirable, but your approach is foolish. The doctrine you have just described to me is the lowly teaching of the Hinayana. That is why the Buddha has set forth eight analogies,15 and why Bodhisattva Manjushrī has described seventeen differences16 between the Hinayana and the Mahayana. The Buddha has said, for example, that the Hinayana is like the light of a firefly compared to the brilliance of the sun, or like plain crystal compared to emerald. Moreover, the teachers of India, China, and Japan have written not a few treatises refuting the Hinayana teachings.

"Next, concerning your reverence for those who observe these practices, a teaching is not necessarily worthy of honor simply because its practitioners are respected. It is for this reason that the Buddha laid down the principle, 'Rely on the Law and not upon persons.'17

"I have heard it said that the sages of ancient times who observed the precepts could not bear even to utter the words 'kill' or 'hoard,' but would substitute some pure-sounding circumlocution, and when they happened to catch sight of a beautiful woman, they would meditate upon the image of a corpse.18 But if we examine the behavior of the priests of today who supposedly observe the precepts, we find that they hoard silks, wealth, and jewels, and concern themselves with lending money at interest. Since their doctrines and their practices differ so greatly, who would think of putting any strong mind of determination in them?

"And as for this matter of building roads and constructing bridges, it only causes people trouble. The charitable activities at the port of Iijima and the collecting of rice at the Mutsura Barrier have brought unhappiness to a great many people, and the setting up of barriers along the seven highways of the various provinces has imposed a hardship upon travelers. These are things that are happening right in front of your eyes. Can't you see what is going on?"

The unenlightened man thereupon flushed with anger and said, "You with your little bit of wisdom have no cause to speak ill of that eminent priest and to defame his teachings! Do you do so knowingly, or are you simply a fool? It is a fearful thing you are doing."

Then the lay believer laughed and said: "Alas, you are the foolish one! Let me briefly explain to you the biased views of that school. You should understand that, when it comes to the Buddhist teaching, there is the Mahayana division and the Hinayana division, and that in terms of schools there are those based upon the provisional teachings and those based upon the true teaching. Long ago, when the Buddha taught the Hinayana doctrines in Deer Park, he was opening the gate to a phantom city.19 But later, when the mats were spread for the teaching of the Lotus Sutra on Eagle Peak, then those earlier doctrines ceased to be of any benefit."

The unenlightened man looked at the lay believer in perplexity and said: "Both the documentary evidence and the evidence of actual fact indeed support what you have said. But then what kind of Buddhist teaching ought one to embrace in order to free oneself from the sufferings of birth and death and quickly attain Buddhahood?"

The other replied: "Although I am only a layman, I have given myself earnestly to the practice of Buddhism, and from the time of my youth, I have listened to the words of many teachers and have done a certain amount of reading in the sacred scriptures. For those of us of this latter age, who have committed all manner of evil, there is p.103nothing that can compare with the Nembutsu teachings that lead to rebirth in the Pure Land. Thus, the Supervisor of Priests Eshin says, 'The teachings and practices that lead to rebirth in the Land of Perfect Bliss are the eyes and feet for those who live in this defiled latter age of ours.'[20] The Honorable Hōnen collected key passages from the various sutras and spread the doctrine of exclusive devotion to the practice of the Nembutsu. In particular, the original vows[21] of the Buddha Amida surpass the vows of all other Buddhas in their worth and importance. From the first vow, that the three evil paths will not exist in his land, down to the last vow, that bodhisattvas will be enabled to attain the three types of perception,[22] all of Amida's compassionate vows are to be greatly welcomed. But the eighteenth vow is particularly effective on our behalf. In addition, even those who have committed the ten evil acts or the five cardinal sins are not excluded, nor is any distinction made between those who have recited the Nembutsu only one time and those who have recited it many times. For this reason, everyone from the ruler on down to the common people favors this school far above the other schools. And how many countless people have gained rebirth in the Pure Land as a result of it!"

The unenlightened man said: "Truly one should be ashamed of the small and yearn for the great, abandon the shallow and embrace the profound. This is not only a principle of Buddhism but a rule of the secular world as well. Therefore, I would like to shift my allegiance without delay to this school you have described. Please explain its principles to me in greater detail. You say that even those who have committed the five cardinal sins or the ten evil acts are not excluded from the Buddha's compassionate vows. What, may I ask, are the five cardinal sins and the ten evil acts?"

The wise lay believer replied: "The five cardinal sins are killing one's father, killing one's mother, killing an arhat, shedding a Buddha's blood, and disrupting the harmony of the Buddhist Order. As for the ten evil acts, there are three acts of the body, four acts of the mouth, and three acts of the mind. The three evil acts of the body are killing, stealing, and unlawful sexual intercourse. The four evil acts of the mouth are lying, flattery, defaming, and duplicity. The three evil acts of the mind are greed, anger, and foolishness."

"Now I understand them," said the unenlightened man. "From this day forward, I will place all my trust in this power of another, of the Buddha Amida, to bring me to rebirth in the Pure Land."

At that time there was a practitioner of the esoteric school who was extraordinarily diligent in upholding its teachings. He too came to call on the unenlightened man to console him. At first he spoke only of "wild words and ornate phrases,"23 but in the end he discoursed on the differences between the two types of Buddhist teachings, those of the exoteric schools and those of the esoteric school. He inquired of the unenlightened man, "What sort of Buddhist doctrines are you practicing, and what sutras and treatises do you read and recite?"

The unenlightened man replied, "Recently, in accordance with the instruction of a lay believer I know, I have been reading the three Pure Land sutras and have come to put profound trust in Amida, the lord of the Western Paradise."

The practitioner said: "There are two kinds of Buddhist teachings, the exoteric teachings and the esoteric teachings. The most profound doctrines of the exoteric teachings cannot compare even to the elementary stages of the esoteric teachings. From what you tell me, it seems that the doctrine you have embraced is the exoteric teaching put forth by Shakyamuni. But the doctrine that I adhere to is the secret teaching of Mahāvairochana, the King of Enlightenment. If you are truly fearful of this burning house that is the threefold world we live in and long for the wonderful Land of Tranquil Light, then you should cast aside the exoteric teachings at once and put strong mind of determination in the esoteric teachings."

The unenlightened man, greatly startled, said: "I have never heard of this distinction between exoteric and esoteric doctrines. What are the exoteric teachings? What are the esoteric teachings?"

The practitioner replied: "I am a hardheaded and foolish person, and am not learned at all. Nevertheless, I would like to cite one or two passages and see if I can dispel your ignorance. The exoteric teachings are the doctrines preached in response to the request of Shāriputra and the other disciples by the Thus Come One of the manifested body. But the esoteric teachings are those that

Mahāvairochana, the Thus Come One of the Dharma body, preached spontaneously out of his boundless joy in the Law, with Vajrasattva as his listener. These teachings constitute the Mahāvairochana Sutra and the others of the three esoteric sutras."24

The unenlightened man said, "What you say stands to reason. I think I should correct my former error and hasten to embrace these more worthy teachings."

There was a mendicant priest who drifted about from province to province like floating grass, who rolled on from district to district like tumbleweed. Before anyone realized it, he appeared on the scene and stood leaning on the pillar of the gate, smiling but saying nothing.

The unenlightened man, wondering at this, asked what he wanted. At first the priest made no reply, but after the question was repeated, he said, "The moon is dim and distant, the wind brisk and blustery." His appearance was quite out of the ordinary and his words made no sense, but when the unenlightened man inquired about the ultimate principle behind them, he found that they represented the Zen teachings as they are expounded in the world today.

He observed the priest's appearance, listened to his words, and asked what he considered a good cause for entering the Buddha way. The mendicant priest replied: "The teachings of the sutras are a finger pointing at the moon. Their doctrinal nets are so much nonsense that has been captured in words. But there is a teaching that enables you to find rest in the essential nature of your own mind—it is called Zen."

"I would like to hear about it," said the unenlightened man.

"If you are truly in earnest," said the priest, "you must face the wall, sit in Zen meditation, and make clear the moon of your original mind. That the Zen lineage of the twenty-eight patriarchs was passed on without break in India, and that the line of transmission was handed down through the six patriarchs25 in China is clear for all to see. It would be pitiful indeed if you should fail to understand what they have taught and remain caught in the nets of doctrine. Since the mind itself is the Buddha, and the Buddha is none other than the mind, what Buddha could there be outside yourself?"

When the unenlightened man heard these words, he began to ponder various things and to quietly consider the principles he had heard. He said: "There are a great many different Buddhist doctrines, and it is very difficult to determine which are sound and which are not. It is only natural that Bodhisattva Ever Wailing should have gone east to inquire about the truth, p.105that the boy Good Treasures should have sought for it in the south, that Bodhisattva Medicine King burned his arms as an offering, and that the ascetic Aspiration for the Law stripped off his skin. A good teacher is truly difficult to find. Some say that one should go by the teachings of the sutras, while others say that the truth lies outside the sutras. In pondering the rights and wrongs of these doctrines, one who has not yet fathomed the depths of Buddhism and stands gazing over the waters of the Law is in doubt as to how deep they may be; one who assesses a teacher does so with all the anxiety of a person walking on thin ice. That is why the Buddha has left us those golden words, 'Rely on the Law and not upon persons,' and why it is said that those who encounter the correct teaching are as few as the grains of earth that can be placed on a fingernail. If there is someone who knows which of the Buddhist teachings are true and which are false, then I must seek him out, make him my teacher, and treat him with appropriate respect."

They say that it is as difficult to be born in the realm of human beings as it is to thread a needle by lowering the thread from the heavens, and as rare to see and hear the Buddha's teachings as it is for a one-eyed turtle to encounter a floating log with a hole just the right size to hold him. Having this in mind and believing that one must regard the body as insignificant and the Law as supreme, the unenlightened man climbed numerous mountains, impelled by his anxiety, going from one temple to another as his feet would carry him. In time he arrived at a rocky cave with green mountains rising sheer behind it. The wind in the pines played a melody of eternity, happiness, true self, and purity, and the emerald stream that bubbled along in front sent its waves striking against the bank with echoes of the perfection of these four virtues. The flowers carpeting the deep valley bloomed with the hue of the true aspect of the Middle Way, and from the plum blossoms just beginning to open in the broad meadow wafted the fragrance of the three thousand realms. Truly it was beyond the power of words to describe, beyond the scope of the mind to imagine. One might have thought it the place where the Four White-Haired Elders of Mount Shang lived, or the site where some ancient Buddha had walked about after meditation. Auspicious clouds rose up at dawn, a mysterious light appeared in the evening. Ah, the mind cannot grasp it nor words set it forth!

The unenlightened man wandered about, pondering what was before him, now pausing in thought, now resuming his steps. Suddenly he came upon a sage. Observing his actions, he saw that the sage was reciting the Lotus Sutra; his voice stirred the seeker deeply. Peering in at the quiet window of the sage's retreat, he found that the sage was resting his elbows on his desk, pondering the sutra's profound meaning.

The sage, divining that the unenlightened man was searching for the Law, asked in a gentle voice, "Why have you come to this cave among these far-off mountains?"

The other replied, "Because I attach little importance to life but great importance to the Law."

"What practices do you follow?" asked the sage.

The unenlightened man answered: "I have lived all my life amid the dust of the secular world and have not yet learned how to free myself from the sufferings of birth and death. As it happened, however, I encountered various good teachers, from whom I learned first the rules of discipline and then the Nembutsu, True Word, and Zen teachings. But though I have learned these teachings, I am unable to determine their truth or falsity."

The sage said: "When I listen to p.106your words, I find that it is indeed just as you have said. To hold life lightly but value the Law is the teaching of the sages of former times, and one that I myself know well.

"From the realm where there is neither thought nor no thought26 above the clouds to the very bottom of hell, is there any being who receives life and yet succeeds in escaping death? Thus, even in the unenlightened secular writings we find it said, 'Though you may set out at dawn on the journey of life with pride in the beauty of your rosy cheeks, by evening you will be no more than a pile of white bones rotting on the moor.'27 Though you may move among the most exalted company of court nobles, your hair done up elegantly like clouds and your sleeves fluttering like eddies of snow, such pleasures, when you stop to consider them, are no more than a dream within a dream. You must come to rest at last under the carpet of weeds at the foot of the hill, and all your jeweled daises and brocade hangings will mean nothing to you on the road to the afterlife. The famed flower-like beauty of Ono no Komachi28 and Soto'ori Hime29 was in time scattered by the winds of impermanence. Fan K'uai and Chang Liang, in spite of their skill in the military arts, in the end suffered beneath the staves of the wardens of hell. That is why men of feeling in former times wrote poems such as these:

How sad, the evening smoke

from Mount Toribe!

Those who see off the dead one—

how long will they remain?30

Dew on the branch tips,

drops on the trunk—

all sooner or later

must vanish from this world.31

"This rule of life, that if one does not die sooner one will surely die later, should not at this late date come as a surprise to you. But the thing that you should desire above all is the way of the Buddha, and what you should continually seek are the teachings of the sutras. Now, from what you have told me about the Buddhist doctrines you have encountered, I can see that some of them belong to the Hinayana division of Buddhism and some to the Mahayana. But, leaving aside for the moment the question of which is superior and which inferior, I can say that, far from bringing you deliverance, the practice of these teachings will lead to rebirth in the evil paths."

At this the unenlightened man exclaimed in surprise: "But were not all the sacred teachings that the Buddha expounded throughout his lifetime designed to benefit living beings? From the time of the preaching of the Flower Garland Sutra at the seven places and eight assemblies, down to the ceremony in which the Nirvana Sutra was expounded on the banks of the Ajitavatī River, all the doctrines were taught by Shakyamuni Buddha himself. Though one may perhaps be able to distinguish certain small degrees of relative merit among them, how could any of them possibly be the cause for rebirth in the evil paths?"

The sage replied: "The sacred teachings that the Thus Come One proclaimed in the course of his lifetime may be divided into the categories of provisional and true, Hinayana and Mahayana. In addition, they may be classified according to the two paths of the exoteric and the esoteric. Thus they are not all of the same sort. Let me for a moment explain the general nature of the teachings and thus relieve you of your misunderstandings.

"When Shakyamuni, the lord of teachings in the threefold world, was nineteen years old, he left the city of Gayā and went into retreat on Mount Dandaka,32 where he carried out various difficult and painful austerities. He p.107attained enlightenment at the age of thirty and, at that time, instantly banished the three categories of illusion and brought to an end the vast night of ignorance. It might appear that he should at that time have preached the one vehicle of the Lotus Sutra of the Wonderful Law in order to fulfill his original vow. But he knew that the people varied greatly in their capacities, and that they did not have the receptivity to understand the Buddha vehicle. Therefore, he devoted the following forty years and more to developing the people's inherent capacity. Then, in the last eight years of his life, he fulfilled the purpose of his advent in the world by preaching the Lotus Sutra of the Wonderful Law.

"Thus it was that, when the Buddha was seventy-two, he preached the Immeasurable Meanings Sutra as an introduction to the Lotus Sutra and therein stated: 'In the past I sat upright in the place of meditation for six years under the bodhi tree and was able to gain supreme perfect enlightenment. With the Buddha eye I observed all phenomena and knew that this enlightenment could not be explained or described. Why? Because I knew that living beings are not alike in their natures and their desires. And because their natures and desires are not alike, I preached the Law in various different ways. Preaching the Law in various different ways, I made use of the power of expedient means. But in these more than forty years, I have not yet revealed the truth.'

"The meaning of this passage is that, when the Buddha was thirty years of age, seated in the place of enlightenment under the bodhi tree, he observed the inner heart of all living beings with the Buddha eye and realized that it was not the proper time to preach to them the Lotus Sutra, which reveals the direct way to the attainment of Buddhahood for all living beings. Therefore, as one would wave an empty fist about to humor a little baby, he resorted to various expedient means, and for the following forty years and more he refrained from revealing the truth. Thus he defined the period of the expedient teachings as clearly as the sun rising in the blue sky or the full moon coming up on a dark night.

"In view of this passage, why should we, with the very same strong mind of determination that could just as easily be directed toward the Lotus Sutra, cling to the provisional teachings of the sutras that preceded the Lotus, those doctrines defined by the Buddha to be empty, and as a result keep returning to the same old dwelling in the threefold world, with which we are already so familiar?

"Therefore, in the 'Expedient Means' chapter in the first volume of the Lotus Sutra, the Buddha says, 'Honestly discarding expedient means, I will preach only the unsurpassed way.' This passage indicates that one should honestly discard the teachings that the Buddha set forth in the various sutras preached in the previous forty-two years, namely, the Nembutsu, True Word, Zen, and Precepts doctrines to which you referred.

"The meaning of this passage is perfectly clear. And, in addition, we have the warning delivered in the 'Simile and Parable' chapter in the second volume, 'desiring only to accept and embrace the sutra of the great vehicle and not accepting a single verse of the other sutras.' This passage is saying that, no matter what year of the Buddha's life a sutra may have been preached in, one should not accept even a single verse from any of the sutras other than the Lotus Sutra.

"The varying doctrines of the eight schools are as numerous as so many orchids and chrysanthemums, and priests and lay believers differ in appearance, yet they all agree in claiming to cherish the Lotus Sutra. But how do they interpret these passages from p.108the Lotus Sutra that I have just cited? These passages speak of 'honestly discarding' the earlier teachings and forbid one to accept so much as a single verse from any of the other sutras. But are the doctrines of Nembutsu, True Word, Zen, and Precepts not based on the 'other sutras'?

"Now this Lotus Sutra of the Wonderful Law I have been speaking of represents the true reason why all Buddhas make their advent in the world and teaches the direct way to the attainment of Buddhahood for all living beings. Shakyamuni Buddha entrusted it to his disciples, Many Treasures Buddha testified to its veracity, and the other Buddhas extended their tongues up to the Brahmā heaven, proclaiming, 'All that you [Shakyamuni] have expounded is the truth!'33 Every single character in this sutra represents the true intention of the Buddhas, and every brushstroke of it is a source of aid to those who repeat the cycle of birth and death. There is not a single word in it that is untrue.

"Is not one who fails to heed the warnings of this sutra in effect cutting off the tongues of the Buddhas and deceiving the worthies and sages? This offense is truly fearful. Thus, in the second volume it says, 'If a person fails to have strong mind of determination but instead slanders this sutra, immediately he will destroy all the seeds for becoming a Buddha in this world.'34 The meaning of this passage is that, if one turns one's back on even one verse or one phrase of this sutra, one is guilty of a crime equal to that of killing all the Buddhas of the ten directions in the three existences of past, present, and future.

"If we use the teachings of the sutras as a mirror in which to examine our present world, we will see that it is a difficult thing to find one who does not betray the Lotus Sutra. And if we understand the true meaning of these matters, we can see that even a person of disbelief cannot avoid being reborn in the hell of incessant suffering. How much more so is this true, then, for someone like the Honorable Hōnen, the founder of the Nembutsu school, who urged people to discard the Lotus Sutra in favor of the Nembutsu! Where, may I ask, in all the five thousand or seven thousand volumes of sutras is there any passage that instructs us to discard the Lotus Sutra?

"The Reverend Shan-tao, who was revered as a practitioner who had gained enlightenment through the attainment of meditation and honored as a living incarnation of Amida Buddha, designated five kinds of sundry practices that are to be discarded, and said of the Lotus Sutra that 'not even one person in a thousand' could be saved by it; by which he meant that if a thousand people put strong mind of determination in that sutra not a single one of them will attain Buddhahood. And yet the Lotus Sutra itself says, 'If there are those who hear the Law, then not a one will fail to attain Buddhahood.'35 This indicates that if they hear this sutra then all beings in the Ten Worlds, along with their environments, will attain the Buddha way. Hence the sutra predicts that Devadatta, though he has committed the five cardinal sins, will in the future become a Buddha called the Thus Come One Heavenly King, and tells how the dragon king's daughter, though as a woman subject to the five obstacles and thought to be incapable of attaining Buddhahood, was able instantly to achieve the Buddha way in the southern realm. Thus even the dung beetle can ascend through the six stages of practice and is in no way excluded from achieving Buddhahood.36

"In fact, Shan-tao's words and the passages of the Lotus Sutra are as far apart as heaven and earth, as different as clouds from mud. Which one are we to follow? If we stop to ponder the logic of the matter, we will realize that p.109Shan-tao is the deadly enemy of all Buddhas and sutras, and the foe of wise priests and humble lay believers alike. If the words of the Lotus Sutra are true, then how can he escape the hell of incessant suffering?"

At these words, the unenlightened man flushed with anger and said: "You are a person of no more than humble station in life, and yet you dare to utter such ugly accusations. I find it very difficult to judge whether you speak out of true understanding or out of delusion, and to tell whether your words stand to reason or not. It behooves us to remember that the Reverend Shan-tao is said to have been a transformed body of Amida the Well Attained37 or of his attendant Bodhisattva Great Power. And the same is said of the Honorable Hōnen, or that he was a reincarnation of Shan-tao. These were both outstanding men of antiquity, and in addition they had acquired extraordinary merit through their religious practices and commanded the most profound degree of understanding. How could they possibly have fallen into the evil paths?"

The sage replied: "What you say is quite correct, and I too had great respect for these men and believed in them as you do. But in matters of Buddhist doctrines one cannot jump to conclusions simply on the basis of the eminence of the person involved. The words of the sutras are what must come first. Do not make light of a teaching just because the person who preaches it is of humble station. The fox of the kingdom of Bima who recited the twelve-character verse that goes, 'There are those who love life and hate death; there are those who love death and hate life,' was hailed as a teacher by the god Shakra,38 and the demon who recited the sixteen-character verse that begins, 'All is changeable, nothing is constant,' was treated with great honor by the boy Snow Mountains. This was done, however, not because the fox or the demon was of such eminence, but simply out of respect for the doctrines they taught.

"Therefore, in the sixth volume of the Nirvana Sutra, his final teaching delivered in the grove of sal trees, our merciful father Shakyamuni Buddha, the lord of teachings, said, 'Rely on the Law and not upon persons.' Even when great bodhisattvas such as Universal Worthy and Manjushrī, men who have returned39 to the stage of near-perfect enlightenment, expound the Buddhist teachings, if they do not do so with the sutra text in hand, then one should not heed them.

"The Great Teacher T'ien-t'ai states, 'That which accords with the sutras is to be written down and made available. But put no strong mind of determination in anything that in word or meaning fails to do so.'40 Here we see that one should accept what is clearly stated in the text of the sutras, but discard anything that cannot be supported by the text. The Great Teacher Dengyō says, 'Depend upon the preachings of the Buddha, and do not put strong mind of determination in traditions handed down orally,'41 which expresses the same idea as the passage from T'ien-t'ai's commentary. And Bodhisattva Nāgārjuna says that one should rely on treatises that are strong mind of determinationful to the sutras, but not rely on those that distort the sutras.42 This passage may be understood to mean that, even among the various sutras, one should discard the provisional teachings put forth prior to the Lotus Sutra and put one's strong mind of determination in this sutra, the Lotus. Thus both sutras and treatises make it perfectly clear that one should discard all scriptures other than the Lotus.

"Nowhere in all the five thousand or seven thousand volumes of sutras listed in the K'ai-yüan era catalog43 do we find a single scriptural passage that expresses disapproval of the Lotus Sutra and advises one to discard it or to cast p.110it aside, nor any passage that says it is to be classified among the sundry practices and abandoned. If you disagree, you had better find some reliable passage from the sutras that will support your view, so that you may rescue Shan-tao and Hōnen from their torments in the hell of incessant suffering.

"The practitioners of the Nembutsu in our present day, priests as well as ordinary lay men and women, not only violate the words of the sutras but also go against the instructions of their own teachers. Shan-tao produced a commentary in which he described five kinds of sundry practices that should be abandoned by practitioners of the Nembutsu. Referring to these sundry practices, The Nembutsu Chosen above All says: '[Shan-tao states as follows:] "Concerning the first of the sundry practices, that of reading and reciting sutras, with the exception of the recitation of the Meditation on the Buddha Infinite Life Sutra and the other sutras that preach rebirth in the Pure Land, the embracing, reading, and recitation of all other sutras, whether Mahayana or Hinayana, exoteric or esoteric, is to be regarded as a sundry practice. . . . Concerning the third of the sundry practices, that of worshiping, with the exception of worshiping the Buddha Amida, the worshiping or honoring of any other Buddha or bodhisattva, or deity of this world is to be regarded as a sundry practice. Concerning the fourth of the sundry practices, that of calling on the name, with the exception of calling on the name of the Buddha Amida, calling on the name of any other Buddha or bodhisattva, or deity of this world is to be regarded as a sundry practice. Concerning the fifth of the sundry practices, that of praising and giving offerings, with the exception of praises and offerings directed to the Buddha Amida, the praising of and giving of offerings to any other Buddha or bodhisattva, or deity of this world is to be regarded as a sundry practice."'

"This passage of commentary is saying that with regard to the first sundry practice, that of reading and reciting sutras, there are fixed rules for priests and lay believers of the Nembutsu, both men and women, concerning which sutras are to be read and which are not to be read. Among the sutras that are not to be read are the Lotus, Benevolent Kings, Medicine Master, Great Collection, Heart, Woman Born as a Man to Become a Buddha, and Life-Prolonging Northern Dipper sutras, and in particular, among the eight volumes of the Lotus Sutra, the so-called Perceiver of the World's Sounds Sutra,44 which is commonly read by so many people. If one reads so much as a single phrase or a single verse of these sutras, then, although one may be a devoted practitioner of the Nembutsu, one is in fact grouped among those who follow sundry practices and cannot be reborn in the Pure Land. Yet now, as I observe the world with my own eyes, among those who chant the Nembutsu I see many people who read these various sutras, thus going against their teachers and thereby committing one of the seven cardinal sins.45

"In addition, in the passage concerning the third kind of sundry practice, that of worshiping, it is said that with the exception of the worship of Amida flanked by two honored bodhisattvas,46 the worshiping or honoring of any of the earlier mentioned Buddhas, bodhisattvas, or heavenly gods and benevolent deities is to be regarded as a sundry practice and is forbidden to practitioners of the Nembutsu. But Japan is a land of the gods. It was created by the august deities Izanagi and Izanami,47 the Sun Goddess deigns to have her dwelling here, and the Mimosuso River48 for many long ages down to the present has continued to flow [through the grounds on which her p.111shrine is located]. How could anyone who was born in this country heed such an erroneous doctrine! In addition, as we have been born under the all-encompassing sky and enjoy the benefits of the three kinds of luminous bodies, the sun, the moon, and the stars, it would be a most fearful thing if we should show disrespect to the gods of these heavenly bodies.

"Again, in the passage concerning the fourth kind of sundry practice, that of calling on the name, it says that there are certain names of Buddhas and bodhisattvas that the Nembutsu believer is to call on, and certain names of Buddhas and bodhisattvas that he is not to call on. The names he is to call on are those of the Buddha Amida and his two honored attendants. The names he is not to call on are those of Shakyamuni, Medicine Master, Mahāvairochana, and the other Buddhas; those of the bodhisattvas Earth Repository, Universal Worthy, and Manjushrī, the gods of the sun, moon, and stars; the deities of the shrines in Izu and Hakone, Mishima Shrine, Kumano Shrine, and Haguro Shrine; the Sun Goddess; and Great Bodhisattva Hachiman. If anyone so much as once recites any of these names, then, although he may recite the Nembutsu a hundred thousand or a million times, because he committed the error of calling on the name of one of these Buddhas, bodhisattvas, the gods of the sun and moon, and other deities, he will fall into the hell of incessant suffering and fail to be reborn in the Pure Land. But when I look about at the world, I find Nembutsu believers who call on the names of these various Buddhas, bodhisattvas, heavenly gods, and benevolent deities. Thus, in this matter as well, they are going against the instructions of their own teachers.

"In the passage concerning the fifth sundry practice, that of praising and giving offerings, the Nembutsu believer is enjoined to make offerings to the Buddha Amida and his two bodhisattva attendants. But if he should offer even a little bit of incense or a few flowers to the earlier mentioned Buddhas, bodhisattvas, or heavenly gods and benevolent deities, then, although the merit he has gained from the Nembutsu practice may be laudable, because of the error he has committed, he is condemned to be classified among those who carry out sundry practices. And yet, when I look around the world, I see the Nembutsu believers paying visits to various shrines and offering streamers of paper or cloth, or entering various Buddhist halls and bowing in reverence there. In this, too, they are going against the instructions of their teachers. If you doubt what I say, then look at the text of Nembutsu Chosen above All. It is very clear on these points.

"Again, The Teaching on Meditation Sutra49 by the Reverend Shan-tao says: 'With regard to intoxicants, meat, and the five strong-flavored foods,50 one must vow never to lay a hand on them, never to let one's mouth taste them. One must pledge, "If I should go against these words, then may foul sores break out on both my body and mouth!"' The meaning of this passage is that the Nembutsu believers, men and women lay believers, nuns and priests alike, must not drink wine and must not eat fish or fowl. In addition, they must not eat any of the five strong-flavored foods, the pungent or strong-smelling foods such as leeks or garlic. If any Nembutsu believers fail to abide by this rule, then in their present life they will find foul sores breaking out on their bodies, and in the next life they will fall into the hell of incessant suffering. In fact, however, we find many Nembutsu laymen and laywomen, nuns and priests, who pay no heed to this prohibition but drink as much wine and eat as much fish and fowl as they please. They are in p.112effect swallowing knives with which to wound themselves, are they not?"

Thereupon the unenlightened man said: "In truth, as I listen to your description of the doctrine, I can see that, even if the Nembutsu teaching could in fact lead one to rebirth in the Pure Land, its observances and practices are very difficult to carry out. And of course, since the sutras and treatises upon which it is based all belong to the category of provisional expositions, it is perfectly clear that it can never lead to rebirth in the Pure Land. But surely there is no reason to repudiate the True Word teachings. The Mahāvairochana Sutra constitutes the secret teaching of Mahāvairochana, the King of Enlightenment. It has been handed down in an unbroken line of transmission from the Thus Come One Mahāvairochana to Shan-wu-wei and Pu-k'ung. And in Japan the Great Teacher Kōbō spread the teachings concerning the mandalas of the Diamond Realm and the Womb Realm. These are secret and arcane teachings that concern the thirty-seven honored ones.51 Therefore, the most profound doctrines of the exoteric teachings cannot compare even to the elementary stages of the esoteric teachings. Hence the Great Teacher Chishō of Gotō-in temple52 stated in his commentary, 'Even the Lotus Sutra cannot compare [to the Mahāvairochana Sutra], much less the other doctrines.'53 Now what is your view on this matter?"

The sage replied: "At first I too placed my trust in the Thus Come One Mahāvairochana and desired to carry out the teachings of the True Word school. But when I investigated the basic doctrines of the school, I found that they are founded on views that in fact are a slander of the correct teaching.

"The Great Teacher Kōbō of Mount Kōya, of whom you have spoken, was a teacher who lived in the time of Emperor Saga. He received a mandate from the emperor directing him to determine and explain the relative profundity of the various Buddhist teachings. In response, he produced a work in ten volumes entitled The Treatise on the Ten Stages of the Mind. Because this work is so broad and comprehensive, he made a condensation of it in three volumes, which bears the title The Precious Key to the Secret Treasury. This work describes ten stages in the development of the mind, from the first stage, the 'mind of lowly man, goatish in its desire,'54 to the last stage, the 'glorious mind, the most secret and sacred.'55 He assigns the Lotus Sutra to the eighth stage, the Flower Garland Sutra to the ninth stage, and the True Word teachings [of the Mahāvairochana Sutra] to the tenth stage. Thus he ranks the Lotus Sutra as inferior even to the Flower Garland Sutra, and as two stages below the Mahāvairochana Sutra. In this work, he writes, 'Each vehicle that is put forward is claimed to be the vehicle of Buddhahood, but when examined from a later stage,56 they are all seen to be mere childish theory.' He also characterizes the Lotus Sutra as a work of 'wild words and ornate phrases,' and disparages Shakyamuni Buddha as being lost in the region of darkness.

"As a result, Kōbō's disciple in a later age, Shōkaku-bō, the founder of Dembō-in temple, was led to write that the Lotus Sutra is not fit even to be a sandal-tender for the Mahāvairochana Sutra, and that Shakyamuni Buddha is not worthy even to serve as an ox-driver for the Thus Come One Mahāvairochana.57

"Still your thoughts and listen to what I say. In all the five thousand or seven thousand volumes of sutras that the Buddha preached during his lifetime, or the three thousand or more volumes of the Confucian and Taoist scriptures, is there anywhere a passage clearly stating that the Lotus Sutra is p.113a doctrine of 'childish theory,' or that it ranks two stages below the Mahāvairochana Sutra, being inferior to the Flower Garland Sutra as well, or that Shakyamuni Buddha is lost in the region of darkness and is not worthy even to serve as an ox-driver to the Thus Come One Mahāvairochana? And even if such a passage did exist, one would certainly have to examine it with great care.

"When the Buddhist sutras and teachings were brought from India to China, the manner of translation depended upon the inclination of the particular translator, and there were no fixed translations for the sutras and treatises. Hence the Tripitaka Master Kumārajīva of the Later Ch'in dynasty always used to say: 'When I examine the Buddhist teachings as they exist in China, I find that in many cases they differ from the Sanskrit originals. If the sutra translations that I have produced are free from error, then, after I am dead and cremated, my body, since it is impure, will no doubt be consumed by the flames, but my tongue alone will not be burned.' And when he was finally cremated, his body was reduced to a pile of bones, but his tongue alone remained, resting on top of a blue lotus blossom and emitting a brilliant light that outshone the rays of the sun. What a wonderful thing!

"Thus it came about that the translation of the Lotus Sutra made by the Tripitaka Master Kumārajīva in particular spread easily throughout China. And that is why, when the Great Teacher Kompon [Dengyō] of Enryaku-ji attacked the teachings of the other schools, he refuted them by saying, 'We have proof in the fact that the tongue of the Tripitaka Master Kumārajīva, the translator of the Lotus Sutra, was not consumed by the flames. The sutras that you rely upon are all in error.'

"Again, in the Nirvana Sutra the Buddha says that, when his teachings are transmitted to other countries, many errors are bound to be introduced into them. Even if among sutra passages we were to find the Lotus Sutra characterized as useless, or Shakyamuni Buddha described as a Buddha lost in the region of darkness, we should inquire very carefully to see whether the text that makes such statements belongs to the provisional teachings or the true teaching, to the Mahayana or the Hinayana, whether it was preached in the earlier or the later part of the Buddha's life, and who the translator was.

"It is said that Lao Tzu and Confucius thought nine times before uttering a single word, or three times before uttering a single word. And Tan, the Duke of Chou, was so eager to receive his callers that he would spit out his food three times in the course of a meal and wring out his hair three times in the course of washing it [in order not to keep them waiting]. If even the people described in the shallow, non-Buddhist writings behaved with such care and circumspection, then how much more so should those who study the profound doctrines of the Buddhist scriptures!

"Now nowhere in the sutras and treatises do we find the slightest evidence to support this contention [that the Lotus Sutra is inferior to the Mahāvairochana Sutra]. The Great Teacher Kōbō's own commentary says that one who slanders persons and disparages the correct teaching will fall into the evil paths.58

A person like Kōbō will invariably fall into hell—there can be no doubt of it."

The unenlightened man seemed to be dazed, and then suddenly began to sigh. After some time, he said: "The Great Teacher Kōbō was an expert in both the Buddhist and non-Buddhist writings and a leader of the masses. In virtuous practices he excelled the others of his time, and his reputation was known everywhere. It is said that when p.114he was in China he hurled a three-pronged diamond-pounder59 all the way across the more than eighty thousand ri of the ocean until it reached Japan, and that when he expounded the meaning of the Heart Sutra so many sufferers from the plague recovered their health that they filled the streets. Thus he was surely no ordinary person, but a manifestation of a great sage in temporal form. We can hardly fail to hold him in esteem and put strong mind of determination in his teachings."

The sage replied: "I at first thought the same way. But after I entered the path of the Buddha's teachings and began to distinguish what accords with its principles from what does not, I realized that the ability to perform miraculous acts at will does not necessarily constitute a basis for determining the truth or falsity of Buddhist teachings. That is why the Buddha laid down the rule that we should 'rely on the Law and not upon persons,' which I mentioned earlier.

"The ascetic Agastya poured the Ganges River into one ear and kept it there for twelve years, the ascetic Jinu drank the great ocean dry in a single day, Chang Chieh exhaled fog, and Luan Pa exhaled clouds.60 But this does not mean that they knew what is correct and what is not in the Buddhist teachings, or that they understood the principle of cause and effect. In China, when the Dharma Teacher Fa-yün lectured on the Lotus Sutra, in no time at all flowers came raining down from the heavens. But the Great Teacher Miao-lo said, 'Though he could bring about a response in this way, his understanding still did not accord with the truth [of the Lotus Sutra].'61 Thus Miao-lo accused him of having failed to understand the truth of Buddhism.

"The Lotus Sutra rejects the three categories of preaching—that done by the Buddha in the past, the present, and the future.62 It refutes the sutras preached before it, saying that in them the Buddha had 'not yet revealed the truth.'63 It attacks the sutras of the same period by declaring itself superior to those 'now being preached,' and repudiates the sutras expounded later by stating that it excels all those 'to be preached.' In fact, the Lotus Sutra is first among all sutras preached in the three periods of past, present, and future.

"In the fourth volume of the Lotus Sutra, we read, 'Medicine King, now I say to you, I have preached various sutras, and among those sutras the Lotus is the foremost!'64 This passage means that at the gathering on Eagle Peak the Buddha addressed Bodhisattva Medicine King and told him that, beginning with the Flower Garland Sutra and ending with the Nirvana Sutra, there were countless sutras numbering as many as the sands of the Ganges, but that among all these the Lotus Sutra that he was then preaching held first place. But evidently the Great Teacher Kōbō took the word 'first' to mean 'third.'

"In the same volume of the Lotus Sutra, the Buddha says, 'For the sake of the Buddha way in immeasurable numbers of lands from the beginning until now I have widely preached many sutras, and among them this sutra is foremost.'65 This passage means that Shakyamuni Buddha has appeared in countless lands, taking different names, and assuming varying life spans. And it establishes that, among all the sutras he has preached in the various forms in which he manifested himself, the Lotus Sutra holds first place.

"In the fifth volume of the Lotus Sutra, it is stated that 'it holds the highest place,'66 making clear that this sutra stands above the Mahāvairochana, Diamond Crown, and all the other countless sutras. But evidently the Great Teacher Kōbō read this as 'it holds the lowest place.' Thus Shakyamuni and Kōbō, the Lotus Sutra and Precious Key to the Secret Treasury, are in fact p.115completely at odds with each other. Do you intend to reject Shakyamuni and follow Kōbō? Or will you reject Kōbō and follow Shakyamuni? Will you go against the text of the sutra and accept the words of an ordinary teacher? Or will you reject the words of an ordinary teacher and honor the golden words of the Buddha? Think carefully before you decide what to accept and what to reject.

"Furthermore, in the 'Medicine King' chapter in volume seven, ten similes are offered in praise of the teachings of the Lotus Sutra. The first simile concerns water, and in it streams and rivers are likened to the other various sutras and the great ocean to the Lotus Sutra. Thus, if anyone should assert that the Mahāvairochana Sutra is superior and the Lotus Sutra inferior, he is in effect saying that the great ocean holds less water than does a little stream. Everyone in the world today understands that the ocean exceeds the various rivers in size, and yet they fail to realize that the Lotus Sutra is the foremost among sutras.

"The second simile concerns mountains. Ordinary mountains are likened to the other sutras and Mount Sumeru to the Lotus Sutra. Mount Sumeru measures 168,000 yojanas from top to bottom; what other mountain could compare with it? To say that the Mahāvairochana Sutra is superior to the Lotus Sutra is like saying that Mount Fuji is bigger than Mount Sumeru.

"The third simile deals with the moon and stars. The other sutras are likened to the stars, and the Lotus Sutra is likened to the moon. Comparing the moon and the stars, can anyone be in doubt as to which is superior?

"Later on in the series of similes, we read, 'This sutra likewise is foremost among all the sutra teachings preached by all the Thus Come Ones, preached by all the bodhisattvas, or preached by all the voice-hearers.'

"This passage tells us that the Lotus Sutra not only is the foremost among all the doctrines preached by Shakyamuni Buddha in the course of his lifetime, but also holds first place among all the teachings and sutras preached by Buddhas such as Mahāvairochana, Medicine Master, or Amida, and by bodhisattvas such as Universal Worthy or Manjushrī. Therefore, if anyone should assert that there exists a sutra superior to the Lotus, you must understand that he is expounding the views of the followers of non-Buddhist teachings or of the heavenly devil.

"Moreover, as to the identity of the Thus Come One Mahāvairochana, when Shakyamuni Buddha, the lord of teachings, who had been enlightened from remote ages past, for forty-two years dimmed his light and mingled with the dust of the world, adapting himself to the capacities of the people of the time, he, a Thus Come One who unites the three bodies in one, temporarily assumed the form of Vairochana.67 Therefore, when Shakyamuni Buddha revealed the true aspect of all phenomena,68 it became clear that Vairochana was a temporary form that Shakyamuni had manifested in response to the capacities of the people. For this reason, the Universal Worthy Sutra says that Shakyamuni Buddha is given the name Vairochana Pervading Everywhere, and that the place where that Buddha lives is called Eternally Tranquil Light.

"Now the Lotus Sutra expounds the doctrines of the mutual possession of the Ten Worlds, a single moment of life comprising the three thousand realms, the unification of the three truths, and the inseparability of the four kinds of lands. Moreover, the very essence of all the sacred teachings expounded by Shakyamuni Buddha in his lifetime—the doctrines that persons of the two vehicles can achieve Buddhahood, and that the Buddha attained p.116enlightenment in the inconceivably remote past—is found only in this one sutra, the Lotus. Is there any mention of these most important matters in the three esoteric sutras you have been talking about, the Mahāvairochana Sutra, the Diamond Crown Sutra, and so forth? Shan-wu-wei and Pu-k'ung stole these most important doctrines from the Lotus Sutra and contrived to make them the essential points of their own sutras. But in fact this is a fraud; their own sutras and treatises contain no trace of these doctrines. You must make haste and remedy your thinking on this point.

"The fact is that the Mahāvairochana Sutra includes each of the four types of teachings69 and expounds the kind of precepts whose benefit is exhausted when the bodily form comes to an end.70 It is a provisional teaching, designated by Chinese teachers71 as a sutra belonging to the Correct and Equal category, the group of sutras that, according to T'ien-t'ai's classification, were preached in the third period. How shameful [to hold it above the Lotus]! If you really have a mind to pursue the way, you must hurry and repent of your past errors. In the final analysis, this Lotus Sutra of the Wonderful Law sums up all the teachings and meditative practices of Shakyamuni Buddha's entire lifetime in a single moment of life, and encompasses all the living beings of the Ten Worlds and their environments in the three thousand realms."

Part Two

AT this, the unenlightened man looked somewhat mollified and said: "The words of the sutra are clear as a mirror; there is no room to doubt or question their meaning. But although the Lotus Sutra surpasses all the other sutras that the Buddha taught before, at the same time, or after, and represents the highest point in his preaching life, still it cannot compare with the single truth of Zen, which cannot be bound by words or confined in the text of a sutra, and which deals with the true nature of our minds. In effect, the realm where the countless doctrines are all cast aside and where words cannot reach is what is called the truth of Zen.

"Thus, on the banks of the Ajitavatī River, in the grove of sal trees, Shakyamuni Buddha stepped out of his golden coffin, twirled a flower, and, when he saw Mahākāshyapa's faint smile, entrusted this teaching of Zen to him. Since then, it has been handed down without any irregularity through a lineage of twenty-eight patriarchs in India, and was widely propagated by a succession of six patriarchs in China. Bodhidharma is the last of the twenty-eight patriarchs of India and the first of the six patriarchs of China. We must not allow this transmission to be lost, and founder in the nets of doctrine.

"So, in the Sutra of the Buddha Answering the Great Heavenly King Brahmā's Questions, the Buddha says: 'I have a subtle teaching concerning the eye and treasury of the correct teaching, the wonderful mind of nirvana, the true aspect of reality that is without characteristics. It represents a separate transmission outside the sutras, independent of words or writing. I entrust it to Mahākāshyapa.'

"Thus we see that this single truth of Zen was transmitted to Mahākāshyapa apart from the sutras. All the teachings of the sutras are like a finger pointing at the moon. Once we have seen the p.117moon, what use do we have for the finger? And once we have understood this single truth of Zen, the true nature of the mind, why should we concern ourselves any longer with the Buddha's teachings? Therefore, a man of past times has said, 'The twelve divisions of the scriptures are all idle writings.'

"If you will open and read The Platform Sutra of Hui-neng, the sixth patriarch of this school, you will see that this is true. Once one has heard even a single word and thereby grasped and understood the truth, what use does one have for the teachings? How do you consider this principle?"

The sage replied: "You must first of all set aside the doctrines for the moment and consider the logic of the matter. Can anyone, without inquiring into the essential meaning of the Buddha's lifetime teachings or investigating the basic principles of the ten schools, presume to admonish the nation and teach others? This Zen that you are talking about is something that I have studied exhaustively for some time. In view of the extreme doctrines that it teaches, I must say that it is a highly distorted affair.

"There are three types of Zen, known respectively as Thus Come One Zen, doctrinal Zen, and patriarchal Zen.72 What you are referring to is patriarchal Zen, and I would therefore like to give you a general idea of it. So listen, and understand what it is about.

"It speaks of transmitting something apart from the teachings. But apart from the teachings there are no principles, and apart from principles there are no teachings. Don't you understand the logic of this, that principles are none other than teachings and teachings none other than principles? This talk about the twirled flower, the faint smile, and something being entrusted to Mahākāshyapa is in itself a teaching, and the four-character phrase about its being 'independent of words or writing' is likewise a teaching and a statement in words. This sort of talk has been around for a long while in both China and Japan. It may appear novel to you, but let me quote one or two passages that will clear up your misconceptions.

"Volume eleven of The Supplement to T'ien-t'ai's Three Major Works states: 'If one says that we are not to hamper ourselves by the use of verbal expressions, then how, for even an instant in this sahā world, can we carry on the Buddha's work? Do the Zen followers themselves not use verbal explanations when they are giving instruction to others? If one sets aside words and phrases, then there is no way to explain the meaning of emancipation, so how can anyone ever hear about it?'

"Farther on, we read: 'It is said that Bodhidharma came from the west and taught the "direct pointing to the mind of man" and "perceiving one's true nature and attaining Buddhahood." But are these same concepts not found in the Flower Garland Sutra and in the other Mahayana sutras? Alas, how can the people of our time be so foolish! You should all put strong mind of determination in the teachings of the Buddha. The Buddhas, the Thus Come Ones, tell no lies!'

"To restate the meaning of this passage: if one objects that we are hampering ourselves with doctrinal writings and tying ourselves down with verbal explanations, and recommends a type of religious practice that is apart from the teachings of the sutras, then by what means are we to carry on the Buddha's work and make good causes in this Saha world of ours? Even the followers of Zen, who advocate these views, themselves make use of words when instructing others. In addition, when one is trying to convey an understanding of the Buddha way, one cannot communicate the meaning if one sets aside words and phrases. Bodhidharma came to China from the west, p.118pointed directly to people's minds, and declared that those minds were Buddha. But this principle is enunciated in various places even in the provisional Mahayana sutras that preceded the Lotus Sutra, such as the Flower Garland, Great Collection, and Great Wisdom sutras. To treat it as such a rare and wonderful thing is too ridiculous for words. Alas, how can the people of our time be so distorted in their thinking! They should put their strong mind of determination in the words of truth spoken by the Thus Come One of perfect enlightenment and complete reward, who embodies the principle of the Middle Way that is the true aspect of all things.

"In addition, the Great Teacher Miao-lo in the first volume of his Annotations on 'Great Concentration and Insight' comments on this situation by saying, 'The people of today look with contempt on the sutra teachings and emphasize only the contemplation of truth, but they are making a great mistake, a great mistake indeed!'

"This passage applies to the people in the world today who put meditation on the mind and various other things first, and do not delve into or study the teachings of the sutras. On the contrary, they despise the teachings and make light of the sutras. This passage is saying that this is a mistake.

"Moreover, I should point out that the Zen followers of the present age are confused as to the teachings of their own school. If we open the pages of The Continued Biographies of Eminent Priests, we find that in the biography of the Great Teacher Bodhidharma, the first patriarch of Zen in China, it states, 'By means of the teachings one can understand the essential meaning.' Therefore, one should study and practice the principles embodied in the sacred teachings preached by the Thus Come One in the course of his lifetime and thereby gain an understanding of the substance of the various doctrines and the nature of the different schools.

"Furthermore, in the biography of Bodhidharma's disciple, Hui-k'o, the second of the six Chinese patriarchs, it states that the Meditation Master Bodhidharma handed over the four volumes of the Lankāvatāra Sutra to Hui-k'o, saying: 'Observing this land of China, I find only this sutra to be of real worth. If you base your practice on it, you will be able to bring salvation to the world.' Here we see that, when the Great Teacher Bodhidharma came from India to China, he brought the four volumes of the Lankāvatāra Sutra and handed them over to Hui-k'o, saying: 'When I observe the situation in this country, I see that this sutra is of outstanding superiority. You should abide by it and put it into practice and become a Buddha.'

"As we have just seen, these patriarch-teachers placed primary emphasis on the sutra texts. But if we therefore say that one must rely on the sutras, then we must take care to inquire whether those sutras belong to the Mahayana or the Hinayana, whether they are the provisional teachings or the true teaching.

"When it comes to making use of sutras, the Zen school relies on such works as the Lankāvatāra Sutra, the Shūramgama Sutra, and the Diamond Wisdom Sutra. These are all provisional teachings that were preached before the Lotus Sutra, doctrines that conceal the truth.

"These various sutras expound partial truths such as 'the mind itself is the Buddha, and the Buddha is none other than the mind.' The Zen followers have allowed themselves to be led astray by one or two such sentences and phrases, failing to inquire whether they represent the Mahayana or the Hinayana, the provisional teachings or the true teaching, the doctrines that reveal the truth or the doctrines that conceal it. They merely advance the p.119principle of nonduality without understanding the principle of duality,73 and commit an act of great arrogance, claiming that they themselves are equal to the Buddha. They are following in the tracks of the Great Arrogant Brahman of India and imitating the old ways of the Meditation Master San-chieh of China. But we should recall that the Great Arrogant Brahman, while still alive, fell into the hell of incessant suffering, and that San-chieh, after he died, turned into a huge snake. How frightful, how frightful indeed!

"Shakyamuni Buddha, with his understanding that had penetrated the three existences, and by the light of the clear wisdom-moon of perfect enlightenment and complete reward, peered into the future and, in the Sutra on Resolving Doubts about the Middle Day of the Law, made this prediction: 'Among the evil monks there will be those who practice meditation and, instead of relying on the sutras and treatises, heed only their own view of things, declaring wrong to be right. Unable to distinguish between what is correct and what is erroneous, all they will do is face monks and lay believers and declare in this fashion, "I can understand what is right, I can see what is right." You should understand that it is people like this who will destroy my teachings in no time at all.'

"This passage is saying that there will be evil monks who put all their strong mind of determination in Zen and do not delve into the sutras and treatises. They will base themselves on distorted views and fail to distinguish between false and true doctrines. Moreover, they will address themselves to men and women believers, monks and nuns, declaring, 'I can understand the doctrines, but other people do not,' in this way working to spread the Zen teachings. But you should understand that these people will destroy the correct teaching of the Buddha. If we examine this passage and observe the state of the world today, we see that the two match each other as perfectly as do the two halves of a tally. Be careful! There is much to fear here.

"You spoke earlier of twenty-eight patriarchs of India who orally transmitted this Zen doctrine, but on what evidence is such a statement based? All the texts I have seen speak of twenty-four or, in some cases, twenty-three persons who transmitted the Buddha's teachings. Where is the translation that establishes the number of patriarchs as twenty-eight? I have never seen such a statement. This matter of the persons who were involved in the line of transmission of the Buddha's teachings is not something that one can simply write about arbitrarily. The Thus Come One himself left a clear record of what the line of transmission would be.

"Thus, in A History of the Buddha's Successors, it states: 'There will be a monk by the name of Āryasimha living in the kingdom of Kashmir who will strive vigorously to accomplish the Buddha's work. At that time the ruler of the kingdom will be named Mirakutsu,74 a man who gives himself up wholly to false views and has no reverence or strong mind of determination in his heart. Throughout the kingdom of Kashmir, he will destroy Buddhist temples and stupas and slaughter monks. He will take a sharp sword and use it to cut off Āryasimha's head. But no blood will spurt from his neck; only milk will come flowing out. With this, the line of persons who transmit the Law will be cut off.'

"To restate this passage: The Buddha says that, after he passes into nirvana, there will be a succession of twenty-four persons who will transmit his teachings. Among these, the last to carry on the line of transmission will be a monk named Āryasimha, who will work to spread the Buddha's teachings throughout the kingdom called Kashmir. The ruler of this state will be a p.120man named King Dammira. He will be a person of false views and profligate ways, who has no strong mind of determination in the Buddha's teachings and no reverence for the monks. He will destroy Buddhist halls and stupas and use a sword to cut off the heads of the monks. And when he cuts off the head of the monk Āryasimha, there will be no blood in his neck; only milk will come flowing out. The Buddha declares that at this time the line of persons who transmit his teachings will be cut off.

"The actual events did not in any way differ from the Buddha's predictions; the Venerable Āryasimha's head was in fact cut off. And as his head fell to the ground, so too did the arm of the king.

"It is a gross error to speak of twenty-eight patriarchs. This is the beginning of the errors of the Zen school. The reason that Hui-neng lists twenty-eight patriarchs in his Platform Sutra is that, when he decided to treat Bodhidharma as the first patriarch of Chinese Zen, he found that there were too many years between the time of Āryasimha and that of Bodhidharma. He therefore arbitrarily inserted the names of three Zen teachers to fill up the interval, so that he could make it seem as though the Law had been transmitted from India to China without any break or irregularity in the line of transmission. It was all a fabrication designed to make people respect the Zen teachings.

"This deception was put forth long ago in China. Thus, the eleventh volume of Three Major Works states: 'In our [T'ien-t'ai] school, we recognize a transmission through twenty-three patriarchs. How could there be any error in this view? Concerning the claim that there were twenty-eight patriarchs, we can find no translation of a source that supports such a view. Recently Zen priests have even produced carvings in stone and wood-block engravings, each with a sacred verse attached, which represent the seven Buddhas and the twenty-eight patriarchs, handing these down to their disciples. Alas, how can there be such blatant falsehoods! If persons of understanding have any power at all, they should do everything they can to correct such abuses.'

"This text is saying that to assert a transmission through a line of twenty-eight patriarchs and to produce stone carvings and wood-block engravings of them to indicate the line of transmission are highly mistaken undertakings, and that anyone who understands this should work to correct such errors. This is why I say that patriarchal Zen is a gravely erroneous affair.

"Earlier, you quoted a passage from the Sutra of the Buddha Answering the Great Heavenly King Brahmā's Questions to prove your contention that Zen is 'a separate transmission outside the sutras.' But by quoting a sutra passage you were already contradicting your own assertion. Moreover, this sutra represents the provisional teachings, and in addition, it is not listed either in the K'ai-yüan or the Chen-yüan era catalog of Buddhist works. Thus we see that it is a work unlisted in the catalogs and a provisional teaching as well. Hence the scholars of our time do not refer to it; it cannot be used to prove anything.

"Coming now to the Lotus Sutra, we should note the groups that benefited when it was preached. When the doctrine of the hundred worlds and thousand factors, or three thousand realms in a single moment of life, was expounded in the theoretical teaching, the people of the two vehicles, who had been likened to rotten seeds, had the seeds of Buddhahood sprout. In the previous forty-two years of the Buddha's preaching, these persons had been condemned as incapable of ever attaining Buddhahood. In every gathering p.121and assembly, they heard nothing but curses and slander spoken against them and were shunned by all those of the human and heavenly realms, until it seemed that they were destined to die of hunger. But now, when the Lotus Sutra was preached, it was predicted that Shāriputra would become the Thus Come One Flower Glow, that Maudgalyāyana would become the Thus Come One Tamalapattra Sandalwood Fragrance, that Ānanda would become Mountain Sea Wisdom Unrestricted Power King Buddha, that Rāhula would become the Thus Come One Stepping on Seven Treasure Flowers, that the five hundred Arhats would become the Thus Come Ones Universal Brightness, and that the two thousand voice-hearers would become the Thus Come Ones Jewel Sign. And on the day when the Buddha's life span from the time he attained enlightenment in the remote past was revealed, the bodhisattvas who were as countless as particles of dust increased in their understanding of the way, discarded their still remaining illusions, and attained the last stage before the level of supreme enlightenment.

"Now, if we examine the commentary of the Great Teacher T'ien-t'ai, it states: 'The other sutras tell us that although the bodhisattvas may become Buddhas those persons of the two vehicles can never do so. Good people can become Buddhas, we are told, but there is no indication that evil ones can do likewise. Men, it is said, can become Buddhas, but women are branded as messengers of hell. Human and heavenly beings can attain Buddhahood, but it is nowhere stated that nonhuman creatures can do so. And yet, in this sutra, it is stated that all of these beings can attain Buddhahood.'75

"What a wonderful thing this is! Though we have been born in the impure world in the Latter Day of the Law, we have committed neither the five cardinal sins nor the three cardinal sins76 as Devadatta did. And yet it was predicted that even Devadatta would in time become the Thus Come One Heavenly King, so how much more should it be possible for persons like us, who have committed no such sins, to attain Buddhahood! And the eight-year-old dragon king's daughter, without changing her reptilian form, attained the wonderful fruit of Buddhahood in the southern realm.77 Therefore, how much more likely is it that women who have been born into the human realm should be able to do so!

"It is most difficult to be born in human form, and extremely rare to encounter the correct teaching. Now, if you want to rid yourself quickly of erroneous beliefs and adhere to what is correct, transform your status as a common mortal and attain that of

Buddhahood, then you should abandon the Nembutsu, True Word, Zen, and Precepts teachings and embrace this wonderful text of the single vehicle.78 If you do so, you will without a doubt be able to shake off the dust and defilement of delusion and impurity, and manifest yourself as a pure embodiment of enlightenment."

Then the unenlightened man said: "Listening to the teachings and admonitions of a sage like you, I find that the misunderstandings I have labored under in recent days are all suddenly dispelled. It is as though inherent wisdom had awakened within me. When right and wrong are made so clear, who could fail to take strong mind of determination?

"And yet, when I look at the world around me, I find that, from the supreme ruler on down to the numberless common people, all place deep trust in the Nembutsu, True Word, Zen, and Precepts teachings. Since I have been born in this land, how could I go against the example of the ruler?

"Moreover, my parents and ancestors all put their strong mind of determination in the principles of p.122the Nembutsu and other teachings, and in that strong mind of determination they ended their lives and vanished into the clouds of the other world.

"Here in Japan, there are, to be sure, a great many people, both eminent and humble. Yet, while those who adhere to the provisional teachings and the schools based upon them are numerous, I have yet to hear the name of a single individual who puts strong mind of determination in the teachings that you have been explaining. Therefore, leaving aside the question of which teachings will lead to good places in the next life and which will lead to bad ones, and not attempting to inquire which teachings are true and which false, we find that the five thousand or seven thousand volumes of the Buddhist scriptures and the three thousand or more volumes of the Confucian and Taoist writings all emphasize the importance of obeying the orders of the ruler and complying with the wishes of one's parents.

"In India, Shakyamuni, the lord of teachings, expounded the principles of carrying out filial conduct and repaying one's obligations, and in China, Confucius set forth the way of giving loyal service to the ruler and honoring one's parents as filial offspring should. Persons who are determined to repay the debt of gratitude they owe to their teachers would not hesitate to slice off a piece of their own flesh or cast their bodies away. Among those who were aware of the debt of gratitude they owed to their lords, Hung Yen cut open his stomach, and Yü Jang fell on his sword. And among those who were truly mindful of their obligations to their parents, Ting Lan fashioned a wooden image of his deceased mother, and Han Po-yü wept [upon realizing how feeble his aged mother had become] when she beat him with her staff. Though Confucianism, Brahmanism, and Buddhism all differ in their doctrines, they are alike in teaching one to repay debts of kindness and give thanks for favors received.

"Thus, if I were to be the first one to place strong mind of determination in a doctrine that neither the ruler, my teacher, nor my parents put strong mind of determination in, I would surely be guilty of the charge of turning against them, would I not? At the same time, the passages from the sutras that you have quoted make perfectly clear the truth of this doctrine, and all my doubts about it have been resolved. And if I do not prepare myself for the life hereafter, then in my next existence I will find myself submerged in suffering. Whether I try to go forward or to retreat, my way is beset by difficulties. What am I to do?"

The sage replied: "You understand this doctrine, and yet you can say a thing like that. Have you failed to comprehend the logic of the matter? Or is it simply beyond your understanding?

"Ever since I began to study the Law handed down from Shakyamuni Buddha and undertook the practice of the Buddhist teachings, I have believed it is most important to understand one's obligations to others, and made it my first duty to repay such debts of kindness. In this world, we owe four debts of gratitude. One who understands this is worthy to be called human, while one who does not is no more than an animal.

"As I wish to assist my father and mother to a better life in their next existence and repay the debt that I owe to my country, I am willing to lay down my life, simply because I understand the debt that I owe them and for no other reason.

"Now let me ask you to close your eyes, still your mind, and apply your thoughts to the logic of the matter. If, knowing the best path, one sees one's parents or sovereign taking an evil path, can one fail to admonish them? If a fool, crazed with wine, is about to p.123drink poison, can one, knowing this, not try to stop him? In the same way, if one understands the truth of the Buddhist teachings and knows the sufferings of fire, blood, and swords,79 can one fail to lament at seeing someone to whom one owes a debt of gratitude about to fall into the evil paths? Rather one should cast away one's body and lay down one's life in an effort to save such a person. One will never grow weary of admonishing him, nor will there be limits to one's grief.

"The sufferings that meet our eyes in this present world are lamentable enough. How much more lamentable are those that one will encounter on the long road of death! How can we fail to be pained at the thought of it? A thing to be boundlessly feared is the life hereafter, a matter of greatest concern is the existence to come.

"And yet you say that, without inquiring into what is right and what is wrong, you will follow your parents' orders; without attempting to determine what is correct and what is erroneous, you will obey the words of the sovereign. To a fool, such conduct may appear to be loyal and filial, but in the opinion of a wise person, there can be no greater disloyalty, no greater departure from filial piety.

"Shakyamuni Buddha, the lord of teachings, was a descendant of wheel-turning kings, the grandson of King Simhahanu, and the heir of King Shuddhodana, and should by rights have become a great ruler of the five regions of India. But he awakened to the truth of the impermanence of life and grew to abhor the world, desiring a way to escape this realm of suffering and attain emancipation. King Shuddhodana, grieving at this, cleverly contrived to have the sights of the four seasons displayed to their best advantage in the four directions so that the prince might be diverted from his intention.

"First, in the east, where a break appeared in the trailing mist, he pointed out the wild geese crying as they made their way back north; the plums blooming by the window, their fragrance wafting through the beaded blinds; the entrancing hues of the flowers; the countless calls of the bush warblers; and the other sights of spring.

"In the south he showed him the crystal colors of the fountains, the deutzia flowers blooming beside the clear-flowing streams, the cuckoos of Shinoda forest,[80] and the other signs of summer.

"In the west there were the autumn-reddened leaves mingling with the evergreens to weave a pattern of brocade, the breezes blowing gently over the reed flowers, or the stormy winds that swept wildly through the pines. And as if to remind one of the departed summer, there were the fireflies glimmering by the swampside, so numerous that one might mistake them for the stars in the heavens, and the repeated voices of the pine cricket and the bell cricket, bringing one to tears.

"And in the north, before one knew it, there was the melancholy color of withered fields, the rims of the ponds sealed with ice, and the sad sound of the little streams in the valley.

"Not only did the king attempt to console his son's mind by presenting the world to him in this way, he also assigned five hundred soldiers to guard each of the four gates of the palace. But, in the end, when the prince was nineteen, at midnight on the eighth day of the second month, he summoned his groom Chandaka, ordered him to saddle his horse, Kanthaka, and made his way out of the city of Gayā.

"He entered Mount Dandaka, where for twelve years he gathered firewood on the high slopes, drew water in the deep valleys, and performed various austerities and difficult practices. At the age of thirty he attained the wonderful fruit of enlightenment, p.124becoming the only one worthy of honor in the threefold world and the lord of all the teachings that he expounded throughout his life. He brought salvation to his father and mother and opened the way for all living beings. Could such a man be called unfilial?

"The ninety-five schools of Brahmanists were the ones who accused the Buddha of being unfilial. But by disobeying the command of his father and mother and entering the realm of the unconditioned, he was, on the contrary, able to lead his father and mother to salvation, thus demonstrating that he was in fact a model of filial piety.

"King Wonderful Adornment, the father of Pure Storehouse and Pure Eye, adhered to the non-Buddhist teachings and turned his back on the teachings of the Buddha. His two sons and heirs disobeyed their father's orders and became disciples of Cloud Thunder Sound King Buddha, but in the end they were able to guide their father so that he became a Buddha called Sal Tree King.81 Could anyone say, then, that these were unfilial sons?

"There is a passage in a sutra that says, 'By renouncing one's obligations and entering the Buddhist life one can truly repay those obligations in full.'82 Thus we see that one who casts aside all bonds of indebtedness and love in this present life and enters into the true path of Buddhism is the one who really understands the meaning of obligations.

"Moreover, I know the depth of the obligation owed to one's ruler far better than you do. If you really wish to show that you understand your debt of gratitude, then you should admonish the ruler from the depths of your heart and forcefully advise him. To follow his orders even when these are contrary to what is right is the act of an utter sycophant and the height of disloyalty.

"King Chou of the Yin dynasty was an evil ruler, and Pi Kan, his loyal minister. When Pi Kan saw that the king was going against what was right in ruling the nation, he vigorously admonished him. As a result, Pi

Kan's breast was ripped open, but after his death, King Chou was overthrown by the king of the Chou. To the present day, Pi Kan has been known as a loyal minister, and King Chou as an evil ruler.

"When Kuan Lung-feng admonished his sovereign, King Chieh of the Hsia dynasty, he was beheaded. But King Chieh has come to be known as an evil ruler, and Kuan Lung-feng as a loyal minister. We are taught that, if one admonishes one's sovereign three times and still one's advice is not heeded, then one should retire to the mountain forests.83 Why do you nevertheless remain silent while the ruler commits misdeeds in your full view?

"I have gathered together a few examples of worthies of ancient times who did in fact retire from the world to dwell in the mountain forests. Open your obstinate ears and listen a moment! During the Yin dynasty, T'ai-kung Wang hid himself in a valley called P'o-ch'i; in the Chou dynasty, Po I and Shu Ch'i secluded themselves on Mount Shou-yang; Ch'i Li-chi84 of the Ch'in dynasty retired to Mount Shang; Yen Kuang85 of the Han dynasty lived in a solitary lodge; and Chieh Tzu-sui86 of the state of Chin became a recluse on Mount Mien-shang. Are we to call these men disloyal? Anyone who would do so is a fool. If you understand what it means to be loyal, you will admonish your sovereign, and if you want to be filial, you must speak up.

"Earlier you said that those who adhere to the provisional teachings and to the schools based on them are very numerous, while those who adhere to the school I have been recommending are few, and you ask why one would abandon the teachings favored by many and take up those favored by few. But p.125the many are not necessarily worthy of honor, nor the few, deserving of contempt.

"People of wisdom and goodness are rare indeed, while fools and evil persons are numerous. A ch'i-lin is the finest of beasts and a phoenix the finest of birds, yet they are very few in number. On the other hand, cows and sheep, crows and pigeons are among the lowlier and commoner of creatures, and yet they are extremely plentiful. If the many are always worthy while the few are to be despised, should one then cast aside a ch'i-lin in favor of cows and sheep, or pass over a phoenix and instead select crows and pigeons?

"The mani jewel and the diamond are the most wondrous of all precious stones. These gems are rare, while shards and rubble, clods of earth and common stones are the most useless of objects, and at the same time abound. Now if one follows your advice, ought one to discard the precious jewels and instead content oneself with shards and rubble? How pitiful and meaningless that would be!

"A sage ruler is a rare thing, appearing only once in a thousand years, while a worthy minister appears once in five hundred years. The mani jewel is so rare that we have only heard of it, and who, for that matter, has ever actually seen a ch'i-lin or a phoenix? In both secular and religious realms, as is plain to see, good persons are rare while evil persons are numerous. Why, then, do you insist upon despising the few and favoring the many? Dirt and sand are plentiful, but rice and other grains are rare. The bark of trees is available in great quantities, but hemp and silk fabrics are hard to come by. You should put the truth of the teaching before everything else; certainly you should not base your judgment on the number of adherents."

The unenlightened man thereupon moved off his mat in a gesture of respect, straightened his sleeves, and said: "I have heard what you stated about the principles of the sacred teachings. Truly it is more difficult to be born as a human being than it is to lower a thread from the heavens above and pass it through the eye of a needle at the bottom of the sea, and it is rarer for one to be able to hear the Law of the Buddha than it is for a one-eyed turtle to encounter a floating log [with a hole in it that fits him exactly]. Now I have already obtained birth in the human realm, something difficult to achieve, and have had the privilege of hearing the Buddhist teachings, which are seldom encountered. If I should pass my present life in idleness, then in what future life could I possibly free myself from the sufferings of birth and death and attain enlightenment?

"Though, in the course of a kalpa, the bones I have left behind in successive existences may pile up higher than a mountain, to this day I have not yet sacrificed so much as a single bone for the sake of the Buddha's Law. And though, in the course of these many lifetimes, I have shed more tears over those I loved or was indebted to than there is water in the sea, I have never spilled so much as a single tear for the sake of my future existences. I am the most stupid of the stupid, truly a fool among fools. Though I may have to cast aside my life and destroy this body of mine, I am determined to hold life lightly and to enter the path of the Buddha's teachings, to assist in bringing about the enlightenment of my father and mother, and to save my own person from the bonds of hell. Please teach me exactly how I should go about it. How should one practice if one takes strong mind of determination in the Lotus Sutra? Of the five practices, which one should I concentrate on first? Please give me careful instruction in your worthy teachings."

The sage replied: "You have been imbued with the fragrance of your orchid-room friend;87 you have become upright like mugwort growing in a field of hemp.88 Truly, the bare tree is not really bare: once spring comes, it bursts into blossom. The withered field is not really withered. With the coming of summer, it turns fresh and green again. If you have repented of your former errors and are ready to adhere to the correct doctrine, then without doubt you can swim in the calm and quiet depths [of nirvana], and dwell at ease in the palace of the unconditioned.

"Now, in widely propagating the Buddhist teachings and bringing salvation to all people, one must first take into consideration the teaching, the capacity of the people, the time, the country, and the sequence of propagation. The reason is as follows. In terms of the time, there are the periods of the Former, the Middle, and the Latter Days of the Law, and in terms of the teachings, there are the Hinayana and the Mahayana doctrines. In terms of the practices to be adopted, there are shōju and shakubuku. It is a mistake to practice shakubuku at a time when shōju is called for, and equally erroneous to practice shōju when shakubuku is appropriate. The first thing to be determined, therefore, is whether the present period is the time for shōju or the time for shakubuku.

"Shōju is to be practiced when throughout the entire country only the Lotus Sutra has spread, and when there is not even a single misguided teacher expounding erroneous doctrines. At such a time, one may retire to the mountain forests, practice meditation, or carry out the five, the six, or the ten practices.89 But the time for shakubuku is very different from this. It is a time when many different sutras and teachings spring up here and there like so many orchids and chrysanthemums, when the various schools command a large following and enjoy renown, when truth and error stand shoulder to shoulder, and when Mahayana and Hinayana dispute which is superior. At such a time, one must set aside all other affairs and devote one's attention to rebuking slander of the correct teaching. This is the practice of shakubuku.

"If, failing to understand this principle, one were to practice shōju or shakubuku at an inappropriate time, then not only would one be unable to attain Buddhahood, but one would fall into the evil paths. This is firmly laid down in the Lotus and Nirvana sutras, and is also clearly stated in the commentaries by T'ien-t'ai and Miao-lo. It is, in fact, an important principle of Buddhist practice.

"We may compare these two kinds of practice to the two ways of the civil and the military used in governing a nation. There is a time when military measures should take precedence, and a time when civil measures ought to be emphasized. When the world is at peace and calm prevails within the country, then civil measures should take precedence. But when the barbarian tribes to the east, south, west, and north, fired by wild ambitions, rise up like hornets, then military measures should come first.

"Though one may understand the importance of both civil and military arts, if one does not understand the time, donning armor and taking up weapons when all countries are calm and peaceful and there is no trouble anywhere throughout the world, then one's actions will be wrong. On the other hand, one who lays aside one's weapons on the battlefield when enemies are marching against one's ruler and instead takes up a writing brush and inkstone is likewise failing to act in accordance with the time.

"The methods of shōju and shakubuku are also like this. When the correct teaching alone is propagated and p.127there are no erroneous doctrines or misguided teachers, then one may enter the deep valleys and live in quiet contentment, devoting one's time to reciting and copying the sutra and to the practice of meditation. This is like taking up a writing brush and inkstone when the world is at peace. But when there are provisional schools or slanderers of the correct teaching in the country, then it is time to set aside other matters and devote oneself to rebuking slander. This is like taking up weapons on the battlefield.

"Therefore, the Great Teacher Chang-an in his commentary on the Nirvana Sutra states: 'In past times the age was peaceful, and the Law spread throughout the country. At that time it was proper to observe the precepts and not to carry staves. But now the age is perilous, and the Law is overshadowed. Therefore, it is proper to carry staves and to disregard the precepts. If both past and present were perilous times, then it would be proper to carry staves in both periods. And if both past and present were peaceful times, then it would be proper to observe the precepts in both of them. You should let your choices be fitting and never adhere solely to one or the other.' The meaning of this passage of commentary is perfectly clear.

"In past times the world was honest, people were upright, and there were no erroneous teachings or erroneous doctrines. Therefore, one could behave in a proper manner and carry out one's religious practices peacefully and amicably. There was no need to take up staves and berate others, no occasion to attack erroneous teachings.

"But the present age is a defiled one. Because the minds of people are warped and twisted, and provisional teachings and slander alone abound, the correct teaching cannot prevail. In times like these, it is useless to practice the reading, reciting, and copying [of the Lotus Sutra] or to devote oneself to the methods and practices of meditation. One should practice only the shakubuku method of propagation, and if one has the capacity, use one's influence and authority to destroy slander of the correct teaching, and one's knowledge of the teachings to refute erroneous doctrines.

"As we have seen, it is said that one should let one's choices be fitting and never adhere solely to one or the other. Therefore, we must look at the world today and consider whether ours is a country in which only the correct doctrine prevails, or a country in which erroneous doctrines flourish.

"In answering this we should note that Hōnen of the Pure Land school says that one should 'discard, close, ignore, and abandon' the Lotus Sutra in favor of the Nembutsu. And Shan-tao in his writings calls the Lotus Sutra a 'sundry practice,' saying that 'not even one person in a thousand' can be saved by it, by which he means that, if a thousand people take strong mind of determination in it, not a single one of them will gain enlightenment.

"Kōbō of the True Word school states in his writings that the Lotus Sutra is inferior even to the Flower Garland Sutra and ranks two steps beneath the Mahāvairochana Sutra, designating it a piece of 'childish theory.' And Shōkaku-bō of the same school declares that the Lotus Sutra is not fit even to serve as the sandal-tender of the Mahāvairochana Sutra, and that Shakyamuni Buddha is not worthy to be an ox-driver to the Thus Come One Mahāvairochana.

"The priests of the Zen school disparage the Lotus Sutra by calling it so much saliva that has been spit out of the mouth, a finger pointing at the moon, or a net of doctrine that serves only to entangle. The priests of the Precepts, a Hinayana school, call the Lotus Sutra an erroneous teaching and label p.128it the preaching of the heavenly devil.

"Are persons such as these not slanderers of the correct teaching? One can never be too severe in condemning them, or admonish them too strongly."

The unenlightened man said: "Throughout the more than sixty provinces of Japan, there are many kinds of people and a variety of Buddhist doctrines. What with the Nembutsu priests, the True Word teachers, and the followers of Zen or the Precepts teachings, there is truly hardly a single person who does not slander the correct teaching. But then, why should I criticize other people? My task, it seems to me, is simply to cherish deep strong mind of determination within my own heart and to look on other people's errors as no concern of mine."

The sage replied: "What you say is quite true, and I would be inclined to hold the same opinion. But when we examine the sutras, we find that they tell us not to begrudge our lives [for the sake of the Law], and also say that [one should spread the Buddha's teachings] even at the cost of one's life.90 The reason they speak in this way is because if one does not hesitate on account of others but propagates the principles of Buddhism just as they are set forth in the sutras, then in an age when there are many people who slander the correct teaching, three types of enemies will invariably appear and in many cases deprive one of life. But if, as the sutras tell us, one observes deviations from the Buddha's teachings and yet fails to censure them or to appeal to the ruler to take measures against them, then one is being untrue to the teachings and is not worthy to be looked on as a disciple of the Buddha.

"The third volume of the Nirvana Sutra says: 'If even a good monk sees someone destroying the teaching and disregards him, failing to reproach him, to oust him, or to punish him for his offense, then you should realize that that monk is betraying the Buddha's teaching. But if he ousts the destroyer of the Law, reproaches him, or punishes him, then he is my disciple and a true voice-hearer.'

"The meaning of this passage is that, if a person striving to propagate the correct teaching of the Buddha should hear and see others propounding the teachings of the sutras in a mistaken manner and fail to reproach them himself or, lacking the power to do that, fail to appeal to the sovereign and in this way take measures to correct them, then he is betraying the Buddha's teaching. But if, as the sutras direct, he is not afraid of others but censures these slanderers himself and appeals to the sovereign to take measures against them, then he may be called a disciple of the Buddha and a true priest.

"Being therefore determined to avoid the charge of 'betraying the Buddha's teaching,' although I have incurred the hatred of others, I have dedicated my life to Shakyamuni Buddha and the Lotus Sutra, extending compassion to all living beings and rebuking slanders of the correct teaching. Those who cannot understand my heart have tightened their lips and glared at me with furious eyes. But if you are truly concerned about your future existence, you should think lightly of your own safety and consider the Law above all. Thus the Great Teacher Chang-an states, "'[A royal envoy . . . would rather], even though it costs him his life, in the end conceal none of the words of his ruler"91 means that one's body is insignificant while the Law is supreme. One should give one's life in order to propagate the Law.'92

"This passage is saying that, even if one must give up one's life, one should not conceal the correct teaching; this is because one's body is insignificant while the Law is supreme. Though one's body be destroyed, one should strive to propagate the Law.

p.129"How sad is this lot of ours, that all who are born must perish! Though one may live to a great age, in the end one cannot escape this impermanence. In this world of ours, life lasts a hundred years or so at most. When we stop to think of it, it is a mere dream within a dream. Even in the heaven where there is neither thought nor no thought, where life lasts eighty thousand years, no one escapes the law of mutability, and in the heaven of the thirty-three gods, too, where life lasts a thousand years, it is swept away at last by the winds of change and decay. How much sadder, then, is the lot of the human beings living on this land of Jambudvīpa, whose life is more fleeting than the dew, more fragile than the plantain leaf, more insubstantial than bubbles or foam! Like the moon reflected in the water, one is not even certain whether one exists or not; like the dew on the grass, one may vanish at any moment.

"Anyone who grasps this principle should know that it is of utmost importance to take thought for the existence to come. In the latter age of the Buddha Joy Increasing, the monk Realization of Virtue propagated the correct teaching. Countless monks who were guilty of violating the precepts deeply resented this votary and attacked him, but the ruler, King Possessor of Virtue, determined to protect the correct teaching, fought with these slanderers. In the end, he lost his life and was reborn in the land of the Buddha Akshobhya, where he became the foremost disciple of that Buddha. Similarly, King Sen'yo, because he honored the Mahayana teachings and punished the slander of five hundred Brahmans, was able to reach the stage of non-regression. How reassuring, that those who respect the monks of the correct teaching and admonish those who are evil and in error receive such blessings as these!

"But if, in our present age, one were to practice shōju [rather than shakubuku], then without doubt that person would fall into the evil paths together with those who slander the correct teaching. The Great Teacher Nan-yüeh in his Four Peaceful Practices states, 'If there should be a bodhisattva who protects evil persons and fails to chastise them . . . then, when his life comes to an end, he will fall into hell along with those evil persons.'

"The meaning of this passage is that, if a practitioner of Buddhism should fail to chastise evil persons who slander the Law but give himself up entirely to meditation and contemplation, not attempting to distinguish between correct and incorrect doctrines, or provisional and true teachings, but rather pretending to be a model of compassion, then such a person will fall into the evil paths along with the other doers of evil. Now a person who fails to correct the True Word, Nembutsu, Zen, and Precepts adherents who are slanderers of the correct teaching and instead pretends to be a model of compassion will meet just such a fate as this."

Thereupon the unenlightened man, cherishing his resolve in mind, spoke out in these words: "To admonish one's sovereign and set one's family on the correct course is the teaching of the worthies of former times and is clearly indicated in the texts you have cited. The non-Buddhist writings all emphasize this point, and the Buddhist scriptures are in no way at variance with it. To see evil and fail to admonish it, to be aware of slander and not combat it, is to go against the words of the sutras and to disobey the Buddhist patriarchs. The punishment for this offense is extremely severe, and therefore, from now on, I will devote myself to strong mind of determination.

"But it is truly difficult to put this sutra, the Lotus, into practice. If there p.130is some essential point to be observed, could you explain it to me?"

The sage replied: "I can tell that your aspiration for the way is very earnest and sincere. The essential thing the Buddhas needed in order to attain the true way or enlightenment is nothing other than the five characters of Myoho-Renge-Kyo. It was solely because of these five characters that King Suzudan relinquished his jeweled throne [and attained Buddhahood], and the dragon king's daughter transformed her reptilian characteristics [into those of a Buddha].93

"When we stop to consider it, we find that the sutra itself says, concerning how much or how little of it is to be embraced, that a single verse or phrase is sufficient, and, concerning the length of practice [necessary to reach enlightenment], that one who rejoices even for a moment on hearing it [is certain to become a Buddha]. The eighty thousand teachings in their vast entirety and the many words and phrases of the eight volumes of the Lotus Sutra were all expounded simply in order to reveal these five characters. When Shakyamuni Buddha in the clouds above the Sacred Mountain, in the mists of Eagle Peak, summed up the essence of the doctrine and entrusted it to the Bodhisattvas of the Earth, what do you suppose that teaching was? It was nothing other than these five characters, the essential Law.

"The six thousand leaves94 of commentary by T'ien-t'ai and Miao-lo, like strings of jewels, and the several scrolls of exegesis by Tao-sui and Hsing-man, like so much gold, do not go beyond the meaning of this teaching. If you truly fear the sufferings of birth and death and yearn for nirvana, if you carry out your strong mind of determination and thirst for the way, then the sufferings of change and impermanence will become no more than yesterday's dream, and the awakening of enlightenment will become today's reality. If only you chant Nam-Myoho-Renge-Kyo, then what offense could fail to be eradicated? What blessing could fail to come? This is the truth, and it is of great profundity. You should believe and accept it."

The unenlightened man, pressing his palms together and kneeling respectfully, said: "These priceless words of yours have moved me deeply, and your instruction has awakened my mind. And yet, in light of the principle that superior things encompass those that are inferior, it would seem that the broad should also encompass the narrow and the many should take in the few. However, when we examine the matter, we find that these five characters you have mentioned are few, while the words in the sutra text are many, and that the Daimoku, or title, of the

Lotus Sutra is narrow, while its eight scrolls are very broad. How then can the two be equal in the blessings that they bring?"

The sage said: "How foolish you are! Your attachment to this belief that one should abandon the few in favor of the many towers higher than Mount Sumeru, and your conviction that the narrow should be despised and the broad honored is deeper than the vast ocean. In the course of our discussion, I have already demonstrated that something is not necessarily worthy of honor simply because it is many in number or despicable simply because it is few. Now I would like to go a step farther and explain how the small can actually encompass the great, and the one be superior to the many.

"The seed of the nyagrodha tree, though one-third the size of a mustard seed, can conceal five hundred carts within itself.95 Is this not a case of the small containing the large? The wish-granting jewel, while only one in number, is able to rain down ten thousand treasures without a single thing lacking. Is this not a case of the few encompassing the many? The popular p.131proverb says that 'one is the mother of ten thousand.' Do you not understand the principle behind these matters? The important thing to consider is whether or not a doctrine conforms with the principle of the true aspect of all things. Do not be blindly attached to the question of many or few!

"But since you are so extremely foolish, let me give you an analogy. Myoho-Renge-Kyo is the Buddha nature of all living beings. The Buddha nature is the Dharma nature, and the Dharma nature is enlightenment. The Buddha nature possessed by Shakyamuni, Many Treasures, and the Buddhas of the ten directions; by Superior Practices, Boundless Practices, and the other Bodhisattvas of the Earth; by Universal Worthy, Manjushrī, Shāriputra Mudgalyāyana, and the others; by the great Brahmā and the lord Shakra; by the deities of the sun and moon, the morning star, the seven stars in the Big Dipper in the northern sky, the twenty-eight constellations, and the countless other stars; by the heavenly gods, the earthly deities, the dragon deities, the eight kinds of nonhuman beings, and the human and heavenly beings who gathered in the great assembly to hear the Buddha's preaching; by King Yama—in short, by all living beings from the realm where there is neither thought nor no thought above the clouds down to the flames in the lowest depths of hell—the Buddha nature that all these beings possess is called by the name Myoho-Renge-Kyo. Therefore, if you recite these words of the Daimoku once, then the Buddha nature of all living beings will be summoned and gather around you. At that time the three bodies of the Dharma nature within you—the Dharma body, the reward body, and the manifested body—will be drawn forth and become manifest. This is called attaining Buddhahood. To illustrate, when a caged bird sings, the many birds flying in the sky all gather around it at once; seeing this, the bird in the cage strives to get out."

The unenlightened man said, "You have now explained to me in detail the benefits of the Daimoku and the significance of the Mystic Law. But I would like to ask whether these matters are explained in this manner in the sutra."

The sage replied: "Since you have already understood the principle involved, there is really no need to go on and inquire what scriptural passages it is based on. However, I will cite a passage from the sutra as you request.

"The 'Dhāraṇī' chapter in the eighth volume of the Lotus Sutra says, 'If you can shield and guard those who accept and uphold the mere name of the Lotus Sutra, your merit will be immeasurable.' In this passage, the Buddha is praising the Mother of Demon Children and the ten demon daughters for their vow to protect the votaries of the Lotus Sutra, and saying that the blessings from their vow to protect those who embrace the Daimoku of the Lotus Sutra are beyond even the Buddha wisdom, which completely comprehends the three existences, to fathom. While by rights nothing should be beyond the grasp of the Buddha wisdom, the Buddha says here that the blessings that accrue from accepting and embracing the Daimoku of the Lotus Sutra are the one thing that wisdom cannot measure.

"The blessings of the entire Lotus Sutra are all contained solely within the five characters of Myoho-Renge-Kyo. While the words in the eight volumes of the Lotus Sutra differ according to the contents of the twenty-eight chapters, the five characters of the Daimoku remain the same throughout. To illustrate, within the two characters for Japan are included the more than sixty provinces and the two islands. Are there any districts or provinces that are not contained within this name?

"If one uses the term 'birds,' people know that one is talking about creatures that fly in the sky; if one says 'beasts,' people understand that one is referring to animals that run over the ground. In all things, names are of great importance precisely because they can convey general meanings in this way. This is what the Great Teacher T'ien-t'ai meant when he said that names convey the basic nature of a thing while phrases describe how it differs from other things, or when he said that names designate the fundamental character of a thing.

"In addition, names have the virtue of being able to summon the things to which they refer, and things as a matter of function respond to the name that refers to them. In similar fashion, the name, or Daimoku, of the Lotus Sutra has the power [to summon the Buddha nature to which it refers]."

The unenlightened man said: "If it is as you say, then the blessings of the Daimoku are very great indeed. But these blessings must differ according to whether or not one understands the significance of the Daimoku. I am a man who carries a bow and arrows and devotes himself to the profession of arms. I have no understanding of the true nature of the Buddhist teachings. How could a person such as I gain any great amount of good fortune?"

The sage replied: "According to the principle of the perfect and immediate enlightenment, there is no essential difference between the earlier and later stages of practice, and the blessings of the advanced stages are inherent in the initial stages as well. To carry out one practice is to carry out all practices, and there is no blessing that is not included therein.

"If the situation were as you say and one could not obtain good fortune until after one had understood the truth of Buddhism, then no one, from the bodhisattvas at the stage of near-perfect enlightenment on down to those at the stage of hearing the name and words of the truth, would be able to obtain any good fortune at all. This is because, as the Lotus Sutra says, the truth can only be understood 'between Buddhas.'96

"In the 'Simile and Parable' chapter of the Lotus Sutra, the Buddha declares, 'Even you, Shāriputra, in the case of this sutra were able to gain entrance through strong mind of determination alone. How much more so, then, the other voice-hearers!'

"This passage is saying that even Shāriputra, who was known for his great wisdom, was, with respect to the Lotus Sutra, able to gain entrance through strong mind of determination and not through the power of his wisdom. How much more so, therefore, does this hold true with the other voice-hearers!

"Thus, with the preaching of the Lotus Sutra, Shāriputra, because he had strong mind of determination, was able to rid himself of the name of one who could never attain Buddhahood and was told that he would in time become the Thus Come One Flower Glow.

"It is like the case of a baby being given milk to drink. Even though the baby may not understand the flavor of milk, the milk naturally nurtures the baby's growth. Similarly, if a physician gives medicine to a sick person, even though the sick person may not know the origin and nature of the medicine, if he takes it, then in the natural course of events his illness will be cured. But if he objects that he does not know the origin of the medicine that the physician gives him and for that reason declines to take it, do you think his illness will ever be cured? Whether he understands the medicine or not, so long as he takes it, he will in either case be cured.

"The Buddha has already been called a skilled physician, and the Law has been likened to good medicine and p.133all living beings to people suffering from illness.97 The Buddha took the teachings that he had preached in the course of his lifetime, ground and sifted them, blended them together, and compounded an excellent medicine, the pill of the Mystic Law. Regardless of whether one understands it or not, so long as one takes the pill, can one fail to be cured of the illness of delusion? Even though the sick person may not understand the medicine or even know the nature of the disease from which he suffers, if he takes the medicine, he is bound to recover.

"It is the same way with the practitioners of the Lotus Sutra. Though they may not understand the principles of Buddhism and may not know that they are suffering from delusion, if only they have strong mind of determination, then without a doubt they will be able to free themselves simultaneously from the illnesses of the three categories of illusion—illusions of thought and desire, illusions innumerable as particles of dust and sand, and illusions about the true nature of existence. They will reach the lands of Actual Reward and Tranquil Light, and cause the three bodies of a Thus Come One that they inherently possess to shine.

"Therefore, the Great Teacher Dengyō says: 'Neither teacher nor disciples need undergo countless kalpas of austere practice in order to attain Buddhahood. Through the power of the Lotus Sutra of the Wonderful Law they can do so in their present form.'98 This means that both the teacher who expounds the principles of the Lotus Sutra and the disciple who receives his teachings will, in no long time, together become Buddhas through the power of the Lotus Sutra.

"The Great Teacher T'ien-t'ai produced The Profound Meaning of the Lotus Sutra, The Words and Phrases of the Lotus Sutra, and Great Concentration and Insight, thirty volumes of commentary on the Lotus Sutra. And the Great Teacher Miao-lo in addition produced the thirty volumes of The Annotations on 'The Profound Meaning of the Lotus Sutra,' The Annotations on 'The Words and Phrases of the Lotus Sutra,' and The Annotations on 'Great Concentration and Insight' to comment on T'ien-t'ai's works. Together these works are known as 'the sixty volumes of the T'ien-t'ai school.'

"In Profound Meaning, T'ien-t'ai established the five major principles of name, entity, quality, function, and teaching, and in their light explained the power and efficacy of the five characters of Myoho-Renge-Kyo. In the section on the third of the five major principles, that dealing with the quality of the Lotus Sutra, he writes, 'When one pulls on the main cord of a net, there are no meshes that do not move, and when one raises a single corner of a robe, there are no threads in the robe that are not lifted up.' The meaning of this passage is that, when one carries out the single practice of exercising strong mind of determination in Myoho-Renge-Kyo, there are no blessings that fail to come to one, and no good karma that does not begin to work on one's behalf. It is like the case of a fishing net: though the net is composed of innumerable small meshes, when one pulls on the main cord of the net, there are no meshes that do not move. Or it is like a garment: though the garment is composed of countless tiny threads, when one pulls on a corner of the garment, there are no threads that are not drawn along.

"In Words and Phrases, T'ien-t'ai explains the various words and phrases in the Lotus Sutra, from the opening words 'This is what I heard' to the final words 'they bowed in obeisance and departed.' He explains them in terms of four categories, namely, causes and conditions, correlated teachings, the theoretical and essential teachings, and the observation of the mind.99

"Next, in Great Concentration and p.134Insight, he expounds the meditation on the region of the unfathomable, namely, on the three thousand realms in a single moment of life, based on his thorough understanding of the Lotus Sutra. This is a practice that derives from the Buddha's original enlightenment and represents a principle of truth inherent in one's being. I will not go into it in detail here.

"What an occasion for rejoicing! Though born into an evil age that is stained with the five impurities, we have been able to see and hear the true words of the one vehicle. We read that a person who has planted roots of good fortune [under Buddhas] equal in number to the sands of the Hiranyavatī or the Ganges River is able to encounter this sutra and take strong mind of determination in it.100 Now you have aroused the mind that rejoices in strong mind of determination. Thus without a doubt, just as a box and its lid fit together, so will your own strong mind of determination evoke the Buddha's compassionate response, and the two will unite as one."

The unenlightened man bowed his head, pressed his palms together, and said: "From now on I will accept and uphold this king of the sutras, the Lotus of the one truth, and revere the Buddha, who in the threefold world is alone worthy of honor, as my true teacher. From my present body as a common mortal until the time when I attain the body of a Buddha, I will never venture to turn aside from this strong mind of determination. Though the clouds of the five cardinal sins should hang heavy above me, I will strive to emulate the example of Devadatta in attaining Buddhahood. Though the waves of the ten evil acts should buffet me, I will desire to be like those who formed a bond with the Lotus Sutra by listening to the princes' preaching."101

The sage said: "The human heart is like water that assumes the shape of whatever vessel it occupies, and the nature of beings is like the reflection of the moon undulating on the waves. Now you insist that you will be firm in this strong mind of determination, but another day you are bound to waver. Though devils and demons may come to tempt you, you must not allow yourself to be distracted. The heavenly devil hates the Buddha's Law, and the non-Buddhist believers resent the path of the Buddhist teachings. But you must be like the golden mountain that glitters more brightly when scraped by the wild boar, like the sea that encompasses all the various streams, like the fire that burns higher when logs are added, or like the kālakula insect that grows bigger when the wind blows. If you follow such examples, then how can the outcome fail to be good?"

Background

This treatise is generally thought to have been written in the second year of Bun'ei (1265). Its recipient is unknown. However, toward the end of the work, the unenlightened man refers to himself as "a man who carries a bow and arrows and devotes himself to the profession of arms," so it has been suggested that Nichiren Shonin may have written it for someone of the samurai class.

The treatise consists of two parts and is written chiefly in question-and-answer form. The "sage" in the title indicates the votary of the Lotus Sutra, or Nichiren Shonin himself, while the "unenlightened man" represents all ordinary people of the Latter Day p.135of the Law. In the first part, the unenlightened man, who has realized life's impermanence and is seeking the truth, is visited in succession by a priest of the Precepts school, a lay believer of the Pure Land school, a practitioner of the True Word school, and a priest of the Zen school. Through their conversations, the Shonin outlines the basic tenets of these four major Buddhist schools of his day.

The Precepts priest, who is the first visitor, asserts that the teachings concerning the precepts are the most important of the eighty thousand sacred teachings of Buddhism. He holds up Ryōkan, the chief priest of Gokuraku-ji temple, as an example and exhorts the unenlightened man to observe the five precepts and the two hundred and fifty precepts and devote himself to charitable works as Ryōkan does.

The next visitor, a Pure Land believer, praises the Nembutsu teachings, which enable one to be reborn in Amida Buddha's Pure Land and thereby gain emancipation from the sufferings of birth and death. He singles out the eighteenth of Amida Buddha's forty-eight vows as the sole source of salvation for ordinary people in the Latter Day and asserts that even persons guilty of the ten evil acts and the five cardinal sins can attain rebirth in the Pure Land by calling on this Buddha's name.

The True Word practitioner, who visits next, says that even the most profound doctrines of the exoteric teachings are no more than an introduction to the esoteric teachings. The exoteric teachings, he says, were expounded by Shakyamuni, the Buddha of the manifested body, in accordance with his disciples' capacities, while the esoteric teachings were preached by Mahāvairochana, the Buddha of the Dharma body, out of his spontaneous joy in the Law. He accordingly urges the unenlightened man to discard the exoteric teachings and take strong mind of determination in the more profound esoteric teachings.

The last to come calling is a mendicant Zen priest. He likens the sutras to a finger pointing at the moon and denounces the doctrines contained in them as so much nonsense, exhorting the unenlightened man to sit in meditation to perceive the true nature of his mind in accordance with the "wordless teaching" of Zen.

Troubled by the contradictions in what he has heard, and determined to discover which teaching is correct, the unenlightened man then sets out on a journey in search of a teacher who can clarify matters for him. After visiting various temples one after another, he finally encounters a sage who embraces the Lotus Sutra. The title Conversation between a Sage and an Unenlightened Man refers to the subsequent dialogue that unfolds between them. The unenlightened man confesses that, although he has learned the teachings of the Precepts, Nembutsu, True Word, and Zen schools, he cannot determine whether or not those teachings are true. In reply, the sage declares that the doctrines of all four schools are the cause for rebirth in the evil paths, because they are based on provisional teachings, while only the true teaching, the Lotus Sutra, enables all people without exception to attain Buddhahood.

This comparison of the true and provisional teachings forms the focus of this treatise. The sage refutes the doctrines of those schools that are based on the provisional teachings and cites sutra passages to demonstrate that the supremacy of the Lotus Sutra was set forth by Shakyamuni Buddha himself. His rebuttal of the Nembutsu and True Word doctrines concludes part one of this treatise. Part two begins with his refutation of Zen.

By this time, the unenlightened man has become convinced of the truth of the Lotus Sutra. But he hesitates to p.136embrace it out of considerations of loyalty and filial piety; he points out that everyone from the ruler on down to the common people has strong mind of determination in other schools, and his own parents and ancestors embraced the Pure Land teachings. The sage replies that one can best repay one's debts of gratitude to one's parents and sovereign by embracing the correct Buddhist teaching and thus leading them to salvation. Next, one should evaluate the Buddhist teachings on their own merits and not according to the number of their adherents. The sage also explains that there are two ways of Buddhist practice—shōju and shakubuku—depending upon the time. The present period, when distorted teachings flourish, is the time for shakubuku, he says.

The unenlightened man now having resolved to embrace the Lotus Sutra, the sage reveals to him that the essence of the sutra lies in the five characters of Myoho-Renge-Kyo that form its title. Myoho-Renge-Kyo, he explains, is the Buddha nature inherent in all beings. When one chants Nam-Myoho-Renge-Kyo, the Buddha nature inherent in all things will be summoned forth, and one's own Buddha nature will simultaneously emerge. Even without profound understanding of the Buddhist teachings, one can by this practice attain Buddhahood in one's present form. The sage concludes by exhorting the unenlightened man to maintain strong mind of determination throughout life, without wavering in his resolve.

Notes

1. The Japanese text could also be construed to mean, "We may be terrified by the prospect of the unknown and lament that the world we are familiar with should pass so quickly."

2. Chuang Tzu, "Knowledge Wandered North": "Man's life between heaven and earth is like the passing of a white colt glimpsed through a crack in the wall—whoosh!—and that's the end."

3. This refers to the great earthquakes, heavy floods, and other disasters that occurred during the Shōka era (1257–1259), claiming many lives.

4. The king of Ch'u is King Huai (r. 328–299 b.c.e.). In a dream he had a romantic encounter with a goddess. When she left, she told the king that she would always be with him as a cloud in the morning and as rain in the evening.

5. In the Yung-p'ing era (c.e. 58–75), during the reign of Emperor Ming, Liu Ch'en lost his way on Mount T'ien-t'ai, where he encountered a female immortal being and lived together with her in bliss. When Liu Ch'en returned home after half a year, he found himself in the time of his descendants of the seventh generation.

6. Which poet the Shonin refers to is uncertain. The implication of the verse alluded to is that, being a lowly woodcutter and therefore ignorant of religion, the poet hopes he will not be called upon to bear great sorrow in life.

7. The hell of burning heat and the hell of great burning heat are the sixth and seventh of the eight hot hells—the eighth being the hell of incessant suffering.

8. The hell of the crimson lotus and the hell of the great crimson lotus are the seventh and eighth of the eight cold hells. In these two hells, the cold is said to make one's flesh crack open, so that it has the appearance of red lotus flowers.

9. The five components of body and mind refer here to the five components of life: form, perception, conception, volition, and consciousness that unite temporarily to form an individual living being.

10. After this opening passage, the text shifts to third-person narrative.

11. Ling Lun was a subject of Huang Ti (the Yellow Emperor), a legendary ruler of ancient China. Endowed with remarkably acute hearing, he is said to have excelled in music and been able to distinguish minute differences in pitch.

12. Li Chu, also called Li Lou, was a legendary figure of ancient China whose sight was so acute that he could see the tip of a hair at a hundred paces.

13. The port of Iijima was the only port p.137 servicing Kamakura in the Shonin's time. The Mutsura Barrier was a checkpoint at Mutsura in what is presently Yokohama in Kanagawa Prefecture.

14. Seven roads leading to Kamakura.

15. Comparisons by which Shakyamuni Buddha emphasized the superiority of the Mahayana precepts over the Hinayana, according to the Pure Monastic Rules Sutra. For example, the Hinayana precepts practiced by voice-hearers do not even produce benefit as small as the print of a cow's hoof, while the Mahayana precepts upheld by bodhisattvas produce benefit as vast as the ocean.

16. "Seventeen differences" refers to the reasons why the Hinayana precepts are inferior to the Mahayana precepts, according to the Pure Monastic Rules Sutra. For example, the Hinayana precepts reflect abhorrence of the threefold world, the realm inhabited by unenlightened beings, while the Mahayana precepts do not; the Hinayana precepts show disdain for benefits, while the Mahayana precepts encompass them all.

17. Nirvana Sutra.

18. One of the five meditations to extinguish miscellaneous thoughts, meditation on a corpse was thought to extinguish sexual desire.

19. The Shonin uses an image from chapter 7 of the Lotus Sutra, in which the provisional teachings are likened to a phantom city magically conjured by a guide to allow his party of weary travelers to rest en route to the treasure land (one Buddha vehicle), which is their true destination.

20. The Essentials of Rebirth in the Pure Land.

21. The forty-eight vows that Amida Buddha is said to have made while still engaged in bodhisattva practice as Bodhisattva Dharma Treasury.

22. The first vow states, "If, after I attain Buddhahood, there are any beings of hell, the realm of hungry spirits, or the realm of animals to be found in my land, then let me not attain supreme enlightenment." So there are said to be no beings of the three evil paths in Amida's Pure Land. The three types of perception are: (1) one understands the truth one hears, (2) one follows the truth, and (3) one realizes the true aspect of things that neither is born nor dies.

23. This refers to a phrase used by the poet Po Chü-i to describe his secular writings. Buddhists and Confucians often used this expression in reference to poetry and prose that were lacking in didactic worth.

24. The three esoteric sutras are the Mahāvairochana, Diamond Crown, and Susiddhikara sutras.

25. The twenty-eight patriarchs inherited and passed on that teaching of Shakyamuni that was not expounded in words but instead was transmitted from mind to mind. The first is Mahākāshyapa, and the last, Bodhidharma, the founder of Chinese Zen. The six patriarchs are Bodhidharma, Hui-k'o, Seng-ts'an, Tao-hsin, Hung-jen, and Hui-neng.

26. This refers to the last of the four realms into which the realm of formlessness is divided, the realm of formlessness being the highest division of the threefold world.

27. A poem by Fujiwara no Yoshitaka, appearing in A Collection of Japanese and Chinese Poems for Singing, compiled around 1013.

28. A poet of the mid-ninth century. Many romantic legends have grown up around her.

29. A legendary woman appearing in The Chronicles of Japan and The Records of Ancient Matters.

30. The original source of this poem is unknown. Mount Toribe, located in Kyoto, was used as a cremation site.

31. A poem by the Administrator of Priests Henjō (816–890), which appears in Japanese and Chinese Poems for Singing.

32. In other writings, the Shonin speaks of the nineteen-year-old Shakyamuni as leaving his father's palace in the capital of Kapilavastu, which description is consistent with the traditional account. It is not certain why he says here that the young prince "left the city of Gayā." However, it is generally held that, after leaving Kapilavastu, Shakyamuni first went south to the kingdom of Magadha where Gayā was located. Mount Dandaka was said to be in Gandhara in northern India.

33. These words are actually spoken by Many Treasures Buddha in the "Treasure Tower" chapter. However, since the Buddhas' act of extending their tongues, described in the "Supernatural Powers" chapter, was also meant to affirm the truth of the sutra, the Shonin attributes this statement to all the Buddhas.

34. Lotus Sutra, chap. 3.

p.13835. Ibid., chap. 2.

36. The statement to this effect appears in Ssu-ming Chih-li's commentary on the Meditation on the Buddha Infinite Life Sutra.

37. The Well Attained is one of the ten honorable titles of a Buddha, meaning one who has gone to the world of enlightenment.

38. This story appears in the Unheard-of Causal Relationship Sutra. Countless kalpas ago, a fox in the country of Bima fell into a well while fleeing from a lion. Faced with the prospect of starvation, he awakened to the impermanence of all things and recited a verse to this effect. Hearing this verse, Shakra came down from heaven and honored the fox as his teacher.

39. The Japanese text reads, "have returned," but it may simply mean to "have reached." The original text of this piece is no longer extant.

40. The Profound Meaning of the Lotus Sutra.

41. The Outstanding Principles of the Lotus Sutra.

42. The Commentary on the Ten Stages Sutra.

43. The K'ai-yüan era catalog refers to The K'ai-yüan Era Catalog of the Buddhist Canon, a comprehensive index of Buddhist texts in Chinese compiled by Chih-sheng and finished in 730, the eighteenth year of the K'ai-yüan

era, during the reign of the T'ang emperor Hsüan-tsung.

44. Another name for the "Perceiver of the World's Sounds" chapter of the Lotus Sutra. It was also used as an independent sutra.

45. Seven cardinal sins: According to The Annotations on "Great Concentration and Insight," killing a priest and killing a teacher, plus the five cardinal sins. The "teachers" referred to here are Shan-tao and Hōnen.

46. Two honored bodhisattvas are Perceiver of the World's Sounds and Great Power.

47. Izanagi and Izanami are a male deity and a female deity who appear in Japanese mythology as the progenitors of Japan and of its gods.

48. A river flowing through the compound of the Inner Shrine of Ise, which is dedicated to the Sun Goddess. That the Mimosuso River has continued to flow implies that the imperial lineage, said to originate with the Sun Goddess, has continued unbroken.

49. Actually it is not a sutra but a work on the benefits gained by meditation on Amida Buddha.

50. The five strong-flavored foods refer to five kinds of pungent roots—leek, scallions, onions, garlic, and ginger. They were said to produce irritability, anger, or sexual desire

and were accordingly forbidden for Buddhist monks and nuns.

51. The thirty-seven honored ones refer to the Buddhas and bodhisattvas who constitute the central section of the Diamond Realm mandala, which is composed of nine sections.

52. Literally Later T'ang Hall, a building that Chishō, the fifth chief priest of Enryaku-ji on Mount Hiei, the head temple of the Tendai school, erected on the grounds of Mii-dera temple in what is now Shiga Prefecture. Tō-in (T'ang Hall) on the grounds of Enryaku-ji, which had been erected earlier by Jikaku, the third chief priest of Enryaku-ji, is referred to as Zentō-in (Former T'ang Hall).

53. The Essentials of the Mahāvairochana Sutra.

54. This refers to the stage of the human mind, before the awakening of moral or religious consciousness, in which one is governed, like an animal, by passions and instincts.

55. This refers to the supreme stage at which one unlocks the immeasurable benefits inherent in one's life through the secret doctrine of Mahāvairochana Buddha.

56. "A later stage" means the tenth and supreme stage of the ten stages of the mind, that is, the stage of realizing the esoteric teaching.

57. The Rules of Rites for Revering the Buddha's Relics.

58. The Precious Key to the Secret Treasury.

59. A ritual implement used for prayers in esoteric True Word Buddhism. This story appears in The Biography of the Great Teacher Kōbō. According to this work, before Kōbō left China, he hurled a three-pronged diamond-pounder into the air. Returning to Japan, he went to Mount Kōya to carry out the practice of the esoteric teachings. There he found the same diamond-pounder resting in a tree's branches.

60. Agastya is an Indian ascetic who practiced the Brahmanistic teachings. His occult powers are mentioned in the p.139Nirvana Sutra. Jinu is another Brahmanist ascetic of India, also mentioned in the Nirvana Sutra. According to The History of the Later Han Dynasty, Chang Chieh of the Later Han dynasty excelled in the occult arts of Taoism and caused a thick fog to appear, extending over five Chinese ri (about 2 km). According to Lives of Saints with Mysterious Powers, Luan Pa of the Later Han dynasty drank wine at a banquet and blew it out facing southwest. He explained that he had done so to extinguish a fire that had broken out in the city of Ch'eng-tu, which lay in that direction. On investigation, it was found that rain, mixed with wine, had

fallen heavily in that city and extinguished a fire there.

61. The Annotations on "The Profound Meaning of the Lotus Sutra."

62. In The Words and Phrases of the Lotus Sutra, T'ien-t'ai interprets those sutras preached in the past as the pre-Lotus Sutra teachings, preached over forty-two years; those preached at the same time as the Immeasurable Meanings Sutra; and those preached in the future as the Nirvana Sutra.

63. Immeasurable Meanings Sutra.

64. Lotus Sutra, chap. 10.

65. Ibid., chap. 11.

66. Ibid., chap. 14.

67. A Buddha mentioned in the Flower Garland, Mahāvairochana, and other sutras. In esoteric True Word Buddhism, he is identified with Mahāvairochana Buddha.

68. A reference to the preaching of the Lotus Sutra.

69. The four types of teachings are the Tripitaka teaching, the connecting teaching, the specific teaching, and the perfect teaching. The point here is that the Mahāvairochana Sutra is not a pure perfect teaching. See eight teachings in Glossary.

70. A reference to the Hinayana precepts.

71. A reference to Kuang-hsiu (771–843) and Wei-chüan (n.d.). Kuang-hsiu was the eighth patriarch in the lineage of the T'ien-t'ai school, and Wei-chüan was his leading disciple.

72. "Thus Come One Zen" refers to the Buddha's meditation as described in the sutras. According to the Laṅkāvatāra Sutra, this meditation gives rise to the mystic powers with which the Buddha saves the people. "Doctrinal Zen" refers to the methods of meditation formulated on the basis of the sutras, and "patriarchal Zen," to the Zen teaching deriving from Bodhidharma, in which enlightenment is said to be transmitted wordlessly from master to disciple.

73. Here "nonduality," as taught by the Zen school, refers to the oneness of the Buddha and the ordinary person. The Shonin says that the Zen followers do not understand "duality," that is, the difference between the Buddha who is awakened to the ultimate truth and ordinary people who are deluded about it.

74. Mirakutsu's Sanskrit name is unknown. King Dammira, mentioned in the subsequent paragraph, is another name for the same individual.

75. Words and Phrases. The Shonin slightly rephrases the original passage. "This sutra" in the quotation refers to the Lotus Sutra.

76. Three of the five cardinal sins: (1) injuring a Buddha, (2) fomenting disunity within the Buddhist Order, and (3) killing an Arhat. Devadatta committed these three.

77. This is described in chapter 12 of the Lotus Sutra.

78. "This wonderful text of the single vehicle" refers to the Lotus Sutra.

79. The sufferings of fire, blood, and swords are the sufferings of the three evil paths, which represent hell, the realm of animals, and the realm of hungry spirits, respectively.

80. A forest on Mount Shinoda in Izumi in the Osaka area of Japan, known for its scenic beauty.

81. This story appears in chapter 27 of the Lotus Sutra.

82. Salvation by Men of Pure Strong mind of determination Sutra, cited in The Forest of Gems in the Garden of the Law. The sutra itself is no longer extant. "The Buddhist life" in the sutra's context means a monastic life, but here the Shonin interprets it as a life based on strong mind of determination in the Mystic Law.

83. This appears in The Book of Rites.

84. Ch'i Li-chi (n.d.) was one of the Four White-Haired Elders who, grieved by the social turmoil at the end of the Ch'in dynasty (221–207 b.c.e.), secluded themselves on Mount Shang. After the Ch'in dynasty was replaced by the Han dynasty, they were invited by Empress Lü, the consort of Emperor Kao-tsu, founder of the Han dynasty, to become advisers to Emperor Hui, who was her son and Kao-tsu's successor.

p.14085. Yen Kuang (39 b.c.e.–c.e. 41) was a companion in study to Liu Hsiu, who later became Emperor Kuang-wu, the first emperor of the Later Han dynasty. After Liu Hsiu became emperor, Yen Kuang changed his name and went into seclusion. Emperor Kuang-wu begrudged the loss of Yen Kuang's abilities and entreated him to serve as his minister. However, Yen Kuang refused and spent the rest of his life in seclusion on Mount Fu-ch'un.

86. Chieh Tzu-sui (n.d.) was a retainer of Duke Wen in the Spring and Autumn period (770–403 b.c.e.), who served the duke in exile for nineteen years. When Duke Wen returned and assumed the rulership of Chin, he gave rewards to those who had followed him in exile. However, he overlooked Chieh Tzu-sui. The latter reproached him by saying that rewards should be dispensed by heaven and not by humans. Then he retired to Mount Mien-shang.

87. An "orchid-room friend" indicates a person of virtue. The implication is that the company of a virtuous person works as a good influence, just as one is imbued with fragrance on entering a room filled with orchids.

88. It is said that mugwort in a field of hemp is supported by the hemp plants and thus grows upright.

89. The six practices, mentioned in The Treatise on the Great Perfection of Wisdom, are accepting, upholding, reading, reciting, teaching, and transcribing. In the five practices, accepting and upholding are combined as one practice. The ten practices, set forth in the Heavenly King Supremacy Wisdom Sutra, are transcribing, making offerings, disseminating and transmitting, listening, reading, bearing in mind, widely preaching, reciting, contemplating, and self-exertion.

90. These admonitions appear in the Lotus and Nirvana sutras.

91. Nirvana Sutra.

92. The Annotations on the Nirvana Sutra.

93. This means that the dragon king's daughter acquired the thirty-two features and eighty characteristics of a Buddha.

94. The six thousand leaves comprise T'ien-t'ai's three major works, Profound Meaning, Words and Phrases, and Great Concentration and Insight, and Miao-lo's commentaries on them.

95. Great Perfection of Wisdom states that the nyagrodha, or banyan tree, is large enough to provide shade for five hundred carts, yet the seed from which it grows is only one-third the size of a mustard seed.

96. Lotus Sutra, chap. 2.

97. The Shonin refers here to the parable of the skilled physician in the "Life Span" chapter of the Lotus Sutra.

98. Outstanding Principles.

99. T'ien-t'ai's four guidelines for interpreting the words and phrases of the Lotus Sutra. "Causes and conditions" means to interpret the words and phrases of the sutra in terms of the causes and conditions that brought the Buddha to expound them. "Correlated teachings" means to interpret the sutra's words and phrases in terms of the four teachings of doctrine and the five periods. "Theoretical and essential teachings" is to interpret them in light of the theoretical and essential teachings of the Lotus Sutra; and "the observation of the mind" is to perceive their truth within one's own life through the practice of meditation.

100. The Shonin slightly modifies the wording of the Nirvana Sutra, which says that one who has aroused the aspiration for enlightenment under Buddhas equal in number to the sands of the Hiranyavatī River will be able to embrace a sutra such as this in the evil age.

101. A reference to the sixteen sons of the Buddha Great Universal Wisdom Excellence, who appears in chapter 7 of the Lotus Sutra.